Cheers for John Feinstein's

OPEN

Inside the Ropes
at Bethpage Black

"Feinstein writes with passion about how the 'Black' was transformed from a sort of seedy public golf course to one called demanding, rigorous, 'one of the toughest par-70 I've ever played in my life.' If you want a great golfing read — here it is."
— Harvey Frommer, Sportsology.net

"Feinstein makes the revitalized course the star of *Open*, along with the people who brought the tournament there. . . . As tournament time nears, Feinstein escorts us not only inside the ropes but also behind the scenes. . . . Passion is what makes the U.S. Open more than just another tournament, and *Open* more than just another golf book."
— Allen St. John, *Washington Post Book World*

"One of the best modern-day sports writers. . . . Feinstein continues his writing magic with *Open*."
— Andrew Blair, *Virginia Golfer*

"A talented and prolific author of sports books . . . Feinstein profiles a large cast of both the famous and the essential going about their jobs to produce a championship event. . . . Recommended for any sports collection."
— John Maxymuk, *Library Journal*

"World-class sportswriter John Feinstein probes the personalities of a small but dedicated group. . . . With characteristic insight and knowledge, Feinstein covers the various trails that lead his diverse cast of characters to Bethpage, with interesting side trips to regional qualifiers and into the lives of the pros."

— Martin Brady, *Bookpage*

"An enlightening tale. . . . This is Feinstein's 12th sports book, and once again he negotiated insider access that enlightens his audience and makes jealous his friends in the media, me included. Security after 9/11; devilish course set-up; devious player pairings; NBC's influence; coordinating nearly 5,000 volunteers: Feinstein was privy to it all."

— David Teel, *San Jose Mercury News*

"The best chronicler in sports journalism."

— Craig Smith, *Seattle Times*

"What comes through is that the Open at Bethpage Black was a seminal moment for Long Island and a turning point for the U.S. Open. . . . Feinstein's *Open* is about the legacy. A year later, the 2002 U.S. Open remains 'the People's Open.'"

— Mark Herrmann, *Newsday*

"Impeccably researched and written with you-are-there clarity."

— *Publishers Weekly*

"It's almost inconceivable that the administrators of a large organization could ever be cast as heroes in the modern world, but that's exactly how bestselling sports reporter John Feinstein portrays the employees of the United States Golf Association in this remarkably compelling portrait of how the 2002 U.S. Open at Bethpage Black came to be. . . . Feinstein tells the story from the points of view of those men and women who made David Fay's dream a reality. . . . Feinstein turns the day-to-day operations of the USGA into the stuff of high drama. It works because the Black was such a dramatic venue. . . . Feinstein does the impossible here: he writes a blue-collar tearjerker about a purportedly blue-blood sport."

— Bill Ott, *Booklist*

OPEN

Inside the Ropes
at Bethpage Black

JOHN
FEINSTEIN

Back Bay Books
Little, Brown and Company
New York   Boston

ALSO BY JOHN FEINSTEIN

Caddy for Life

The Punch

The Last Amateurs

The Majors

A March to Madness

A Civil War

A Good Walk Spoiled

Play Ball

Hard Courts

Forever's Team

A Season Inside

A Season on the Brink

Running Mates
(A Mystery)

Winter Games
(A Mystery)

Back Bay Books / Little, Brown and Company
Time Warner Book Group
1271 Avenue of the Americas, New York, NY 10020
Visit our Web site at www.twbookmark.com

Originally published in hardcover by Little, Brown and Company, May 2003
First Back Bay paperback edition, April 2004

ISBN 0-316-17003-8 (hc) / 0-316-77852-4 (pb)
LCCN 2003101414

10 9 8 7 6 5 4 3 2 1
Q-MB
Printed in the United States of America

This is for Ken Denlinger and Dave Kindred. Mentors. Friends. Role models. As journalists and as people.

Introduction

WHEN I FIRST began covering golf in 1993, my vision of the United States Golf Association was pretty similar to the description once offered by Lee Trevino of the typical USGA officer: "Get yourself a blue blazer and some dandruff and you can be a part of the USGA, too." To me, the USGA was a bunch of rich guys with gold buttons, putting on the U.S. Open at gorgeous country clubs filled with their fellow patricians.

My stereotype received a jolt on the last day of the Open in 1994 at Oakmont. The heat in Pittsburgh that week was brutal, the humidity on the golf course thick enough to peel.

On the final afternoon, I was searching for shade — there was none — on the 11th hole when I noticed Grant Spaeth, a onetime USGA president who was on the golf course as a walking rules official. His blue USGA shirt and tie were completely soaked through, and he looked even more miserable than I felt.

"You know," I said to Spaeth, "it might help you guys a little bit if you wore white shirts instead of that blue."

Spaeth shook his head. "No, can't do that," he said. "At the USGA we like to think of ourselves as a blue-collar organization."

Now *that* was funny.

At that moment, I liked the USGA a little bit more.

As time went on, I found other reasons to like the USGA. One was Frank Hannigan, the former senior executive director of the organization. I have often described Hannigan as my favorite curmudgeon. He can find darkness in the sun, treachery in the sale of

Girl Scout cookies. He is also as bright as they come, generous with his time and his ideas, and in spite of his inexplicable fascination with the NBA, one of my favorite people.

It was Hannigan who figured out how to get the U.S. Open played at Shinnecock, and it was the Open at Shinnecock that led to the Open at Bethpage Black. It was also Hannigan who decided to promote David B. Fay over several others to the number two position in the USGA and Hannigan who pushed for Fay's hiring as his successor in 1989 when many on the executive board wanted to go outside and hire a "name."

Fay looks like he would fit comfortably into a USGA blazer. He often wears a bow tie and he was educated at Colgate and Stanford. But he's also the son of a steamship captain who grew up as a caddy and played most of his teenage golf at a nine-hole municipal course. He only wears the bow tie because he has a penchant for spilling food — usually from a greasy-spoon diner because that's where he's most comfortable — on the expensive ties his wife buys him.

Meeting Fay was something of a revelation to me. One of the first things he said to me was, "I love golf, enjoy its traditions as much as anyone, but if you don't love baseball you have no soul."

My kind of guy. It was Fay who first decided that making caddies wear long pants in 90-degree weather was foolish, putting them in shorts for the 1998 Open. "I wouldn't care if the players wear shorts when it's that hot," he said, no doubt sending a tremor through the entire golf establishment.

Fay is, if nothing else, unorthodox. It was that sense of wanting to be different that led him to Bethpage. He believed the USGA needed to make some sort of statement about the importance of public golf, that it needed to get away from always staging its signature championship at havens for the very rich. He remembered the Black Course from his days as a kid and went to check on it one cold afternoon in November and came away convinced that it could be great again.

The Duke of York, credited by many with introducing golf in Great Britain, brought the game to the United States. He and his friend Thomas Powell supposedly played golf on the land that would later become Bethpage State Park in 1688. Powell, who purchased the tract of land that came to become known as Bethpage, also gave it the name.

As the area grew, it went through name changes — for a while it was called Central Park, long before Manhattan's Central Park came into existence — and was passed to Powell's heirs and eventually was bought early in the twentieth century by a railroad tycoon named Benjamin F. Yoakum. It was Yoakum who developed Lenox Hills, first as a housing development and then as a private golf club.

Yoakum died in 1929, shortly after the stock market crashed. As part of the Works Progress Administration program created by the government for the purpose of putting people back to work, the Yoakum estate was leased and later purchased by the state of New York. It was Robert Moses who proposed the idea of building a state park on the Yoakum estate. The name Lenox Hills was changed to Bethpage Golf Club and it was opened to the public — much to the horror of the membership at Lenox Hills, which sought an injunction preventing the sale of the land to the state. The injunction was denied, and eventually, the project went forward.

When the new club opened to the public in 1932, an 18-hole round cost a dollar on weekdays, two dollars on weekends. The course was so popular that Moses began making plans to build others. Within four years, three new courses had been built. Moses' masterstroke was to hire the renowned golf course architect A. W. Tillinghast to design two of the courses — the Red and the Black. To this day there is controversy about just how involved Tillinghast was in the project and just why the Black took shape as it did. There are stories claiming that Tillinghast and Moses fell out before the project was finished, thus explaining why the routing of the course and the bunkering of the course look very much like other Tillinghast designs but the greens do not. Some people speculate that Tillinghast made the greens smaller and easier because the course was part of a public park and he didn't want it to be too difficult. But given that there were three other courses at the time, the Black was clearly built to be the most challenging.

Most recently, Joseph Burbeck, the son of the park's first superintendent, David Burbeck, has claimed that it was his father who actually designed the Black Course, that Tillinghast disappeared from the project soon after it began. Joseph Burbeck was four when the clubhouse had its official opening in 1935, and there are pictures of him alongside his father, formally opening the lock to the front door of the new building.

No one disputes the elder Burbeck's importance in the development of the park or that he played a major role in getting the golf courses constructed. But most Bethpagers will always see the Black as one of Tillinghast's masterpieces. From the day it opened in 1936, it was considered one of the great public golf courses and one of the best layouts anywhere. But as the years went by, even though golfers always talked about it, the course began to fade away. Lack of funds, lack of interest on the part of the state, and the constant pounding the course took because of all the play on it — even with no golf carts allowed — had beaten it down into a state of sad disrepair when David Fay had his crazy idea.

Fay's staff had serious doubts. "You could see the genius in the routing," Mike Davis, one of Fay's key lieutenants, said. "But, God, was it in horrible condition. I mean truly horrible. Part of me thought that David was out of his mind. But the look on his face that day told me that didn't matter. He wanted to do this. It was up to [assistant executive director] Mike Butz and me to figure out how to get it done."

It took a great deal of cajoling and wheedling and politicking for Fay to get the USGA executive board to go along. He put himself on the line, because if the event had failed in any way it would have been seen as his failure. One can see the easy headlines now: FAY'S FOLLY. Instead, it will go down as FAY'S LEGACY.

It was Fay at the beginning but so many others along the way. Perhaps that's what gave me the idea for this book. It struck me that the Open at the Black would be like no other because it was a public golf course; because the "membership" of this club consisted of the state of New York and thousands of public golfers. This was the largest Open ever staged in every way — most fans, most corporate tents, most sprawling venue, longest legal contract, most pretournament meetings — everything.

With the help of Fay first and then his remarkably patient staff later, I have attempted here to explain what it is like to put on an Open and what it was like to put on *this* Open. We all have a sense of what happens in a major championship on the golf course because television does an excellent job of showing us the players and their shot-making. What I have attempted to do here is show you how they got there; the work that goes into the golf course to look the way it does; what goes on behind the scenes in the days and months leading up to the championship and then during the event itself.

That's not to say this book isn't about golfers. After all, Mike Butz, Fay's number two man, likes to say, "When you sort it all out, the bottom line is that the U.S. Open is about 156 guys trying to win a championship." All the hours of work that go into making the Open what it is don't matter if nobody plays. You will read here about a lot of those 156 guys, ranging from Tiger Woods to Felix Casas (who finished 155th because one player withdrew after the first round). You will also read about some of the 8,468 who entered the Open in 2002 who didn't make it to Bethpage. Among them were past Open champions, rising young stars, and top amateurs. Also among them were thousands of players who are symbolized in many ways by my brother Bobby, who at the age of forty earned the right to play in an Open qualifier for the first time in his life. Bobby didn't make it through his local qualifier — most players don't — but being able to claim that he was part of the Open, even as a participant in a local, had great meaning for him.

Which is why it is called the Open. Tiger Woods can play and so can my brother. And thousands in between.

This is a book about all of them and about the people who make it possible for the Open to take place. To most golf fans, the symbol of this Open will always be Woods, holding the championship trophy, adding another major title notch to his belt.

To me, the symbol of this Open will always be Dave Catalano, the man who runs Bethpage State Park, standing on the 18th green a few feet from Woods with a huge smile on his face, clearly filled with pride because of what everyone associated with *his* park had accomplished.

"I was thinking," he said, "that a lot of people who said a bunch of state employees could never pull this off had been proven just a little bit wrong. I was thinking, hey, everyone, guess what — we did it!"

Indeed they did. All of them — from the blue blazers at the USGA (and there are some of them) to the state employees — gave body and soul to make the Open at the Black happen.

What follows is the story of how they did it.

OPEN

1

Like No Other Open

AS SOON AS he saw the policeman standing in the middle of the road, waving him to a stop, Scott McCarron knew he had made a mistake. He had decided that morning to let his wife use the courtesy car that the United States Golf Association had provided him for the week of the 2002 U.S. Open. Jennifer was going into Manhattan, and McCarron thought she would be better off in an SUV.

McCarron took the smaller rental car to the golf course. But as he pulled up to the policeman, he remembered that his Contestant Parking sticker was in the SUV. Like everyone else who had already set foot on the grounds of Bethpage State Park, McCarron knew that security at this Open was unlike security at any other Open. Bethpage is located smack in the middle of Long Island, only thirty-five miles from Ground Zero.

Neither the USGA nor the New York State Police were taking any chances. For the first time in history, the Open was being played at a true public facility, one owned not by a corporation but by a state agency. Bethpage Black was one of five golf courses located inside Bethpage State Park. It was open to anyone with thirty-one dollars and a great deal of patience. Both the tenant for the week — the USGA — and the owner — New York State —

wanted the event to go off without a hitch or a glitch, and certainly without any kind of serious incident.

The atmosphere at the Open was best described on Monday morning, the first day the public was allowed onto the grounds, by Tony Zirpoli, a USGA employee who had once been a school-teacher in the Fort Apache area of the South Bronx. He knew all about tough neighborhoods and police presence, but by the time he made it from his hotel to the clubhouse early on Monday morning, Zirpoli had learned something new. "I think now I know what it must have been like going through Checkpoint Charlie," he said, referencing the Berlin border crossing from East Germany to West Germany during the Cold War era.

Now, McCarron was approaching Checkpoint Charlie without his papers — specifically, his parking pass. He did have his player ID, as did his caddy, Ryan Scott, who was with him. He had golf clubs with his name on them and any other ID the police might want.

"I knew," he said, "it was going to take a while to get to the club-house — if I was lucky."

With his player ID and numerous mea culpas, he managed to get through the first two checkpoints. At the third, though, with nirvana — the parking lot — in sight, the policeman told him he would have to check with the state police command center before letting him pass. The policeman was apologetic. "Scott, I know who you are," he said. "But I gotta check."

Finally, word came back: McCarron could park the unstickered car in the lot today. If he showed up in it again the next day, he would be turned away. McCarron offered his thanks and promised not to make the same mistake twice. He was about to drive away when the policeman stopped him again. "Scott, before you go, can I just ask you one thing?" he said.

McCarron sighed, prepared to sign an autograph or perhaps be lectured once again about why security had to be so tight. But he had no choice. "Sure," he said. "What's up?"

"I was just wondering," the policeman said, a bit hesitant. "On number three . . . have you been trying to land the ball short of the flagstick and hope it rolls up? Or are you playing to the back of the green? I never know how to play that hole. If I land short, the ball dies, and I have a long, long putt. If I go for the back, if I miss it just a little, it rolls over, and then I'm dead. What do you do?"

McCarron stifled a laugh and explained that he was hoping to land short of the flagstick and get a bounce close to the hole. If not, he'd take a par happily and move to the fourth tee.

"Yeah, that sounds good," the cop said, a huge smile on his face. "Nothing wrong with par on this golf course, right?"

"You got it," McCarron said, saying a final thank-you and, at last, wheeling his car into the player lot.

As he and Scott were pulling his clubs out of the trunk, McCarron thought about that conversation. "I realized," he said, "that this had to be the first U.S. Open in history where the cops guarding the golf course had actually played it more often — a lot more often probably — than the players in the event had played it.

"There's never been a U.S. Open where you could say that before. In fact, there's never been an Open anything like this before."

Not even close.

It began on a cold November day in 1994 with a late afternoon walk.

David B. Fay, the executive director of the USGA, was meeting his wife at a dinner party on Long Island and found himself with some extra time. His drive from the USGA offices in New Jersey hadn't taken as long as he had anticipated, and on a whim as much as anything else, he decided to make a stop at Bethpage State Park.

Like almost anyone who had played golf in the metropolitan New York area, Fay was familiar with Bethpage. He had grown up north of Westchester, in the town of Tuxedo Park, and had spent his boyhood working at the tony Tuxedo Club as a caddy, on the grounds crew, and in the golf shop. On Mondays, as at most private clubs, the employees got to play the golf course. The rest of the time when he wanted to play golf, Fay did so at a nine-hole municipal course called Central Valley. It was there that he first heard people talk about Bethpage, specifically the legendary Black Course, the one with the sign on the first tee that read, "Warning: The Black Course Is an Extremely Difficult Course Which We Recommend Only for Highly Skilled Golfers."

By the time he was in high school, Fay knew he had to see the Black for himself. As a teenager with a single digit handicap, he and three friends made the drive south into Queens and then east onto Long Island. They arrived at Bethpage before dawn, knowing that was the only way to ensure a tee time. If you wanted to play one of the other four golf courses in the park, you could come later. Not so for the Black.

"Even back then it was a little beat up," Fay said, talking about the mid-1960s. "With all the play they got out there and with not much money being spent on upkeep, it looked the way most munis look. But it was still a fantastic golf course. Hard, really hard."

Fay and friends made the trip once or twice a summer during high school and college. Fay ended up going to Colgate, where he walked onto the golf team — he was a two-handicapper by then — let his hair grow long, and returned summers to work at Tuxedo. He did spend part of one summer working on the S.S. *United States,* a job arranged for him by his father, a steamship captain. Fay was supposed to go to staterooms when the ride got a bit too rough and clean up after the passengers. Midway through the summer, he thanked his father for the opportunity and went back to work at the golf club.

After college, Fay leapfrogged jobs until landing at the USGA in 1978. By 1989, he had become the executive director. "In the back of my mind, almost from the day I took the job at the USGA, was the notion that someday I'd like to see the Open played on a real public golf course," he said. "I wasn't thinking Pebble Beach, which is a place for the rich, but a place where the guys who played were like the guys I grew up around at Central Valley. But for a long time, it was nothing more than a pipe dream, there was no tangible plan in my mind at all."

Bethpage had been on the USGA's radar screen in the past —

but not as an Open site. In the mid-1980s, Frank Hannigan, Fay's predecessor and mentor, who had grown up playing municipal golf courses on Staten Island, had thought Bethpage would be a good place to hold the U.S. Public Links championship. The Pub Links is one of thirteen championships the USGA conducts every year and is open to amateur players with handicaps of eight or lower who do not hold membership in any private club. As you might expect, it is held at public venues each year. Hannigan, who had taken over the USGA in 1983, thought the Black Course was a natural to host the Pub Links, and he opened negotiations with the state of New York to bring the event there.

But in 1985, Hannigan and Tom Meeks, a member of the USGA's rules and competition committee, were invited to play an outing at the Black. They came away from the day with serious concerns: the golf course was in far worse condition than they had imagined. There were other problems, too. Everywhere they looked there were signs that said "Welcome to Chuck Workman's Bethpage Black." Workman was the golf pro at Bethpage, and he had literally put his signature all over the golf course. "Every bench on every tee box, it was there," Meeks remembered. "It was as if the actual name of the golf course was Chuck Workman's Bethpage Black. I remember saying to Frank that day that I thought we were going to have problems getting this contract done."

If there was any hope left to bring the Pub Links to the Black, it died when Meeks took a phone call from someone working for the state Department of Parks in Albany. The state needed to know how the greens fees — then twenty-three dollars — for the event would be handled: Would the USGA pay or would the players themselves pay?

Meeks, who is never speechless, was about as close as he gets. "No one is going to pay a greens fee," he said when he finally found his voice. "This is a national championship being conducted. There are no greens fees."

On a New York State–owned facility there are *always* greens fees, Meeks was told. Meeks hung up the phone, walked into Hannigan's office, and told him he didn't see any way this was going to get done. Hannigan agreed. The notion of the Pub Links at the Black died there.

Four years later, the Black Course did host a golf tournament: the Met Open, which is put on annually by the MGA. The executive director of the MGA then, as now, was Jay Mottola, who also happens to be David Fay's oldest friend.

"We probably first played together in the cradle," Mottola said. "Our parents were friends, and we've known each other for as long as either of us can remember."

In fact, they were high school teammates in basketball (Mottola went on to be a star at Lafayette and spent several years as a college coach, assisting, among others, future Maryland coach Gary Williams when Williams was at American University) and in golf and worked together at the Tuxedo Club. On at least one occasion, they made the trip to Long Island together to play the Black.

Taking the Met Open to the Black was no small thing. Traditionally, it had been played at some of the famous posh private clubs that dot the area, like Winged Foot and Baltusrol, both traditional U.S. Open sites. Like the USGA, Mottola found himself confronted with the greens fee issue.

"We aren't the USGA, we aren't conducting a national championship," Mottola said. "We were able to work out a compromise with the state: we would pay greens fees for the Pro-Am and for one of the three days of actual competition. For whatever reason, that worked for them and it worked for us."

And so, in 1989, the Met Open went to the Black, the first time *it* had been played at a public facility. One of the competitors in the Met that year was George Zahringer, a top amateur player from the area. Zahringer had been a private course guy most of his life. His family had belonged to Westchester Country Club when he was a boy growing up in Rye, New York, and thanks to a successful career on Wall Street, he belonged to the Deepdale Golf Club on Long Island and the Stanwich Country Club in Greenwich, Connecticut. Deepdale isn't that far from Bethpage, but, as Fay puts it, "the two places don't play home and home a lot."

In short, Zahringer had never seen Bethpage. He had heard about it, knew about the legendary sign and about players sleeping in their cars to get tee times. Even so, he wasn't prepared for what he found when he first set foot on the Black.

"Whatever I had heard about it couldn't begin to do justice to the real thing," he said. "It was sensational, just spectacular. Sure, it was beat up. But to me, it was like looking at a great house that's fallen into disrepair. You could see that the bones were there. It just struck me right away."

Mottola was reminded as he watched the tournament go on how special the Black was. That winter, playing in a foursome during a USGA outing in Florida that included Fay and two members of the executive board, Reg Murphy and Jerry Stahl, Mottola brought up the subject of the Black.

"I remember saying they ought to take a look at it again some-day, and not for the Pub Links," he said. "I knew Reg and Jerry didn't know much about it, but David did. I didn't make a big deal of it, but I brought it up to at least get it into David's thinking, if only just a little bit."

Fay certainly respected his old pal's opinions, but he didn't really give any serious thought to that conversation until he received a letter from Zahringer. Neither man is certain exactly when Zahringer wrote to Fay, and Fay, one of the world's worst record keepers, no longer has a copy of the letter. But both remember the gist of the message: Give the Black some serious thought as a future Open site.

"The Black," Fay remembers Zahringer writing, "is as good as it gets. There is genius in the design."

People are constantly letting Fay know about unknown gems that the USGA needs to consider. But this was a little bit different. Fay respected Zahringer both as a good player and as someone who understood golf and golf courses. Plus, he knew the Black well from his younger days, even though he hadn't been there for years.

"It was one of those letters you read twice," he said later. "It wasn't as if I started thinking seriously about going there that day or even thought about it very often. But I did think to myself, I wonder if . . ."

Two phone calls kept the Black on Fay's brain: one came from Zahringer, following up on his letter. The second came from Mottola in the fall of 1994 after the MGA had conducted another of its championships — The Ike — at the Black. "Jay just wanted to remind me that the Black was still out there and still worthy of consideration," Fay said. "Again, it wasn't as if I jumped out of my chair and said, I've got to go see the Black for myself, but it did simmer, just as the letter from George did. These were two guys whose opinions I respected telling me that the Black was still an extraordinary test of golf and if I was looking somewhere down the line to do something a little different with the Open, I should at least take a look at it at some point."

That point arrived sooner than Fay had thought it might when he found himself driving on the Southern State Parkway on that chilly November day with time to spare and the exit for Bethpage State Parkway looming ahead. Why not? he thought to himself and swung the car onto the exit ramp and in the direction of the park.

Ten minutes later, he pulled into the parking lot. It was late afternoon, it was blustery, and it was November, but there were still cars in the lot and golfers on the golf courses. He knew from experience that the last group would have teed off the Black a couple of hours earlier because it would be dark by shortly after five o'clock and people didn't like to play nine-hole rounds there since the 10th tee was about as far from the clubhouse as you can get.

He parked his car and walked around the old clubhouse, built in the 1930s as part of the WPA project that had funded the park, and three of the current five golf courses. He didn't want to go into the clubhouse or the pro shop because he didn't want to bump into Workman, who would recognize him and wonder what he was doing there. He knew he was unlikely to be spotted by anyone else and that the first tee would be empty with only about an hour of daylight left.

"I've always enjoyed sneaking onto golf courses," he said. "We did it all the time when I was a kid, and for years, a friend of mine and I traditionally played our first round of the spring at Canoe Brook [a posh club near Fay's home in Summit, New Jersey]. We would park in a corner of the lot, jump on the south course, and if anyone said anything to us we were prepared to just say, Oh, this isn't Summit Municipal? We must have taken a wrong turn."

Fay didn't have any golf clubs and he had no intention of playing. All he wanted to do was take a look-around stroll. He glanced at the famous sign and looked down from the elevated first tee at the first fairway. He stuck his hands in his pockets and started walking. He wasn't interested in the condition of the golf course at that moment nor in reminiscing about the rounds he had played there as a teenager. What he was trying to do was put himself in the shoes of the top pros and try to see what they might see, walking the golf course.

"If I'm good at anything, it is making myself into the player that's going to be playing a course when I look at it," he said. "It doesn't matter even a little bit how I would play the golf course or what I would find appealing or unappealing about it. What mattered in this case was how Nick Price [then the number one player in the world] would play it."

Fay walked down number one, veering right at the dogleg and pausing on the green. He remembered then that the least impressive part of the Black was the greens — most were relatively small and flat — unlike those on other courses created by A. W. Tillinghast, the famous architect who had designed the Black.

Hardly overwhelmed by number one, Fay walked off the green and crossed Round Swamp Road to the second tee. A tunnel for golfers runs under Round Swamp, but it occurred to Fay that at a U.S. Open spectators would have to cross the road since it would be impossible to funnel all of them through the underground passage. He also knew that there was another point on the golf course (between 14 green and 15 tee) where everyone came back across the road.

"Right away, I saw problems," he said. "To begin with, I wasn't all that impressed with number one as a championship-level hole. But that was okay. On most golf courses the first hole is pretty ordinary. But when I walked across Round Swamp I was thinking that any notion of holding an Open there would go straight out the window if you couldn't get the road closed down for the entire week. I figured regardless of anything else, that was going to be a major hurdle."

Fay walked to the second tee and down the relatively short par-four and up onto the elevated green. Another okay hole. He turned right and paused on the third tee. From there he saw a par-three that most pros would play with a middle iron. Not a bad hole — there was some deep bunkering around the green and trouble behind it — but still nothing that would make him think this was a place to bring the U.S. Open.

Fay circled the third green and walked down the hill leading to the fourth tee. Starting to feel a bit chilled, he walked onto the tee of the first par-five on the golf course and came to a dead stop.

"That's when I knew," he said. "Right there, it hit me. It all came back."

The fourth tee at the Black is one of those magic golf places that golfers talk about forever. It isn't as scenic as the 18th tee at Pebble Beach or the ninth at Turnberry because there's no water any-where in sight. It isn't as daunting as the 17th at the TPC at Saw-grass or as historic as the Road Hole at St. Andrews.

But it is breathtaking, with Tillinghast's famous cross bunkers in front of you, an elevated fairway on the other side of them, and trees left and right to make you pay for a mistake. For a golf hole built in the 1930s, it stands up remarkably well to the technology of today. Even a perfect drive leaves a top player with decisions to make about how to play his second shot. That comes later, though. On the tee, one just stands there and pays homage to Tillinghast.

Now, Fay thought, I get it. Now I understand what Zahringer and Mottola are talking about. He walked the length of the fourth, glancing at all the trouble that loomed behind the green for an overly aggressive player, then walked back several steps to the fifth tee. Another signature hole, a difficult par-four with trouble left and right for any kind of wayward drive or second shot.

Fay is not an emotional or overly sentimental man. Having survived a serious bout with cancer at the age of thirty-six, he doesn't take anything about golf or his job all that seriously. The only sport that truly gets a rise out of him is baseball, his boyhood passion for the New York Yankees still intact. Now, though, he was excited.

By the time he reached the fifth green, it was almost dark, and he was in serious danger of being late for his party. Since the 12th hole runs directly behind the sixth tee, he made his way up 12, remembering it as one of the most difficult par-fours he had ever played. He crossed the road again and walked up 15 — another bear of a par-four — and then made his way back to the clubhouse. He took note of the natural amphitheater around the par-three 17th and remembered that 18 was not an overwhelming finishing hole. Still, he had seen enough.

"It was a long, long way from being anywhere close to reality," he said. "But I can remember getting back into the car thinking that this was doable. I mean, there were about a million ifs, but the potential was there. It *was* a great golf course. That's always going to be the ultimate question — is it a golf course worthy of a United States Open? If the answer's no, you walk away no matter what else may come into play. If the answer's yes, then you have to go and find out what else is in play. I knew there would be a lot to overcome.

"But I thought I knew the answer to the most important question: Was the Black a U.S. Open golf course? In my heart, I was absolutely convinced that day that the answer was yes."

2

Tony's Bridge

IF DAVID FAY had taken his walk around Bethpage Black in 1974 or even in 1984, he could have seen exactly the same golf course, been just as impressed, and yet, realistically, would have walked back to his car thinking, well, it might have been nice to put on an Open here, it's just not something we can do.

One of the reasons for that thinking would have been money. The USGA was a much smaller organization in the '70s and '80s than in the '90s or today, and even though it is nonprofit now as it was then, it simply didn't have the kind of funds available that it has now.

But money would not have been the most pressing issue. Until 1986, the USGA was in charge of the U.S. Open, but it only played a role in actually putting it on. The way it worked was this: The USGA would select a course to host an Open and reach an agreement with the club. Most contracts were straightforward: the USGA got 65 percent of the gate, the host club 35 percent plus any sales it made on clubhouse badges and most (87.5 percent) of the program sales. The USGA got all the TV revenue and concession money. The club pro would run the merchandising operation, and any profit was his to keep. The club appointed a general chairman from its membership, and he put together the various committees that ran the championship, ranging from marshals to player hospitality to housing for players, media, and officials.

In short, the USGA ran the Open inside the ropes, the host club ran it outside the ropes.

That began to change in the early 1980s. In 1978, the executive board had decided to shake up the leadership of its staff. The man in charge of the day-to-day operation at the time was P. J. Boatwright, a legendary golf figure who was far more interested in running golf championships than in being an administrator. Frank Hannigan by then had grown tired of office life and had arranged it so he still made the TV deals and played a major role in golf course selection but left the rest to others. His place as full-time assistant to the executive director had been taken by John Laupheimer. The board decided someone needed to be in charge, so it created the job of senior executive director. It gave the job to Harry Easterly, a former USGA president. Boatwright contented himself with running all the championships, and Hannigan continued in his part-time role.

Unfortunately, the new arrangement didn't work out. Easterly was fired early in 1983, and the board all but begged Hannigan to succeed him, which Hannigan agreed to do in return for a substantial raise. But before all that occurred, Easterly did get one of his dreams put into motion: Shinnecock.

Easterly had always been a huge fan of Shinnecock Hills, the revered links course on the eastern end of Long Island, which had history, tradition, and the sort of layout that would make it different from any other place where the Open had ever been contested. Shinnecock *had* hosted an Open — in 1896. The world had changed considerably since then. No one argued Shinnecock's pedigree or its ability to challenge the world's best players. In fact, the USGA had staged a Walker Cup there in 1977, and both Easterly and Hannigan had come away convinced Shinnecock was one of the great tests of golf anywhere in the world. But hosting an amateur team match between the U.S. and Great Britain and Ireland was one thing. Hosting a U.S. Open was quite another.

The problem was logistics. Shinnecock is a seasonal golf club, open only from April to October, with a membership that isn't around in the off-season. There was no central heating in the clubhouse. Most Shinnecock members considered it their second club, a summer playground they used while on vacation. That meant there was no membership base in place to form the committees necessary to run an Open. Easterly understood all this. So he went to Hannigan and said, "Isn't there *some* way to take an Open to Shinnecock?"

Hannigan's answer was a definite maybe. "We might be able to do it," he said, "if we ran the whole thing ourselves."

On March 2, 1981, Hannigan sent Easterly a ten-page single-spaced memo detailing exactly what would have to be done for the USGA to undertake an Open at Shinnecock. Hannigan had asked Fay, who was then the advance man on all USGA events, to do a detailed financial study of the 1980 Open, which had been held at Baltusrol in New Jersey, and compare it to how the finances would break down if the USGA went to a contract that was a straight rental with all risks and rewards falling in the lap of the USGA. Fay's conclusion was direct: We'll make money if we take over running the event. His conservative estimate was an extra $600,000 added to the bottom line. Armed with the Fay financial breakdown and the Hannigan memo detailing how each committee would be staffed, Easterly set up a meeting with Shinnecock board members. Offered the chance to host an Open with a guaranteed profit and almost no responsibility for the membership, Shinnecock accepted.

"Actually, the easy part was the staffing," Hannigan said, years later. "Volunteers are vastly overrated. It meant doing some juggling and moving people into jobs they hadn't done before. That wasn't hard. I had no doubt we could run the championship. The hard part was dealing with the politics of eastern Long Island."

Once Easterly and Hannigan had decided that the Open could be run in-house and sold the idea to Shinnecock, they had to sell it to the executive board. There was some skepticism, mostly about traffic and housing, but the board was willing to put Easterly and Hannigan out on a limb if they wanted to crawl out there. Shinnecock was offered a unique deal: the USGA would pay the club a straight rental fee of $400,000. Any profits — or losses — would be the USGA's. The club agreed.

Late in the fall of 1983, Hannigan, who had succeeded Easterly as senior executive director the previous winter, called Tony Zirpoli into his office. Zirpoli had been with the USGA as an administrator since 1980. Prior to coming to the USGA, Zirpoli had supplemented his income as a junior high school social studies teacher by caddying at a Long Island club called the Creek during summers and on weekends. One of the members he became friendly with there was Joseph C. Dey, who had once been the USGA's executive director. When things began to slide badly in the city school system in the late '70s, Zirpoli asked Dey if he knew anyone in golf who might help him find work. Dey sent him to P. J. Boatwright, who had succeeded Dey as the USGA's executive director in 1968, and Boatwright hired Zirpoli as an administrator working in the areas of amateur golf and public golf.

Hannigan wasn't the least bit interested in Zirpoli's skills as an administrator in either area when he called him into his office. "You're a Long Island guy," he said to him. "Take a drive out to Shinnecock and look around. Find out what we're going to have to do and who we're going to have to get to in order to do this."

Zirpoli understood. Although Hannigan didn't know it, he wasn't *just* a Long Island guy — he was a Long Island guy with connections. He and his family had been friendly for years with Joe Margiotta, the longtime chairman of the Republican Party in Nassau County. Even though Shinnecock was in Suffolk County, Margiotta would know who Zirpoli needed to connect with and could help him connect.

It helped, too, that Zirpoli was friends with Peter Smith, the golf course superintendent at Shinnecock. Smith wasn't just the superintendent at Shinnecock, he was a full-blooded Shinnecock Indian, and Hannigan knew that some of the parking that would be needed to put on the Open could be found on the Shinnecock Reservation.

So, shortly before Thanksgiving, Zirpoli took his Hannigan-ordered drive out Route 27 to Shinnecock. When he reported back to Hannigan he was straightforward: we need the college, we need the train station, and most important, we need a bridge.

The college in question was Southampton College, which was located directly across Route 27 from the golf club. There was also a train station there. The college could potentially be used for parking, as a staging area for shuttle buses, and if the Long Island Rail Road would cooperate, as a dropping off point for fans who would come by rail. All of that could probably be negotiated with the various groups in question. The problem then was getting them from Southampton or the train station across Route 27 to the golf course. Stopping traffic to let thousands of golf fans cross the one road that connected the Hamptons to most of the outside world was simply out of the question. There was only one answer — a bridge. "Get it done," Hannigan said.

Easier said than done. Margiotta was able to get Zirpoli to Suffolk County executive Peter Cohalan to plead his case. Cohalan had larger problems on his mind at the time than a bridge for the USGA, specifically the problems at the Shoreham Nuclear Power Station, which was ready to come on-line and produce a much-needed new power supply but was being held up by environmental protests. Cohalan told Zirpoli to take his plan to the Commissioner of Public Works. Zirpoli did. The answer he got back was direct: No.

Zirpoli knew that no wasn't going to fly with Hannigan and that without the bridge the number of tickets the USGA would be able to sell would probably be cut in half. Already, Hannigan was only planning to sell 14,500 tickets because of the potential housing and traffic problems. If the number went much lower than that, a financial disaster was possible.

Zirpoli knew that the USGA had no fallback position with only two years to go until the championship. But Cohalan didn't know that. Zirpoli was able to finally get a face-to-face meeting with Cohalan. "Without the bridge," he said, "we may not be able to hold the championship. It's that important."

Cohalan went back to his guy at Public Works. "Build it," he told him.

The bridge was built. It had to be twenty-seven feet high at its apex so it would go over the train station as well as Route 27. When it was completed, some friends of Zirpoli made a small sign that they placed at one end of it: The Tony Zirpoli Memorial Bridge.

"I didn't like the part," he said, "about it being a memorial."

Zirpoli was very much alive when the Open came to Shinnecock in 1986, and so was Hannigan. The other major hurdle was cutting a deal with the Shinnecocks on the parking. Even with the support of Smith, this wasn't easy, either. After one meeting, Zirpoli reported back to Hannigan that he had been personally blamed for 300 years of racial subjugation.

"He accepted the blame," Hannigan said, "and then got the deal done."

The event was a huge success. Hannigan didn't push the envelope too far, limiting ticket sales to 14,500 spectators daily. But that was more than enough to make the golf course look crowded and to ensure a considerable profit. Fans arrived by car, bus, and train. The bridge worked wonderfully, though most who used it never noticed the Zirpoli sign.

Most important, perhaps, almost everyone raved about the golf course, a true links setup unlike any other course the Open had been played on in the past. The players loved it. The fans loved it. TV loved it because it was so spectacularly visual. One of the few skeptics was four-time Open champion Jack Nicklaus, who was employed at the time as a part-time commentator for ABC. One of the reasons this arrangement existed was that Terry Jastrow, the executive producer of ABC's golf telecasts, was Nicklaus's partner in Nicklaus's TV production company.

Nicklaus was riding about as high as possible coming into the Open that year, having just pulled off his miraculous victory at the

Masters, becoming at age forty-six the oldest man in history to win the event. He didn't play poorly at Shinnecock — he finished tied for eighth — but was not as enamored of the golf course as most others were. Perhaps it had something to do with the fact that he lost a ball on the 10th hole on the first day — the first lost ball he could remember in his storied career. When he arrived in the ABC booth late Sunday for his stint, he told Jastrow and director Chuck Howard that he thought Shinnecock was overrated and intended to declare it a nice members course when asked about it on air.

To his everlasting credit, Jastrow immediately turned to Hannigan, who was also in the booth as the USGA liaison and rules expert, and asked him if he would like to debate Nicklaus on air on the merits of the golf course. Absolutely, Hannigan answered. At that point Nicklaus said, "Oh, let's just forget about it."

Raymond Floyd broke out of a remarkable eight-way tie on the back nine that afternoon and won the championship. Almost everyone talked about what a breakthrough it was to take the Open to a great links like Shinnecock and pull off the week with a minimum of logistical problems. Could the USGA have made more money by going to a more traditional venue, executing the old contract, and selling 25,000 tickets a day? Yes. But it still made a tidy profit at Shinnecock and was the toast of the golf world for going there.

The next day, at a USGA executive board meeting at the neighboring National Golf Links of America, the board voted a huge bonus package for the staff, to be distributed by Hannigan. When someone asked then-USGA president Bill Williams how the money would be divided up, Williams said, "That is strictly up to Frank."

"We found out," Fay said later, "that we could do a lot more ourselves than we had thought. And the more we did ourselves, the more freedom we had to try new things. And, potentially, down the road, there was the chance to make the Open bigger and better than it had ever been before."

And more profitable.

All of which would lead, eventually, to Bethpage.

Shinnecock was a breakthrough. The golf course was so good it was made a part of the informal Open rota forever, returning in 1995 and due to return again in 2004. In 1995, confident that the logistics were now controllable, the USGA paid the club $2 million in rent and sold 22,500 tickets a day. For 2004, the numbers will be $5 million and 25,000 people.

"Harry Easterly, who could not have successfully put on a two-car funeral, deserves credit for wanting to go to Shinnecock. The vision was his. The execution was mine — with considerable help from Zirpoli. They're getting five million bucks in '04. You would think, by now, the SOBs would have offered to make Tony and me honorary members, wouldn't you?"

As he spoke those words, Frank Hannigan giggled at both his audacity and lack of modesty. They are two of his more endearing traits. He loves to write, often sending long letters to friends describing his exploits and adventures. Sometimes he will break in while telling a story to say "Boy, was I good!" or to comment on the lack of education, social or literary, of one of his compatriots or competitors.

Hannigan turned seventy-one shortly before the Open came to Bethpage. He had left the USGA in 1989, but given that the work he had done at Shinnecock and his mentoring of David Fay played a large role in the event going there, one might have thought he would be on the grounds throughout the week, reveling in what he had wrought.

Not exactly.

"Background check!" he screamed when he learned that everyone with any kind of credential — staff, media, vendor — had to submit to a screening in the wake of 9/11. "I will *not* submit to a background check. I'm too damn old for that kind of crap. I'll stay home and watch it on TV. Background check, my ass."

Vintage Hannigan. To describe him as opinionated or obstreperous doesn't begin to do him justice. Curmudgeon, which gets close, is incomplete. He will tell you quite proudly that he would much rather spend an evening at a Broadway show than at Shinnecock or Pebble Beach and will then explain why the *least* important people at a United States Open Championship are the players.

"They played the thing before Hogan and after Hogan, before Nicklaus and after Nicklaus, and believe it or not, before Tiger Woods and someday after Tiger Woods," he will say. "Players, no matter how great, come and go. The championship lives on." And then, just to prove he isn't as eloquent as you might think, he will add, "Even if those stupid SOBs running the USGA do everything they can to fuck it up."

Hannigan grew up on Staten Island, the son of a shipyard electrician who later became a member of the New York State Assembly. His first connection to sports came through his maternal grandmother, a Polish immigrant who loved the Brooklyn Dodgers and took him by ferry to Ebbets Field where she rooted for the Dodgers — except when Stan Musial came to town with the Cardinals.

Frank was a good baseball player, the best twelve-year-old (in his humble opinion) on Staten Island, but by the time he was fourteen he had skipped three grades and was too small to compete with his older classmates. "The only reason I was a good student was because my mother told me the better I did in school, the less I would have to go," he said.

At fourteen, just when he was finding that baseball was passing him by, Hannigan's family moved into a house near Silver Lake, a municipal golf course that cost fifty cents to play. He began playing and working there, cutting the grass and cutting holes while hitting balls in his spare time.

"I was fascinated by the whole scene," he said. "I liked the golf, I liked working on the course, I liked the people I met there, so I spent a lot of time there."

After graduating from high school shortly after turning sixteen, he ended up at Wagner College. Wagner was on Staten Island and not a financial burden on his parents, especially since he lived at home and made the thirty-minute commute by bus to school every day. He got a degree in English — "worthless," he calls it now — and went to work at the local paper, *The Staten Island Advance*. He started in the pressroom, but thanks to his golf background was given the local golf beat when the paper's longtime golf writer died.

He combined that job with some publicity work at his alma mater and some writing for trade magazines for several years (stories on breakthroughs in *American Druggist* were a specialty). On New Year's Eve in 1960 he went to the old Madison Square Garden for the traditional triple-header that climaxed the then eight-team Holiday Festival. "Ohio State beat St. Bonaventure in the final," he remembered. "Double overtime. Great game."

On his way to the ferry that would take him home, he picked up an early *New York Times* in the ferry terminal and sat inside on the frigid winter night paging through the want ads, something he did on occasion. Under G was a small ad that said simply, Golf Editor Wanted. An employment agency's name, phone number, and address were listed. Two days later, Hannigan presented himself in person at the employment agency. Impressed, the man behind the desk sent him directly to a five-story limestone building at 40 East 38th Street, where he was instructed to see Mr. Dey.

Joseph C. Dey was then executive director of the USGA, and he needed someone to edit the USGA's bimonthly magazine; be curator of the small museum that was housed in the limestone building, and do a little public relations work, especially during the one championship that received serious media coverage, the U.S. Open. Back then, everyone at the USGA had more than one assignment, since there was a total of twenty employees. Today, there are close to three hundred.

Hannigan got the job at a salary of $7,500 a year but kept his golf-writing job with the *Advance* just in case things didn't work out. His first Open was that summer at Oakland Hills, outside

Detroit, the course where Ben Hogan had won in 1951 and famously declared, "I slayed the monster." Gene Littler, that year's champion, wasn't nearly as well known as Hogan, but Hannigan did get to meet one of his literary heroes, Herb Wind, who was still working for *Sports Illustrated* at the time. When Hannigan introduced himself to Wind, he complimented him on a piece he had written that winter on Boston Celtics guard Bob Cousy.

"You know your stuff," Wind told Hannigan. "That was a good piece."

A lifelong friendship was born on the spot.

By the following year, Hannigan had been named tournament relations manager, which is a fancy way of saying he advanced the USGA's events, getting to town early to help set up the golf course, find the needed volunteers, and deal with any and all logistics. In the case of the Open, that meant arriving on-site two months in advance. Three years later, several members of the PGA's Player Relations Committee approached him about coming over to run the tour. This was before the players had broken away from the PGA of America to form the PGA Tour, and Hannigan decided he didn't want to jump into that political mosh pit. Instead, he leveraged the PGA offer into a promotion to assistant executive director, a job he shared at the time with P. J. Boatwright. Three years later, when Dey left to become the first commissioner of the newly formed PGA Tour, Boatwright became the executive director and Hannigan was made his number two man.

The timing was perfect for Hannigan, who was now married — to Janet Carter, a graduate, as he proudly points out, of Yale Drama School — and had two young children. He was no longer an advance man. In fact, in 1965, he had been assigned to negotiate the Open's TV contract, which had been with NBC for several years. Hannigan managed to get ABC to commit $60,000 a year for five years, beginning in 1966. He also insisted that it be written into the contract that ABC's top two voices, Jim McKay and Chris Schenkel, would be part of the telecasts. It was the beginning of a twenty-nine-year relationship between the network and the USGA.

Hannigan's other big project as assistant director was moving the

USGA out of Manhattan. The five-story building on 38th Street was no longer big enough to house the rapidly growing organization, and prices in the city for real estate were oppressive. "I remember [then NFL commissioner] Pete Rozelle telling me you can't be a big-time organization unless you are headquartered in New York," Hannigan said. "I didn't buy it."

After a flirtation with Columbus, Ohio (where an insurance company was willing to give the USGA a golf course and the land for a new headquarters), Hannigan found — via a tip from the wife of the great course designer Robert Trent Jones — an old estate in Far Hills, New Jersey. The USGA purchased the estate and the grounds — sixty-two acres — for $450,000. It has since purchased the adjoining land — formerly owned by Cyrus Vance — and the building that was headquarters became the museum. Next to it is a sprawling four-story building that houses the current staff.

Hannigan almost left the USGA in 1978 when he didn't get the senior executive job but stayed on because he enjoyed doing the TV work — on camera and off — and because he had cut a deal that allowed him to work away from the office most of the time. When Easterly was fired, he was quickly offered the job and took it. He was a controversial figure during his six years on the job: outspoken, quick-witted, and different from what most people were used to in those who ran golf organizations.

Hannigan was a liberal Democrat in a world of conservative Republicans. To this day, he likes to point out that he has never voted for a Republican in his life and that Fay, also a Democrat, has. "He voted for [Senator Jacob] Javits when he lived in New York," Hannigan likes to say derisively.

"Guilty," admits Fay with a smile.

Hannigan and Fay became close friends during Hannigan's tenure. In spite of Fay's past political crimes, they had a similar view of the world; each was a little off center in his own way. Hannigan loves to quote literature, to the point where Fay often refers to him as Mencken Jr. Fay would rather quote Joe Torre, but both men have a similar view of golf and golfers: They respect both without revering either.

Fay came to the USGA in 1978 after two years as communications director for the Metropolitan Golf Association, a job he found after a brief, unproductive and — his word — boring career as an investment counselor. In 1979, shortly after he and his fiancée, Joan McAnaney, had set their wedding date for early June, Fay found out he had been promoted to Hannigan's old tournament relations job — meaning he would be leaving for Toledo right after his wedding to advance that year's U.S. Open at the Inverness Club.

When Joan learned where her husband was going right after the wedding, she insisted on making a change in the wedding announcement that was to run in the local newspapers in Westchester. The last line of the announcement read, "The couple will honeymoon in Toledo."

The marriage survived northwest Ohio and two years of USGA advance work before Fay, for all intents and purposes, threatened to quit if he wasn't taken off the road. Eventually, Hannigan promoted him to assistant executive director, passing over several more experienced people to do so, and quietly began grooming him to take his place.

All of that hit a major snag late in 1985 when Fay was diagnosed with Burkitt's lymphoma, an unusual and aggressive form of stomach cancer. Since Burkitt's is often found in those of West African descent, Fay has often kidded that getting the disease was certainly a difficult way to learn that he may have had ancestors from the Ivory Coast. But the disease itself was no joke. Fay spent most of six months in a New Jersey hospital, large chunks of that period in isolation. It was a scary time. He was thirty-six, with daughters who were four and two. Hannigan, who gets queasy whenever he sets foot in a hospital, forced himself to visit on several occasions. He hated being there, he hated the way the chemo made Fay look, and he hated thinking about what the possible outcome of the illness might be.

Fay's goal was to get out of the hospital in time for Shinnecock. The doctors had told him they thought the disease had been caught early enough so that with very aggressive treatment he could beat it. More than anything else, Fay's concern during that period was about what would happen to Joan, Katie, and Molly if he wasn't around.

"I'm not a big sentimentalist or anything," he said. "I don't sit around and say I'm blessed by this or blessed by that. But I wanted to live, and I wanted to be healthy."

He did both. He left the hospital the day before the Open began at Shinnecock. A week later he was back. He had left too soon and he got sick again immediately — a fever attacked his weakened immune system. That meant another month in the hospital. He got out in July in time for the girls' junior championships in Marysville, California, having lost a total of forty-five pounds. But this time he was out for good. He spent the week in Marysville eating Mexican food and ice cream and put sixteen pounds back on in seven days.

Three years later, Hannigan, having seen the Open at Shinnecock and his other prized location — the Country Club in Brookline, Massachusetts — decided he'd had enough of USGA politics. He accepted an offer to work at ABC full time, both as a writer and an on-air rules expert, and also made a deal to write for *Golf Magazine*. There were some on the executive committee who wanted to go outside the organization to hire his replacement. The headhunter that had been hired was pushing Tom Butters, the athletic director at Duke, who was a whiz at fund-raising. Hannigan still had the ear of people on the executive committee, though, and he insisted Fay should get the job.

Fay was chosen to succeed Hannigan early in 1989. He was completely recovered from the cancer, and he had a lot of ideas about changing the organization. And, based on what he had seen at Shinnecock, a lot of ideas about changing the U.S. Open.

3

As Easy as . . . NBC

ALMOST FROM THE beginning, one of the keys to the USGA–New York State marriage was money. The USGA was willing to make enough of a financial commitment to the state that Governor George Pataki, facing an ongoing budget crisis, could easily make the case that the coming of the Open to Bethpage was a low-risk venture with huge potential as a moneymaker for the state parks system.

One of the reasons the USGA could make that sort of financial commitment was that it was flush. Even though it is a 501(c)3 non-profit, tax-exempt organization, the USGA has increased in size and in revenue flow by leaps and bounds during the last twenty years. A quick look at the size of the staff is a tip-off to how the USGA has grown: in 1982, the first year anyone even bothered to keep a record, the USGA had 102 employees around the country. In 1990, that number had grown to 160. By 2000, the number was at 283 — and counting.

"When I first came on board in 1990, we didn't have a single lawyer working for us," said Mark Carlson. "If we needed something done, we went to outside counsel or got a board member who was a lawyer to do it for us. Now, we have seven lawyers. Seven!"

"And we need every single one of them," David Fay says quickly when the subject comes up.

According to Fay, one of the people responsible for the USGA's financial growth in the late twentieth and early twenty-first centuries is Carlson. A small-town kid from western Pennsylvania who grew up in the shadow of Penn State, Carlson, who is now fifty-five, is passionate about Florida State football (he was the school's sports information director for seven years); the Final Four (he worked at CBS for eight years); and protecting the interests of the USGA and the USGA's TV partners (i.e., the networks that pay the USGA millions of dollars a year). He has a round face, white hair, and the easy smile and outgoing nature of a lifelong public relations man — which he is. Carlson joined the USGA thirteen years ago, about a week, he figures, before he was going to be let go by CBS Sports, where he had been the head of the PR department.

Back then, working with the USGA's TV network, ABC, was a part of the PR department's job. There really wasn't that much to do. ABC had owned the USGA contract since 1966, and every few years, Sandy Tatum, an ex-USGA president, would fly in from his law offices in San Francisco, spend some time with the folks from ABC, and emerge with a new three- or four-year deal. Occasionally, someone inside the organization would raise the specter of putting the contract out for bid to CBS and NBC, but the idea would die very quickly and ABC would re-up again.

"It was very easy and very cozy," Fay said. "But we were getting to the point where I was pretty sure it wasn't the best thing in the world for us."

Shortly after Carlson's arrival at Golf House, Fay decided to free him of most of his PR duties and let him focus on television since he had network experience. ABC's contract was due to expire at the end of 1994, and Fay wanted Carlson to put together a memo exploring the best way to maximize the USGA's TV package.

At that point ABC was paying about $8 million annually for the rights to all USGA properties. The important one, of course, was the Open, but it also televised the Senior Open and the Women's

Open, and farmed the U.S. Amateur out to ESPN. "But the package wasn't really worth $8 million, because we were still paying all the production costs on everything except the last two days of the Open," Carlson said. "When you added that in, we were netting about $5 million from the package."

Carlson eventually presented Fay with a fifty-six-page memo that was part history, part number crunching, and part battle plan. His conclusion, when Fay finally waded through all the paper, was direct: put this thing out to bid.

Fay and Carlson knew that getting a serious bid from CBS was unlikely. The network already owned the rights to two majors — the Masters and the PGA — but more importantly probably would not want to do anything that might possibly upset the Lords of Augusta, who always insisted on one-year contracts and kept CBS on a very short leash, knowing how important their product was to the network. Coming on the heels of CBS losing the NFL, there was almost no way the network was going to risk losing the Masters for what was no better than a one-in-three shot to get the Open.

"Which meant," Carlson said, "the other player in the game almost certainly had to be NBC."

For many years, golf had not really been a priority at NBC. It hadn't owned the rights to a major championship since the early 1960s, when it televised the Open before ABC took over the rights in 1966. NBC golf was just this side of hit-and-giggle for most of the 1970s and 1980s, with the Bob Hope Desert Classic usually the centerpiece of its golf coverage. Once the baseball game of the week began in April, golf was nothing more than a four-letter word to NBC.

"Almost everyone who did golf on NBC did it as a second sport," said Tommy Roy, now NBC's executive producer. "A lot of the announcers were pro athletes from other sports, like Bob Trumpy and Tom Seaver. It just wasn't a big deal."

That had started to change when NBC first began televising the Players Championship, an event that then-PGA commissioner Deane Beman (and his successor, Tim Finchem) insisted be treated by the network as if it were a major. It also began to change when the network hired Johnny Miller as its top golf analyst in 1991. Miller was completely different from anyone else who had ever sat in a tower behind the 18th green. His golfing pedigree — twenty-four titles, including wins in both the U.S. and British Opens — was impeccable. But unlike almost every other ex-player who had ever strapped on a microphone, Miller wasn't still trying to be one of the boys. He first-guessed shots, second-guessed shots, and used the dreaded "choke" word on the air.

By the end of his first year, Miller was an absolute, complete hit with golf fans because he told them exactly what he was thinking and they loved it. He was also ready to quit.

"I couldn't believe how angry I made the guys," he said. "I mean, they saw me as some kind of a traitor. All I was trying to do was be true to the shot. If a guy hit a bad shot, I didn't just say bad shot, I tried to explain what he needed to do to make it a good shot. I remember [past PGA champion and longtime commentator] Dave Marr once saying that he was being paid good money to gild the lily on the air. Well, I guess the way I looked at it was that in any great recipe you need some tart berries to mix with the sweet, sugary syrup."

Miller got people's attention right away when, on the last hole of that year's Bob Hope, he speculated about the possibility of his good friend Peter Jacobsen choking as he stood over a difficult second shot with a one-shot lead on the 18th hole on Sunday. "He had a downhill lie, trying to hit a high shot over water, with the tournament on the line," Miller said. "I just commented this was the kind of situation in which guys sometimes choke.

"The next thing I know, Peter, one of my best friends on tour, doesn't speak to me for six months. Finally, late in the fall, he walks up to me somewhere and says, 'You know, I finally saw the tape of the Hope, and you didn't say anything wrong. People told me you said I was going to choke. You didn't say that.' You see, that was part of the problem. Guys were hearing bits and pieces of what I was saying from friends or wives and not the whole thing. Even so, by the end of the year my attitude was, I don't need this. If I'm pissing everybody off, I'll just go home."

So Miller told NBC he wouldn't be coming back the next year. Thanks for the memories.

The next day, NBC Sports president Dick Ebersol flew out to Napa to meet with Miller. "I had plans for what I thought we could become in golf," Ebersol said. "The Ryder Cup had become huge, and I knew as soon as I could free Tommy Roy up [from the NBA] and put him on golf, we would improve in leaps and bounds. But I needed Johnny to be part of the package."

Miller was surprised by how ardently Ebersol argued that he had to return. "I was just an announcer," he said. "And golf wasn't a big thing with NBC. But he kept saying I had to come back. He made it sound like the network would go bust if I didn't come back. I guess that's what makes a good salesman."

"Yup," Ebersol says with a smile. "I was definitely selling that day."

Miller came back. And a year later, in 1993, Roy became the network's golf producer. "Tommy's like a mad professor in the truck," Miller said. "But that's because he loves golf so much."

With good reason. The son of a club pro, Roy had grown up in Tucson, Arizona, surrounded by the game, though he never played seriously until he was sixteen because, in his view, "golf wasn't cool."

His attitude changed when he figured out as a high school junior that he probably wasn't destined for the NBA, the NFL, or the major leagues. Once he began working seriously at the game, he quickly became a top junior player.

"I started playing well a little too late to be seriously recruited by any of the major programs," he said. "I could have gone to junior college, but I decided to stay home and go to Arizona, even though I knew it had one of the top programs in the country and walking onto the team would be difficult. I figured at worst I'd still get to play a lot."

Which he did — though not on the golf team. As a sophomore,

he volunteered to work at the Tucson Open, which was televised by NBC. When he reported for work, he was offered one of two jobs: work in a bar out on the golf course selling drinks or work as a runner for the NBC cameramen, bringing them coffee and donuts and whatever else they needed. "A friend of mine had done that the year before and he told me they gave him a really nice rental car to drive around in all week and a big tip when the tournament was over," Roy said. "So I took the NBC job."

By the weekend, the NBC people realized that Roy could be helpful in the truck. He knew all the players on sight, which made him an ideal spotter. At the conclusion of the tournament, the NBC production people were impressed enough with his work that they asked him to come and work at the Bob Hope the following week. A week later, they asked him to stay on for the rest of their golf season. That meant dropping out of school, which he did, much to the dismay of his parents.

"I was absolutely hooked," he said. "That week was right after all the big college bowl games, and in those days NBC had the Orange Bowl and the Rose Bowl and the Fiesta Bowl, and all the techs who came to work in Tucson showed up wearing gear from all the bowl games and talking about this coach or that coach or something that had happened during the game. The next week a lot of them were going to the AFC Championship game and then the Super Bowl after that. Plus, I was on the inside, really on the inside, at a golf tournament. I just thought it was the coolest thing I'd ever seen. Right then, I knew when I got out of college this was what I wanted to do — work for a TV network. I had no real clue exactly what I wanted to do, I just knew I wanted to be involved that way."

Roy returned to school in the fall, but that winter NBC came back to Tucson and again offered Roy work for its entire West Coast swing. Again, he said yes and dropped out. He eventually made it back long enough to get his degree in 1981, but he was locked in with NBC long before he graduated.

"Actually, my first summer after graduation, they sent me to

Europe to help out producing the Tour de France," he said. "By the time it was over, the baseball players were getting ready to go on strike, and with no game of the week, they were desperate for programming, so they just left me over there to do various events out of Europe the rest of the summer. It was a great learning experience."

Roy quickly became a fast-track guy on the production end at NBC Sports. The only thing that slowed him down was golf — his golf. He had continued to be a serious amateur player through college and after college and kept improving, especially when he played competitively.

"For a long time I was a good player with a penchant for choking," he said. "Whether it was in a money match with friends or in some kind of tournament, I tended to choke when it mattered most. But that began to change in my twenties. Part of it, believe it or not, may have been working in TV. When you're in the truck doing live TV, you're under the gun all the time, making decisions or getting things done, and you really can't choke. You just have to do it. Coincidence or not, after I started working TV full-time, I began to become a much better player under pressure."

By the summer of 1986, what had started as a pipe dream in the far reaches of his brain had become something he wanted to at least give a shot: trying to make it to the PGA Tour. "Long shot, absolutely a long shot," he said. "But I thought I was still young enough — twenty-seven — to give it a try. So I went in and told Mike Weisman that I was going to leave NBC and see what I could do."

Weisman, who was then the network's sports executive producer, wished Roy the best and told him if things didn't work out, there would be a place waiting for him at NBC. That was nice to hear, but even if Weisman hadn't said it, Roy's mind was made up. He worked out a deal with Raycom, a Charlotte, North Carolina–based syndicator, to produce Pacific-10 football games for them that fall. That would allow him to be based on the West Coast, in a warm-weather venue. The plan was to work on his game hard for a year, then try Qualifying School in the fall of 1987.

He never got that far.

A couple of weeks after leaving NBC, he was driving home from a party in Tucson one night after a couple drinks too many when he decided to roll open the roof of the 280Z he was driving. "It was something I did all the time without any problem," he said, "when I was sober."

This time, as he reached back to pull the roof open, his arm got stuck and his shoulder was wrenched painfully, so painfully that he was fortunate to be able to pull his arm down and get the car pulled over without doing any further damage. He had torn muscles in his shoulder. The doctors told him he had two options: surgery, which would mean no golf for at least six to eight months, or rehab, which meant no golf for at least six to eight months.

Hearing about the accident, Weisman called to let Roy know the door at NBC was still open. Roy quickly accepted the offer to return and as he started his rehab sessions jumped right back onto the NBC fast track. When NBC outbid CBS for the rights to the NBA in 1990, Ebersol and Terry O'Neil, who had succeeded Weisman as executive producer, made him the coordinating producer for the NBA package at the tender age of thirty-one. The only disappointing part of the promotion was that it meant not doing golf, since the basketball season ran concurrent with NBC's golf schedule.

"I loved doing the basketball," Roy said. "But I really missed the golf. It's in my blood."

Ebersol knew that and always planned to move Roy back to golf. In fact, in his pitch to Miller in the fall of 1991, he mentioned that he had plans to improve NBC's still weak golf coverage and that part of the plan was to move "this kid," as he called Roy, back to the golf package as producer within a year or two. Ebersol made that move in 1993, and Roy was delighted. That summer, he got a call from Ebersol one day saying he urgently needed to see him that afternoon.

"I had absolutely no clue what it could possibly be about," he said.

It was about Terry O'Neil. According to Ebersol, he had offered O'Neil a new contract, they had agreed on it, and then NBC had won the rights to the Atlanta Olympics. "Terry wanted more money because we'd gotten Atlanta," Ebersol said. "I thought I had done very well by him and told him this was the deal, take it or leave it. He left it."

Which was why Ebersol called Roy. Even though Roy was still just thirty-four and no one that young had ever been the executive producer for a network's sports division, Ebersol was convinced he was the right man to replace O'Neil. Roy walked into Ebersol's fifteenth-floor office at 30 Rockefeller Plaza at three o'clock on a Thursday afternoon as a golf producer and walked out as the network's executive producer.

Sort of.

"Tommy's first reaction was that he didn't want to do it," Ebersol remembered. "He loved working in the truck, he thought he was too young, he wasn't sure he was ready to deal with everything that came with the job. I knew he could do it and I wanted him to do it. When he left, I had him talked into it."

Roy did agree that afternoon to take the job. He called his wife, Anne, whom he had first met when he worked at NBC as a college student during the summer and she worked there as a page, and told her he might be a little late getting to the Jimmy Buffett concert they had tickets for that night at Jones Beach. After he had given her the news, he settled in to watch the concert.

"At some point that night, I decided I didn't want the job," he said. "I appreciated Dick's faith in me, I understood the opportunity, but I just didn't think I wanted to do it."

The next morning, Roy went straight in to see Ebersol to tell him he had changed his mind. As he had done with Miller two years earlier, Ebersol went into his salesman routine. The magic worked again. He convinced Roy that not only was he the man to be executive director but that there was no reason why he couldn't continue to produce golf for as long as he saw fit. That helped. More than anything, Roy just wasn't ready to give up the truck.

"It's like a drug to me," he said. "I love being in there, making decisions, figuring out what to do next. I didn't want to leave it behind, at least not then."

As soon as Roy had reagreed to take the job, Ebersol walked him out of his office, down the circular stairs that led to his office, and into the common area at the foot of the steps. He called everyone on the staff together and announced that Roy was the new executive producer.

"I wasn't going to give him a chance to change his mind again," Ebersol said.

All of Ebersol's sales work — convincing Miller to stay; getting Roy in place as his golf producer and executive producer; and the hiring of golfers like Roger Maltbie, Mark Rolfing, Gary Koch, and later, Bob Murphy, as announcers — set up the phone call in March 1994 that would change life at the USGA — and at NBC — forever.

It was the opening morning at the Players Championship in March 1994, and Jon Miller — no relation to Johnny Miller — was sitting in his hotel room getting some work done before heading over to the NBC trucks to monitor that afternoon's telecast. Miller is NBC's senior vice president for programming, a role in which he does most of the nuts-and-bolts negotiating when NBC acquires the rights to televise events, whether they be the Olympics, the NBA, or rodeo.

Miller's phone rang and he picked up, expecting it to be someone calling from across the street where the tournament was being held. Instead, he heard an unfamiliar voice introducing himself as Mark Carlson, head of broadcasting for the USGA. Miller had no idea who Carlson was, which was apt, since Carlson had no idea who Miller was.

"I had been a CBS guy, " he said. "I knew no one at NBC. Someone told me Jon Miller was the place to start a dialogue with NBC."

Carlson explained to Miller that the USGA's TV package was coming up for bid in a couple of months, that the contract with ABC was up at the end of 1994. Would NBC be interested, he asked, in bidding on the package?

Miller was taken aback by the out-of-the-blue question. He knew that ABC had owned the rights to the U.S. Open forever. He also knew that Arthur Watson, who had been president of NBC Sports in the '80s, had made an attempt to bid on the package and had gotten nowhere.

"I'm going to have to get back to you," he told Carlson. "I'll need to talk to Dick [Ebersol] and see how he feels. My guess is he won't want to deal with it until we're back in New York next week."

"Fine," Carlson said. "I'll wait to hear from you."

Still unsure exactly what was going on, Miller headed over to the trucks a few minutes later and found Ebersol. "Call the guy back right away," Ebersol said. "And tell him we're extremely interested."

Ebersol and Miller both had to consider the possibility that NBC was being used as a stalking horse to get ABC to up the ante on the rights fee. But Ebersol was just as convinced that NBC had to take its best shot at any opening that might lead to his network getting its hands on a major championship.

Two weeks later, on the day before that year's Masters began, Ebersol, Miller, Tommy Roy, and an NBC lawyer named Gary Zinkel met in San Francisco with Sandy Tatum and Carlson.

Carlson had already briefed the NBC Four on how important Tatum would be in the process. It wasn't just that he had negotiated with ABC through all the years, but his closeness to the ABC people. "I think [ABC golf producer] Terry Jastrow thought of himself as being like a son to Sandy," Carlson said. "Which is why no one there ever really thought we'd go anyplace else with the package."

Each network would submit a sealed bid, complete with an unsigned contract. The USGA would then decide which one to accept. No negotiating, no counteroffers. "I thought that was important to make it clear to the other networks that we were serious about giving everyone a fair chance," Carlson said. "Sandy was opposed to the idea because he loved to negotiate. But eventually David [Fay] and [USGA president] Reg Murphy agreed this was the way to go."

Carlson had also contacted his old friends at CBS. He knew from his own experience there that they would be convinced, regardless of how the bidding was to be handled, that they were being used to get ABC to come up with more money.

"We had gone after the Open the last time [1989] when I was still at CBS," Carlson said. "I remember Neal Pilson [then the president of CBS Sports] telling me there was no doubt we were a stalking horse — and he was right. Plus, after what had happened the last time, they weren't going to risk upsetting the folks at Augusta on a bid they didn't think they could win anyway."

Carlson's understanding of his old network proved accurate. After initially agreeing to fly to San Francisco for a similar meeting with Tatum, the CBS people had pulled out, saying simply, "This isn't for us."

So, as Carlson had suspected, the race would be between NBC and ABC.

"I honestly didn't know if we had a real chance at it or not," Ebersol said. "But we were going to go after it with everything we had, and I knew we had to put a lot of money on the table to convince them how serious we were. I went to [GE chairman and CEO] Jack Welch and told him I thought this could be a very important package for us. I pointed out that the first three Opens we would do if we got the package would be in New York, Detroit, and Washington — the financial center of the country, the hub of the automobile industry, and the center of government and diplomacy for the country and the world. Places where you could really do some big-time corporate business in addition to the golf tournament.

"I had put together a bid that was three years at $12 million a year, with options for two more years. He looked at it and said, 'You're low, add $1 million a year.' So I did."

The final step in the process came in late May. On the Wednesday before Memorial Day, Fay, Tatum, and Carlson went to ABC's offices in Manhattan and met with Dennis Swanson, who was their sports president, executive producer Dennis Lewin, and Jastrow and Jim Jennett, the producer and director of the golf package. They listened to them talk about the tradition built through twenty-nine years, the presence that men like Jim McKay and Peter Alliss brought to the telecasts, and how important the USGA was to them.

The next morning they had a similar meeting at 30 Rock with the same foursome who had met with Tatum and Carlson in San Francisco. This time, though, NBC had brought an extra person to the meeting: Johnny Miller.

Ebersol had asked Miller to fly in to talk to the USGA threesome about what it would mean to him personally to broadcast the U.S. Open. Miller had grown up as a U.S. Open kid, someone who, when he was playing with his dad, would end the day by saying, "This putt is to win the U.S. Open." He had gone on to win the Open in 1973 at Oakmont by shooting a historic 63 on the final day.

Miller talked about what the Open had meant to him as a boy, its role in his relationship with his father and, later, with his own sons. He talked about what it meant to win it and how much he would love to broadcast it. As he spoke, he became more and more emotional, finally breaking down.

"It wasn't as if we were going to hand the rights to NBC because Johnny started to cry," Fay said later. "But it certainly got our attention, especially Sandy's."

"I get emotional a lot," Miller said. "I certainly didn't go in there intending for that to happen. I *did* really want us to get the Open. A lot of people had said to me through the years, Hey, you're a good announcer, but what are you announcing that really matters? When I started to talk about the Open and all those memories flooded back, I just lost it."

The meeting broke up at about ten-thirty. Both ABC and NBC had been asked to have their bids ready at one P.M.

Fay, Tatum, and Carlson left NBC but stayed in Rockefeller Center for lunch. While they ate, Tatum suggested they all pick a network and a number. "By then, I was really getting nervous," Carlson said. "I mean, if we had gone through all of this and the number didn't go up considerably, I was going to look pretty bad. I went low — I think I picked $9 million and ABC."

Fay took $10 million and NBC.

Tatum, who had been the skeptic at the start, went for $11 million and NBC.

By the time they had finished dessert, Carlson was shaking with nerves and anticipation. The three separated, Tatum going to the nearby offices of McKinsey and Company, where USGA board member Ron Daniels was a partner. He had reserved a conference room for them. Carlson went back across the street to NBC to pick up their bid. Fay went to ABC. The ABC people had already picked Carlson out as the bad guy in the process, so Fay decided it was best if he went back there.

Carlson arrived first, holding the NBC envelope. He and Tatum waited for Fay before opening it. Shortly before two, Fay walked in with ABC's bid. "I still remember Swanson handing me the envelope and saying, 'We worked really hard to make this right for you guys,' " Fay said. "I thought, Okay, we'll see."

They opened ABC's envelope first, since they were the rights holder. Carlson had, as it turned out, called their bid almost perfectly: a little less than $9 million per year for four years. Then they opened the NBC envelope, and there it was: $13 million a year for three years, with USGA options for the next two years, meaning the USGA without any further negotiation or bidding was guaranteed at least $65 million for five years. The number of hours that would be telecast was increased, not only for the Open but for the other USGA events as well.

"Jackpot," Carlson said.

"It was an absolute no-brainer at that point," Fay said. "If we had not accepted the NBC bid, we would have failed to meet our fiduciary responsibility to the organization."

They decided to wait until the end of the upcoming three-day weekend before going public with what had happened. The only other person brought into the loop at that point was Murphy, the USGA president, who was overnighted both offers.

All of which made the NBC people crazy.

"The last thing they said on Thursday morning was, 'We'll let you know when we have a decision,'" Jon Miller said. "The message was pretty clear: Don't call us, we'll call you. But all weekend Dick kept calling me, saying, 'What do you think? Is the delay good for us or bad for us? It must mean they're at least thinking about us, right?' Finally, I called Mark, looking for a hint or *something*. I couldn't get a thing out of him."

On Tuesday morning, the executive committee quickly voted to accept NBC's offer. Tatum was dispatched to call Dennis Swanson to officially give him the news. "One of the most difficult things I ever had to do," he said. "I knew they would be devastated."

Shortly after that, Fay called Ebersol to tell him. The celebrating at NBC soon began. "It was a giant breakthrough for us," Ebersol said. "It made us a big-time player in golf because it meant we had two of the three most important events in the game: the Open and the Ryder Cup."

The reaction at ABC was a mixture of shock and anger. When Carlson arrived three weeks later at Oakmont for that year's Open, someone from ABC took him aside and quietly told him that it would be better if he stayed away from the ABC compound that week.

By the end of the week, the acrimony between ABC and the USGA was off the charts, in large part because of a rules incident the last day that would prove to be the beginning of the end of the friendship between Fay and Frank Hannigan. How angry was Fay with ABC at that point?

"Put it this way," he said. "If NBC had come to us after the '94 Open and said, 'You know, we've changed our mind, we just can't do this,' I'd have given the rights to the Home Shopping Network before I would have gone back to ABC."

NBC wasn't about to pull out. The deal was done. Now, the USGA was wealthier than it had ever been, armed with the kind of money it had never had in the past. The kind of money that helped make the renovation of Bethpage Black possible.

4

"I Have a Dream"

DAVID FAY DIDN'T linger in the Bethpage parking lot after his walk on that November afternoon in 1994. It was dark by the time he walked off the 18th green, and he was late for the dinner party that had brought him to Long Island in the first place. On the drive over, his brain was racing, turning over what he had just seen and wondering, as he put it later, "if I was completely out of my mind."

There was only one way to find the answer to that question, and that was to ask other people. Fay isn't exactly certain what he did next. In his memory, he composed a memo that he sent to several trusted staff members. According to Fay, the memo began with the words, "I have a dream." He then went on to outline his thoughts on Bethpage and his belief that the Black Course might — *might* — be a place where a U.S. Open could be staged. According to Fay, he sent the memo to at least two people: Mike Butz and Mike Davis. Butz is Fay's number two man, the assistant executive director. Davis is the day-to-day point man for the Open, technically the tournament director.

If Fay sent the memo, neither Butz nor Davis nor any of the other people he may have sent it to can remember it in any detail. None of them have the memo in their files, and Butz and Davis are notoriously careful record keepers. Fay claims the memo exists somewhere in the closet in the corner of his office. Finding something in that closet would be only slightly more difficult than finding the lost city of Atlantis.

So there may or may not have been an "I Have a Dream" memo. "Maybe I dreamed it," Fay said, laughing. "But I swear I remember writing it."

What Butz and Davis do remember, memo or no memo, is a day when Fay walked into each of their offices and shut the door. "By itself, that tells you something is up," Butz said. "David is not a closed-door guy. It has to be something important for him to close the door."

This *was* important. Fay told both his lieutenants what he was thinking. Butz and Davis both grew up in Chambersburg, Pennsylvania. Both were — and are — low-handicap players. Neither of them knew very much about Bethpage Black.

"I had heard about it," Davis said. "I knew there was a state park out there on Long Island that we went past on the way to Shinnecock with a bunch of courses and that one of them was a Tillinghast with a great reputation but that it was very badly run down. That was it. If I hadn't studied a lot of golf course architecture I wouldn't have known anything about it at all."

What he did know put him well ahead of Butz. "I had no idea what David was talking about," he said. "I had never heard of the place."

Fay explained the history of the golf course to them and explained that it was in a public park that had five golf courses in all. That would make the logistics very workable. Still, the golf course was beaten up and to go there would mean dealing with the state of New York. Fay had no idea how that would work out. George Pataki was about to succeed Mario Cuomo as governor, so there was no way to get a read on who they might be dealing with in a new administration.

"He understood there were a lot of hurdles involved," Davis said. "But you could see he was excited. David doesn't get excited about that many things. When he does, it gets your attention."

Once he had clued his staff to what he was thinking, Fay thought the next step was to let them see what he was talking about. Even before he did that, Fay placed a phone call to Richard Spear, the golf course superintendent at Piping Rock, a private club on Long Island that wasn't that far from Bethpage.

Spear and Fay had first become friends when Spear worked at another nearby club, Plandome, in the 1980s. A college classmate of Fay's was a member, and Fay often played there with him. Spear was a very good player and had been a professional briefly before deciding to concentrate on, as superintendents put it, turf. He was also bright and funny, the kind of person Fay enjoyed spending time with. Fay could also see, first at Plandome, then at Piping Rock, that Spear knew his business.

"I want you to do me a favor," Fay told Spear. "Take a drive over to Bethpage and look at the Black. Don't say anything to anyone. I know the golf course is in awful condition. But I want you to look at it and tell me, if the money was spent, if, agronomically, it can be a great golf course again."

Spear knew enough about Bethpage to believe, without looking, that the answer to Fay's question was yes. But he agreed to go over, take a closer look, and get back to Fay.

"If Richard had called me back and said, 'No way, you just can't do it,' that would have been the end of it," Fay said. "I trusted him implicitly, especially as someone who understood Long Island agronomically from having been there so long."

When Spear called Fay back, his report was brief and to the point. "There is absolutely no question," he said, "that if the money is there, this can be a great golf course again."

That was what Fay expected to hear. It was also what he wanted to hear.

Fay claims that the legendary I Have a Dream memo contained a suggestion that they all drive to the Black before dawn one morning, sleep in their cars, and play the golf course, hoping to get in and out unannounced and unnoticed.

That was not the way it happened. Fay ended up putting together a group of twelve people for the trip to the Black. In addition to himself, Butz, Davis, and Spear, he invited Tim Moraghan, who is the USGA's tournament agronomist; Rees Jones, the architect known as "the Open Doctor"; David Eger, who was in charge of rules and competition and was the best player on staff; Tom Meeks, also a key rules and competition person; Tony Zirpoli; Brett Avery, who runs publications for the USGA and is also an excellent player; Fay's old pal Jay Mottola; and Rabbi Marc Gellman.

The person who would seem to least belong among the twelve was Gellman. Gellman, along with Father Tom Hartman, is half of the now-famous God Squad. They host their own syndicated TV show and have become well known for their appearances on the nationally syndicated *Imus in the Morning* radio show. Gellman and Fay had become friends through the years, often running into each other at charity banquets and dinners.

Gellman was also an avid golfer, a six-handicapper who played Bethpage often and, like a lot of those who frequent the course, had come to see the Black as an almost mystical place. "It was dying, though," he said. "It was becoming a black hole because the state of New York not only wasn't putting money into Bethpage, it was taking the money Bethpage made and putting it into other park projects around the state."

Gellman had come to Long Island more than twenty years earlier, after growing up in Milwaukee. He had learned to play on municipal courses around Milwaukee and became a good player, the captain of his high school team as a senior. It was during that senior year that he had a revelation which, he says, changed his life.

"Sandy Koufax not pitching the first game of the World Series because it fell on Yom Kippur," he said. "I found that inspiring. I was trying to decide what I wanted to do with myself. Koufax showed me you could be committed spiritually and morally and still be part of the real world, have connections and commitments."

Gellman went to the University of Wisconsin, where he concentrated in Hebrew and Semitic studies. He spent his senior year in Israel and was ordained a rabbi in 1971. He was a chaplain at Northwestern, where he got a Ph.D. in philosophy and medical ethics. "Eventually, I realized that if you're going to be a serious rabbi, you have to know more than Milwaukee and Chicago," he said. "A serious Jew has to confront New York City at some point."

He landed in Teaneck, New Jersey, for three years before moving to Temple Beth Torah in Melville, a few miles from Bethpage. By this time it was 1982, and Gellman hadn't touched a golf club since the 1965 Wisconsin high school state championships. "I was in Herman's World of Sporting Goods one day buying a soccer ball for my son," he said. "All of a sudden, I heard the golf clubs talking to me. It was like Circe and the Sirens calling out to Ulysses in the *Odyssey*. They were telling me it was time to try golf again."

Rather than set out on a boat to sail around the world, Gellman got in his car, drove two exits down the Long Island Expressway to Round Swamp Road, and presented himself to Joe Rehor, the longtime pro at Bethpage. Rehor took him out for a lesson. "I hit one five-iron, high, true, and perfect," Gellman said. "I was back."

All the way back, waking up predawn to get on the car line to play both the Black and the almost-as-difficult Red Course. His handicap got down to as low as four, and Bethpage became his second temple. He worshiped there, too, albeit in a different way.

By 1986, Gellman was restless again. He had an offer to move to a temple in Miami, another of those places a Jew needs to confront. But he wasn't sure if it was the right move for his family or for him. As Passover approached that year, he asked God to send him a sign that would tell him what to do.

God sent him a priest.

"Easter and the first day of Passover fell on the same day that year," he said. "News 12 [Long Island] called and asked me if I would come on with this priest named Tom Hartman to talk about the differences and, maybe more important, the similarities in our two religions. We spent two minutes together talking on the air. Then we spent the next two hours talking in the parking lot."

By the time the two men were finished talking, Gellman knew he wasn't going to Miami. "Tommy said to me, 'God isn't finished with you here on Long Island,' and he was right," Gellman said. "Tom was the sign."

The two men became partners, appearing together at charity lunches and outings. Bernadette Castro, who was then a big-time Republican fund-raiser in New York, asked them to speak at a luncheon that she had invited her friend Don Imus to in 1987. Imus loved the act and started inviting them to appear regularly on his show. That led, eventually, to the TV show.

It was during this period that he first met Fay. Gellman and Hartman appeared often at Met Golf Association functions, and Fay, first as assistant executive director, then as executive director, often attended. "He became my unofficial religious adviser," Fay said.

One year when the Senior Amateur was scheduled for the Atlantic Golf Club, a predominantly Jewish club on the eastern end of Long Island, Fay contacted Gellman to make sure Yom Kippur didn't fall the week of the event. "I found out later that the members at Atlantic would have had no problem with us playing on Yom Kippur," he said. "But I didn't know that at the time."

Gellman began sending Fay the religious calendar each year so he would have a guide to work with when scheduling championships. In 1994, when the USGA scheduled its gala hundredth anniversary bash at the Metropolitan Museum of Art, Fay asked Gellman and Hartman to appear.

It was that night that Gellman brought up Bethpage to Fay. By then, Fay had taken his walk around Bethpage and either written or dreamed his I Have a Dream memo. He told Gellman he was well aware of Bethpage and its potential and said nothing more. Gellman, a man who listens to talking golf clubs and looks for signs from God that appear in the form of a priest, told Fay he had a vision of the Open at Bethpage.

"I had this vision," he said. "I would stand on the car line with my buddies and I would say, Someday, they're going to play a U.S. Open here. They're going to play it at *our* golf course. I remembered my father, who played golf and never had any money, and I had this recurring dream, even though I was wide awake when I had it. The last round of the U.S. Open is being played at the Black

Course, and some father, someone like my dad, who never had any money but loved golf, is sitting on the couch with his son. Someone is lining up a critical putt, and the father shakes his head and says, 'That putt breaks more to the left than he thinks.' And his son looks at him and says, 'Dad, you played that golf course? You know what that putt is going to do?'

"And the father looks at his son and says, 'Oh, yeah, son, I played the Black. I've played it a lot.'

"I told David that was my dream."

Fay, who was already dreaming a similar dream, said nothing.

A couple of months later, Gellman got a phone call. Could he make it to Bethpage on May first to play the Black with Fay and a few guys from the USGA? Absolutely, he could make it. "One thing, Marc," Fay said. "Keep this quiet. No publicity. We just want to come out there and take a look around."

"Absolutely, David. I understand."

On May first, the USGA Twelve arrived at Bethpage. "I don't think there was a soul on Long Island who didn't know we were coming," Fay said. "They did everything but put up a sign that said Welcome, USGA. I had no doubt in my mind who the culprit was."

"David should know by now," Gellman said, years later. "You never ask a Jew to keep a secret."

The memo that they all still have in their files was short and to the point: "We are going to go out to Bethpage on May first and play the golf course. We need to decide if this is something worth pursuing . . . David."

And so, on that morning, they all pulled into the parking lot in front of the old clubhouse, pulled their clubs from their trunks, and proceeded to the first tee. They did not, as Fay had envisioned, have to sleep in their cars. Once word had gotten around that they were coming, officials from the state of New York had set aside a block of three tee times for them.

"I was in the third foursome," Brett Avery remembered. "By the time we got on the tee, there must have been about a hundred people gathered around. They all knew who we were and, presumably, why we were there. I was nervous with all those people watching."

Mike Butz remembers being struck by how run-down the place was: the clubhouse, the putting green, the driving range — and that was before he laid eyes on the golf course. "It was actually good to understand right away that we weren't at one of the ritzy clubs where the Open was usually played," he said. "We had been at Baltusrol and Oakmont the previous two years. This was a long way from either one of them. It really was a muni, and it had that feel from the minute you got out of your car."

It felt that way even more when they got on the course itself. Even with Fay's warnings about the conditioning, they were taken aback by what they saw. "Mostly it was the bunkers," Mike Davis said. "I mean, you noticed that the tees and greens were kind of chewed up, but that's the kind of thing that can be fixed pretty quickly. The bunkers, though, had more sand in them than most deserts."

All twelve were good players, ranging from Eger, who is now on the Senior Tour, to Zirpoli, the only one in the group who was not quite a single-digit handicapper. But none of them was completely prepared for the Black from the back tees — specifically, none of them was prepared for the bunkers.

Everyone in the group has a story about the bunkers that day. But the person whose bunker adventure everyone remembers to this moment was Tom Meeks. There are few people on earth who love to play golf more than Meeks. A solid six-handicapper, Meeks was enjoying himself until he reached the third green. There, he missed the green to the left and found himself in one of the deep bunkers.

Meeks entered the bunker and took one swipe at the ball. Then another. And another and another. The only thing he succeeded in doing was moving a lot of sand, a good deal of which ended up on him. As Meeks flailed away, his playing partners heard him wailing, "I will be goddamned if the United States Open Championship will *ever* be played on *this* golf course!"

"I think," said Tim Moraghan, who was in Meeks's foursome, "the ball is still in there."

Standing on the tee, Davis and Fay saw Meeks flailing and heard him wailing. They got a good laugh from the sight and the sounds until each found himself in the same bunker a few minutes later. "I'm a good bunker player," Davis said. "I *like* being in bunkers. I had absolutely no chance to get my ball out of there. Neither did David."

There was no doubting the fact that the bunkers at number three were in serious disrepair. Even so, as the twelve made their way around the golf course, they could see why Fay had brought them there.

"Logistically, it was all there, that was easy to see," Davis said. "There was so much space. Even so, there were all sorts of questions in my mind, both about the golf course — which clearly had great potential — and about what it would be like to deal with the state. To be honest, I can remember thinking that day that, as much as I respected David, I thought he had taken leave of his senses just a little bit."

Butz, to whom the nitty-gritty details of any contract would fall, wasn't quite as skeptical. "The first thing is always the golf course," he said. "But there are some places we go where, yeah, you might like the golf course but there's no way to get everything that comes with a U.S. Open on the property. Or you look around and say, 'Well, we could squeeze this here and that there and maybe get it done.' With Bethpage, it was a no-brainer that we could make it work."

Thanks to Gellman, deputy parks superintendent Ed Wankel had arranged for an informal lunch following the round. Naturally, everyone from the parks department and the state wanted to know exactly when the U.S. Open would be coming to Bethpage. Fay tried to low-key the entire thing, but it wasn't working. In fact, within a few weeks of the outing there was a rumor making the rounds — including in the local newspapers — that the USGA and Shinnecock were having some kind of falling out and the '95 Open would be coming to Bethpage.

Of course, there was absolutely no way for anything like that to happen. But once the day at Bethpage had been completed, there was no doubt in anyone's mind that Fay wanted an Open to be played there someday. Even Meeks, once he finally escaped the bunker at number three, was impressed by what he saw. "It clearly had the potential to be a U.S. Open course," he said. "It was that good."

Butz and Davis saw the look in their boss's eye that day and knew what they had to do. Shortly after the trip, they huddled and came up with a list of things that would have to happen if the Open was to be played on the Black. "We knew David wanted this to happen," Davis said. "We also knew that a lot of things had to take place in order for it to actually happen. The first few steps were up to David. After that, the rest of us would get involved."

Step one for Fay was a call to Bernadette Castro, by now the superintendent of parks for the state of New York. Castro was fully aware of the USGA outing at the Black. She had even gone so far as to report the outing and the USGA's "desire" to play the Open at Bethpage during one of her periodic appearances on *Imus in the Morning*. Fay, an Imus listener, had heard Castro rattling on about the U.S. Open coming to Bethpage while en route to work one morning and almost drove off the road. "Fortunately, Imus didn't take the bait," he said. "When Bernadette said my name, Imus said, 'Isn't that the guy who just got caned in Singapore?' And just went right on from there."

Undeterred, Fay contacted Castro and asked if they could meet. Castro almost never played golf and wasn't a golf fan, but she had been exposed to golf as a girl and understood that a call from the executive director of the USGA was worth taking. She, Fay, and Ed Wankel met in the Bethpage clubhouse soon after the May expedition.

Fay's pitch was direct: He wanted to hold a U.S. Open at Bethpage at some point in the future. Open sites had been selected through 2000, so the earliest date would be 2001. If the state agreed, the USGA would rebuild the Black Course — pay for the costs of a redesign and refurbishing. Fay estimated the cost would be about $3 million. That $3 million would be the rental fee. In return, the state would agree to maintain the course once it had been spruced up, which would mean spending more money on maintenance. There were a lot of details to work out if and when an actual contract was signed, but those were the basics: the USGA would give the state the Black in pristine condition, and the state would cooperate in the staging of a U.S. Open.

Castro thought from the very beginning that the offer was a no-brainer. "I couldn't see any downside to it," she said. "They would pay to give us the Black in the kind of condition we couldn't possibly afford to get it in. Then they would bring worldwide attention to it for an entire week, and when the tournament was over, we would still have this great golf course for all our public golfers."

Castro took Fay's offer to two people: Governor George Pataki and his chief of staff, Bradford Race. Their response was the same as hers: How can we say no? Like Castro, Pataki was only an occasional golfer, but he immediately recognized what the deal could mean for the state. Race, on the other hand, was a serious golfer, a member at Winged Foot who was hoping the USGA would bring the Open back there in the near future. "The best thing about the whole deal was that, for once, there were absolutely no politics involved," he said, years later. "The leader of the state Senate's a Republican; the leader of the House of Delegates is a Democrat. Both are avid golfers. Right from the beginning, everyone in Albany was on board with this."

Castro quickly relayed the state's answer to Fay: We accept. Now it was up to Fay to convince his bosses — the USGA's executive committee — that the time for an Open at a municipal golf course had arrived.

David Fay and his staff had met with the executive board one morning during the USGA's semiannual meetings, which were being held in New York in January of 1996. There wasn't much doubt about where the 2001 U.S. Open was going to be held. Judy Bell was the incoming president, and being a midwesterner, she had made it clear to Fay and everyone on the board that she wanted an Open awarded to the Midwest. The Open had been played at Medinah, outside Chicago, in 1990 and at Hazeltine, outside Minneapolis, in 1991. But only one of the next nine sites — Oakland Hills, coming up later in 1996 — was in the Midwest. Tulsa's Southern Hills had been on the USGA's radar for several years. It had been an Open site before — in 1977 — and had hosted the PGA in 1994. There was little doubt that Southern Hills was going to get the Open in 2001.

"That's the way you had to play the game," Frank Hannigan said. "I remember when I wanted to go to the Country Club [in 1988] there was opposition on the board. But there were a couple of guys who badly wanted to go to Oakland Hills [in 1985], which I wasn't crazy about. Basically, I got them to give me the Country Club in return for Oakland Hills, and I threw in Shinnecock while I was at it."

Fay had a similar plan in 1996. He knew Bell needed to announce Southern Hills to get her presidency off to a flying start. In return, he began looking for support for his dream — the Black in '02. He found an important ally in Eric Gleacher.

Gleacher was a very successful mergers and acquisitions entrepreneur who happened to be a scratch golfer, having played college golf at Northwestern. Gleacher, a nominee to the USGA executive board in January 1996, was also a New Yorker who was familiar with Bethpage State Park and the Black Course.

"Not only did I know the course, but I had played in a tournament there [the MGA's Ike Invitational] that summer," Gleacher said. "I agreed with David that if the money was spent it could be a great golf course again."

Fay had made an impassioned plea for an Open at Bethpage at that day's meetings. Staffers remember that it was unusual, because he did all the talking. Normally, when a golf course is presented to the board, Butz, Davis, and Meeks will chip in with comments. Butz will talk about the contract; Davis the logistics around the golf course; Meeks the way the course will set up for an Open. All will have seen it and studied the area. This time, though, Fay covered the bases.

There was skepticism in the room. But according to Gleacher, who remained in the room after the staff had left, it wasn't based so much on newness as lack of familiarity. "I had a strong sense as we talked that they were close to taking Bethpage off the board and moving on to other courses that had been presented," Gleacher said. "It occurred to me that I was the only person in the room who had ever seen or played the golf course. So I suggested that before any decisions were made about it we try to make arrangements to actually see it and play it. We didn't have to select an '02 site that day. So why not see the place before judging it?"

Reed Mackenzie, who was a board member then, agrees that Gleacher might very well have saved the project. "I was very skeptical," he said. "I'm a member at a club [Hazeltine] that has hosted the Open, and I know how difficult it is to pull off an Open. David had made a very eloquent plea and that was why I think we all considered the idea quite seriously. But certainly the fact that most of us did not know the golf course was working against the concept."

Mackenzie smiled. "Fortunately, the people in the room chose to listen to Eric and [former president] Bill Williams, who both thought the idea was at least worth investigating further."

An excursion to Bethpage was arranged for early spring. As luck would have it, the weather that day was awful. Gleacher was afraid the bad weather might set a tone and keep the other board members from seeing what he knew was there.

"The weather didn't matter," Mackenzie said. "Once you cross the road [from one green to two tee], you start to see why the place is special. Then when you get to four, like David says, you say, 'Oh, yes, now I see why people rave about the place.'"

After the trip to Bethpage, the board met again before that year's Open. This time they were unanimous: The Open would go to the Black in '02 if Fay could guarantee cooperation from the state and some kind of guarantee that there would be a nonpolitical point person whose presence after 1998 would be assured, regardless of the outcome of the elections.

Fay wasn't concerned about finding that point man. In fact, the state had already put him in place before the end of 1995. His name was Dave Catalano.

5

Changing Times

ON AUGUST 28, 1996, it became official: The 2002 U.S. Open would be played at Bethpage Black.

The announcement was made with great fanfare, behind the clubhouse at Bethpage, a few yards away from the first tee of the Black Course. George Pataki was there, along with Bernadette Castro and Brad Race and a number of other representatives from the state. The USGA was represented by President Judy Bell, by newly minted executive board member Eric Gleacher, and by David Fay.

It was the first time Fay had actually come face-to-face with Pataki, and even though the two men were at opposite ends of the political spectrum, Fay liked the governor immediately. He was self-assured and confident and minced no words. After all the speeches were over and everyone had congratulated everyone else, Fay and Pataki had a few moments alone.

"He looked me right in the eye and said, 'David, I can assure you, we will not fuck this up.' That was good for me to hear for a couple reasons. First of all, the way he phrased it told me he was a real person, someone you could communicate with. Second, I took that as an assurance that if we got bogged down in any red tape, we could go straight to him or Race and get help."

That doesn't mean there wasn't a good deal of trepidation on the part of those on Fay's staff who would be charged with making the project happen. Fay is one of those idea guys who leaves the nuts-and-bolts work to the people who work for him, in part because he's not any good at details, in part because he knows the people who work for him are. Already Mike Butz was in the throes of try-ing to hammer out the most detailed U.S. Open contract in history.

"Everything had to be included," he said. "It wasn't enough to say we'll put in bleachers. We had to specify how many bleachers, where they would go, how large they would be, what their poten-tial environmental impact might be. There were no approxima-tions on anything. Everything had to be absolutely exact."

In fact, it would be June 1998 before the entire contract — all seventy-five pages, as opposed to the average Open contract of thirty-five pages — would be completed and signed. It wasn't that either side ever had any intention of turning back, it was just that both wanted to make sure who would do what — and who would spend what — was absolutely clear.

One person who was present at the grand announcement but did not take part in any of the speech making was Dave Catalano. Which was exactly the way he wanted it. Speech making, standing in the glare of the public spotlight, calling attention to himself had never been a part of his MO. Catalano was two weeks short of turn-ing forty-nine the day the announcement was made and had spent large chunks of his life in and around Bethpage State Park.

He had grown up in the Village of Bethpage, the oldest son of Charlie and Shirley Catalano. Charlie Catalano worked full-time at the old air base at Mitchell Field before the government closed it and then became a parts analyst at Grumman. He also had a week-end job at Bethpage. "He worked in the picnic area when I was a kid, opening the place up in the mornings, keeping it as clean and neat as possible during the day," Dave remembered. "My first memories of the place are going up there with him to help out when I was a kid."

Growing up, Catalano spent a lot of time in the park. He played golf there, occasionally venturing on to the Black Course, caddied quite a bit, worked in the picnic area, and cut grass on the golf courses.

While he was in college at SUNY Potsdam, Catalano worked summers in the park, first doing the same kind of work his father did in the picnic area, then becoming a full-time member of the crew that took care of the golf courses. To him, Bethpage always was a special place. When he was offered a full-time job working on the golf course before his senior year of college, he accepted.

"At that point, there was no master plan in terms of what I was going to do after college," he said. "So when I was offered the chance to do something I really enjoyed, I figured why not give it a shot and see what develops."

He never made it back to Potsdam. He worked his way up at Bethpage, eventually becoming superintendent of the Blue Course — "Back then we were called greenskeepers," he said — and then took the civil service test that would allow him to become an administrator. He passed and, in 1978, was given his own park, a few miles from Bethpage, to run. A year later he was promoted again, this time being put in charge of Sunken Meadow, one of Long Island's larger parks.

"Even then, my dream was to go back to Bethpage and run it someday," he said. "But that's all it was at the time, a dream."

The dream came true, at least in part because he and Ed Wankel didn't see eye to eye on a lot of things. In 1981, Catalano moved to the parks office in Babylon. He worked his way steadily up the ranks until he was director of operations, reporting directly to Wankel.

"We had different styles that didn't mesh," Catalano said. "I think Ed always thought I got the job done, and I always respected him, but we were never all that comfortable working together."

It is to Wankel's credit that in spite of his differences with Cata-lano, he recognized his talent. In the fall of 1995, with rumors swirling that the USGA might want to bring the Open to Bethpage, he suggested a job switch between Catalano and Ed Meade, who was then running Bethpage.

"To say I jumped at it would be a huge understatement," Catalano said.

By October of 1995, Catalano was back at Bethpage. If he wasn't yet sure who did what in the USGA, there was no doubt in the minds of the USGA people what Catalano did, who he was, and what his role would be.

"I think we all had some doubts about dealing with a state agency, especially in the beginning," Mike Butz remembered. "Meeting Dave and understanding he was going to be our go-to guy throughout was a huge relief. There are some people you meet who you can tell right away know what they're doing and aren't going to BS you on anything. Dave is one of those rare people."

Catalano is, in many ways, a classic New Yorker: What you see is what you get. He has slicked back black hair, a thin mustache, and when you first meet him, a let's-get-right-to-business demeanor. He almost always has a Diet Coke in one hand and a pack of Camel cigarettes in his shirt pocket. When he is in a place where he can smoke — which does not include his office — he is likely to be smoking. Thus the nickname Smokey Dave.

Jon Barker, who arrived at Bethpage in the fall of 1998 to be the USGA's on-site liaison with the state of New York and to begin rounding up volunteers for the championship, never called Catalano by that nickname. He opted instead for Boss.

"Dave is one of those guys who make it clear the minute you meet him that he's going to be completely honest with you and he expects the same from you," Barker said. "If you ask him to do something and he can get it done, he will. If he can't, he'll tell you why he can't. And if you're ever dishonest with him, two things will probably happen: He'll never trust you again, and in all likelihood, he'll take you around back someplace and kick your butt."

But Catalano has a sentimental side, too. He talks about his park almost the way one would talk about a firstborn child, and he talks about Craig Currier, the superintendent of the five golf courses, as if he *is* his firstborn child. He is intensely loyal and intensely proud of the people who work for him.

"If you were to invent the perfect boss," Currier often says, "it would be Dave."

Currier was working at Garden City Men's Club, twenty miles from Bethpage, as an assistant superintendent when the USGA made the announcement that the Open was coming. He was twenty-five at the time and had graduated from SUNY Cobeskill with a degree in agronomics. He had grown up on a dairy farm in upstate New York and had spent a lot of time around a golf course, both playing and working.

After college, he had talked himself into an internship at the Piping Rock Club with Richard Spear, having no idea that he was going to work for a man who was the unofficial agronomic guru to David Fay. Spear had helped him get the job at Garden City, and Currier had also spent some time in the winters working at Augusta. "For a guy my age, it was the perfect life," Currier said. "I spent the summers on Long Island, the winters in Augusta. What could be better?"

Then Pete Evans, the superintendent at Bethpage, decided to retire. Evans had been supervising what amounted to a skeleton staff and had no desire to stick around for what everyone knew would be a sea change in the day-to-day responsibilities of all those connected with Bethpage. Evans's retirement meant Bethpage needed a new superintendent.

"We knew," Catalano said, "that whomever we chose, it would probably be as important as any decision we had ever made, given what the golf course was about to go through."

It would not be a decision made without input from the USGA. Fay called Spear and asked him for a recommendation. "I'll give you one name," Spear answered, "Craig Currier."

Years later, Spear laughed when asked why he recommended Currier. "Well, first, he had the smarts and the attitude," he said. "He had a lot of energy and was always mature beyond his years. Plus, he had this kind of unshakable confidence in himself that I thought would be important."

Ever since his days at SUNY Cobeskill, where Currier got an

associate's degree and then a bachelor's degree in turf, he had intended to become a golf course superintendent.

"I just found the whole deal fascinating," he said. "The way different grasses made golf courses play differently, all the work that went into making a course look and play the way people wanted it to." He was a good player, an athlete who, at 6 feet 5 and 225 pounds, could hit the ball about as long as anyone he played with.

"I'll never forget the way he walked into my office for the interview," Catalano said. "He had this bounce to him, this, I don't what to call it — aura. You don't expect that in someone on a job interview, especially someone so young."

Currier, who understood the magnitude of the opportunity — take a beat-up municipal golf course and get it in shape for a U.S. Open — was convinced that, even with Spear's blessing, he had an uphill battle to get the job because he was only twenty-six.

"I sort of went in there as if I had nothing to lose," he said, "because that's the way I had it figured. But deep down, I really wanted it."

He decided to raise the age issue right off the bat. "I hope you won't hold my age against me," he said.

Catalano laughed. "Right now," he said, "that may be the only thing working *for* you."

He was joking. And by the time Currier left his office, Catalano was convinced he had found the right man for what he thought might be the most important hire he would ever make. "I interviewed the other people," he said. "But I was convinced no one was going to make the impression Craig had. I was right."

In May of 1997, Currier was named the superintendent of golf courses for Bethpage State Park. He started his new job the first week in June. His first assignment was to take a drive to Bethesda, Maryland, to observe that year's U.S. Open so he could get some idea what an Open course looked like during Open week and so he could meet some of the USGA people he would be working with during the next five years.

One of the first people Currier met was Tim Moraghan, the

USGA's tournament agronomist. In a sense, Moraghan would be Currier's boss, since any changes to the golf course would have to be approved by the USGA. Currier and Moraghan hit it off right away. Both were good players — each about a three-handicapper — and had a passion for ice hockey. Currier was a fan of the New York Islanders, Moraghan a New York Rangers fan, so there was plenty to argue about.

One week after the Open, Moraghan made a trip to Bethpage to walk the golf course with Currier and talk about what they thought could and could not be done during the next few years. Standing on the 12th tee, looking at what both men knew was a great golf hole that would need a lot of work, Moraghan, wanting to make certain Currier didn't think the job ahead was too daunting, said, "You know, Craig, we're not expecting you to turn this place into Congressional. We're realistic."

"Sure, Tim," said Currier, who didn't feel daunted in the least by what he was facing. "I know what you're saying."

What Currier was thinking at that moment was a lot different from what he was saying. Damn right, this place won't be Congressional, he thought. By the time 2002 rolls around, it's going to be *better*.

Before Currier could really get to work on making his golf course better than Congressional, he was going to need a lot of help.

The first step was the redesign. Fay knew that it was going to take more than money to remake Bethpage. It was also going to take the right architect. And there was little doubt in Fay's mind who that architect was: Rees Jones. That was why he had invited Jones to join the group that had played the golf course on that day in May 1995.

Jones knew that. In fact, his presence that morning had fueled the rumors that the USGA wasn't out at Bethpage just for a day of golf. Jones was already known by then as the Open doctor. The younger son of the famous architect Robert Trent Jones, Rees

Jones had followed both his older brother — Robert Trent Jr. — and his father into the business. He had first been asked to work on a future Open golf course prior to the Open's return to the Country Club in 1988 and had also worked on redesigns of Open courses at Hazeltine (1991), Baltusrol (1993), and Congressional (1997).

All of those projects had been different from this one because all had been country club courses where conditioning wasn't the issue. They needed nips and tucks and some new tees and extra length to make them a challenge for the modern golfer and for modern equipment, but that was pretty much it. Bethpage would need a lot more than nips and tucks.

The last thing Fay wanted, though, was a brand new golf course. "I didn't want it to be Bethpage Black by Rees Jones, with prior input from A. W. Tillinghast," he said. "I wanted it to be Tillinghast's golf course with Rees's modernizations. From the outset, Rees understood that."

Jones may have understood that, but he was a bit nonplussed when he and Fay — good friends for many years — sat down to discuss the project and negotiate the fee.

"Because it's a public golf course and I know you guys are picking up all the costs, I'll give you a discount on my normal fee," Jones told Fay. His normal fee was about $1 million.

"Damn right, you'll give us a discount," Fay said. "I'm not going to pay you."

Fay laughs as he retells the story. "Once he picked himself up off the floor, I think he got it right away," he said. "I told him it was already going to cost at least $3 million just to move all the earth around. Plus, I said it would enhance his reputation not only as the Open doctor, because this was the ultimate redesign project, but because he had been so magnanimous in donating his services. It would be great PR for him all the way around.

"I may also have said something about a lot of other architects being more than ready and willing to do it for nothing if he didn't want to do it. Which was a complete lie. I hadn't talked to anyone else and had no plans to."

Whether Jones bought Fay's bluff or not, he quickly came around to the idea. "Just so I can say you didn't get me for nothing," he said, "you have to buy me a really good dinner in return for this."

"Hell," Fay said, "I'll buy you two."

And so, for the price of two (expensive) dinners, the Open doctor went to work. Under orders from Fay, he began with a trip to Winged Foot, another of Tillinghast's famous designs and a past Open site. "I wanted him to look at the bunkering," Fay said. "To me, Tillinghast's signature was always the bunkers, and there was no question that what needed the most work at Bethpage was the bunkers. Rees knew that and understood that, but I wanted him to be reminded of Tillinghast at his best in that area because I thought that was going to be the most important aspect of the redesign."

Jones, having played the golf course and, as an architect, being familiar with Tillinghast, didn't disagree. But once he had examined the bunkers at Winged Foot and then again looked at the bunkers at the Black, he told Fay that he would have to make a choice between enlarging the greens or enlarging the bunkers.

"The bunkers didn't reach the greens," Fay said. "Through the years, parts of them had been lost, which is one of the reasons why they were relatively small. Rees wanted to make the greens larger, put some undulation in them, and extend them to reach the bunkers. I said no. For one thing, I didn't think that was the way Tillinghast intended the greens to be. For another, to be completely honest, the cost of extending the greens that way would have been prohibitive. So I told Rees to extend the bunkers and if the winning score is 16 under par because the greens are too small and too flat, I'll take the hit."

Jones told Fay he would extend the bunkers. After all, he wanted to make sure he got his money's worth out of the deal.

On July 21, 1997, the Black Course was closed to begin the redesign.

The redesign by itself wasn't going to be enough. Once the $3 million of USGA money had been spent, it would be up to the state to invest in maintaining the golf course, before, during, and after the playing of the Open. That meant more equipment and more people.

"The first day I was on the job, I had one guy available to me to work on the Black Course," Currier remembered. "I mean, we were way down in terms of personnel. I think we had a total of twenty-six people working on all five golf courses, not all of them full-time employees and none of them with turf degrees. Paying money to bring in new equipment was fine, but we needed people to work on that equipment."

Currier was told he would be given the budget to hire more people. His first hire was Garrett Boddington, a friend from Garden City, who, like Currier, was young and eager and had gone to college fully intending to be a golf course superintendent. Boddington was hired to oversee the Black Course on a full-time basis. Currier would be there a good deal, but he also had responsibility for the other four courses. Boddington would just work the Black.

The redesign took just under eleven months to complete. On June 9, 1998, the first event on the new Black Course, an annual charity outing, was staged on the reborn golf course. The next day it opened to the public once again. The raves for the condition of the course and the changes Jones had made began to roll in shortly thereafter.

A golf course redesign takes place in several stages. In the case of the Black, a large chunk of the work was basic maintenance. The teeing areas had to be reseeded because many had grown so hard that placing a tee in the ground was almost impossible. The greens also had to be redone with new grasses because of their condition. The same was true of the bunkers, which, in addition to all the extra sand, often had trees and weeds all over them. Thousands of trees around the course were removed, some because they interfered with play in places where they shouldn't; some to create different shots at holes; and some because they blocked vistas without ever coming into play. Craig Currier was still removing trees just months before the Open was played.

In a sense, that was the easy part because there would be little disagreement that the work needed to be done. The next step, much more difficult, was reshaping a golf course built in 1932 at a little more than 6,900 yards to challenge the pros of 2002 and their modern equipment. This involved moving a number of tees back or to a different spot to make the tee shot more difficult, forcing the golfers to shape their shots to find the fairway rather than just blast away. By the time he was finished, Jones had added 300 yards in length to the course but had also made it feel longer than that by moving tee boxes, bringing more rough into play at almost every hole — the fairways in most places were much wider than the USGA wanted — and adding subtle touches to the bunkers.

There were also places where Jones made the golf course more fair. At number four, the signature par-five, he added a collection area behind the green that would stop balls that hit on the green and bounced over. Before the redesign, any ball that went over the fourth green had no choice but to go all the way down the hill, often rolling to an almost impossible spot next to the fifth fairway. By adding what amounted to a backstop, Jones gave players a legitimate chance to play for the green in two. Without the change, trying to reach the green in two was almost suicidal, since it involved a long iron that would be difficult to stop on the green, meaning the player would be virtually dead down the hill. The new hole would still penalize a player who flew the green, but a player who hit a shot just a little too hard would still have a chance to get up and down. That added considerable suspense to the players' decision making at the fourth.

The one hole that Fay and Jones agreed had to be completely redone was the 18th. "It just wasn't a finishing hole worthy of the rest of the golf course or of a major championship," Fay said. "I told Rees to just have at it."

Which he did, building a new tee, bringing the rough way in, reshaping the bunkers in the fairway and by the green to make them more severe. Still not a great hole, but by the time he was finished, a hole that would make a player nervous standing on the tee on Sunday with a one-shot lead.

Jones and Fay went round and round on the issue of the bunkers and the greens, finally deciding (Fay) to leave the greens as they were in spite of the concerns about their flatness. Fay was greatly influenced by both Moraghan and Currier, who told him the greens had a lot more contour in them than they appeared to the average player.

Jones worked on the Black lovingly, almost like a parent nurturing his child. He took Fay's request to keep the heart of Tillinghast's design in the golf course very seriously, and when the new Black was unveiled, it was clear that he had done what Fay wanted: It was still very much Tillinghast, the bunkering practically screaming his name, but modernized to make it a challenge to new-age equipment and twenty-first-century golfers.

"Rees was worth every penny I paid him," Fay joked.

The Open at Bethpage Black was now four years away. The idyllic dream born from a chilled November walk was still a way off. But it was now very real.

6

Getting Ready

ONCE THE USGA had decided to hold the Open at Bethpage, the first matter of business was the redesign of the golf course. Once that was completed in the summer of 1998, five men were, for all intents and purposes, in charge of getting the golf course into perfect condition for the playing of the Open four years hence. Craig Currier and Garrett Boddington were there every day throughout the process. As 2002 approached, they were visited more and more frequently by Tim Moraghan, Tom Meeks, and Rees Jones, who was consulted often about the condition of the greens and the bunkers and about any further changes.

Others from the USGA made occasional visits to see how the golf course was progressing, but those five men were in constant contact, making decisions about what to change and what not to change.

Often, they argued. Currier and Boddington built a new tee for the 15th hole that would have made a long, tough hole even longer and tougher. They were thrilled by the notion of what the pros would have to do from their new tee to get the ball into a position where they might have a shot at the green.

Tom Meeks wasn't as thrilled. He thought the hole was already hard enough. What's more, when he asked tournament director Mike Davis to take a look, Davis pointed out that the new tee would make spectator access to and from the 17th tee almost nonexistent. If Meeks had any thoughts about giving in to Currier and Boddington on the issue, they ended when Davis made that point.

As a result, on Meeks's frequent tours of the golf course, Currier and Boddington took to referring to 15 as "the hole where Tom Meeks decided to wear a dress."

"At a private club, once they're committed to hosting an Open, all sorts of committees immediately spring up," said Mike Butz. "There's a general chairman, and he assigns committee chairmen: player hospitality, transportation, marshals, merchandise, parking, you name it. Their job is to round up the volunteers who will be needed, and then we come in a few weeks before the event and train them. This time was different. Dave [Catalano] became, in effect, our general chairman. But we certainly couldn't go to him and say, round up the usual suspects as committee chairmen."

That job, instead, fell to Jonathan Barker, who arrived at Bethpage Black in the fall of 1998 to become the USGA's on-site point man. Barker was a part of the USGA's evolution that had begun at Shinnecock in 1986. After that success, the USGA began to take more and more control of the Open with each passing year. As it negotiated new contracts, it did so with less club involvement written into the contracts. The once nonexistent legal department began with Romaney Berson's arrival in 1992 and grew from that moment on. Prior to the 1993 Open at Baltusrol, two full-time operations people, Steve Worthy and Frank Bussey, were hired. In 1995, when the Open returned to Shinnecock, the USGA took control of merchandising for the first time, hiring Mary Lopuszynski, first on a part-time basis for that event, later as a full-timer.

For that same event (Shinnecock '95), the USGA decided to send in a full-time employee well in advance of the event for the first time. For many years, advancing a U.S. Open fell to whomever held the "tournament relations" job — David Fay, followed by

Mike Butz, followed by Mike Davis. But as the championship continued to grow, it became apparent that two months of advance work simply wasn't enough.

Barker was the first person hired to be a true advance man for the USGA when he was sent to Shinnecock in 1993 to begin preparing for the 1995 Open. Barker was all of twenty-four when he arrived at Shinnecock, barely out of Penn State and still a little bit stunned by what had occurred to land him on the eastern end of Long Island as the USGA's eyes and ears.

Barker had spent most of his early years in the small English seaside town of Woodbridge. His family had also lived briefly in Northern Ireland when he was a young boy, because his father, a chemical engineer, had been offered a very good job there. The job ended one morning when John Barker, en route to work, wandered into the crossfire of a pitched battle between the IRA and local Protestants and survived only because the bullet that was fired into his car buried itself behind him in the seat and just grazed his back.

"He came home that day and said, 'That's it, we're out of here,' " Barker said. "He had three children (Jon is the youngest of three boys), and he wasn't taking any chances with any of us anymore. It was just too close a call. So we went back to England."

Jon Barker was like most middle-class English kids. He grew up loving soccer and cricket, with little knowledge or understanding of golf. "In Scotland, everyone plays golf," he said. "In England, at least where I came from, it was a game for the rich. I never touched a golf club as a kid. Every day I came home from school and played soccer. I might have known who Jack Nicklaus and Arnold Palmer were, but that was it for golf."

In 1981, when Jon was twelve, his father decided to move his family to the United States. Again, a job offer played a role, but so did the future of his three sons. John Barker was convinced all would be better off if they finished their schooling — particularly college — in the U.S. "If you were going to get into Oxford or Cambridge, there weren't two universities anyplace in the world that were better," Jon Barker said. "But my dad figured — correctly — that we weren't quite smart enough and he wasn't wealthy enough for us to end up there. That said, he knew there were a lot of different choices in the States, places that were known around the world. We weren't going to go over there and get into Harvard or Yale, but we'd end up someplace pretty good."

That place turned out to be Penn State. The Barkers ended up in Allentown, Pennsylvania, because that's where the company John Barker went to work for was located. Jon quickly learned to love American sports, especially football and baseball. His first memory of a football game was the 1982 NFC Championship game between the San Francisco 49ers and the Dallas Cowboys. That was the game in which Joe Montana drove the 49ers to the winning score in the final seconds, finding Dwight Clark in the back of the end zone for what became known as "The Catch."

"I felt so bad for the Cowboys that day that I became a fan of theirs for life," he said. "I had no idea they were America's team or about their championships or Tom Landry or anything else. I just wanted to see them do well." And so he did: Barker became a card-carrying lunatic fan, road-tripping to Dallas in January 1993 when the Cowboys made it back to the Super Bowl just to be there while the team was playing in San Diego. "Greatest weekend of my life," he said. "And, of course, we won."

Barker ended up following brothers Tim and Anthony to Penn State and, as a senior, worked as a student assistant in the sports information department. His plan was to graduate and become president of NBC Television. He figured it might take a year or two; five tops.

"I've always been fascinated by television, by the influence it has on our lives," he said. "It is so important to so many people. When I was a kid, we watched NBC, don't ask me why. We were a [Tom] Brokaw household. So I got it in my mind that I wanted to run NBC."

En route to the tower suite at 30 Rock, he was asked in the fall of 1991 to find a speaker for the Penn State women's basketball team preseason banquet. He decided that the best person to get was Mimi Griffin. Griffin was a big name in the Lehigh Valley, which is where Allentown is. She had been a star player at Pittsburgh in the late 1970s, had married Bill Griffin, who had been Lehigh's all-time leading scorer, and started her own marketing company that often handled major golf tournaments. What's more, she had become ESPN's top color commentator as it began expanding its coverage of the women's game.

For a women's basketball banquet, Mimi Griffin was a perfect choice.

There was one problem.

"She wouldn't return my phone calls," Barker said.

Griffin was just a tad busy at the time. She was pregnant with her second child, she was preparing to run both the Senior U.S. Open at Saucon Valley Country Club (in nearby Bethlehem) and the Women's Open at the Broadmoor in Colorado the following summer, and she was still doing TV for ESPN.

"I just didn't have time to deal with some kid calling me from Penn State," Griffin said.

Barker was not about to be deterred by a few unreturned phone calls. He kept calling. And calling. And calling. "Must have called her thirty times," he said.

"More like fifty," Griffin said.

At some point, standing in her office when yet another call came in from Barker, Griffin grabbed the phone from an assistant. "You have to be the single most persistent human being in the history of the world," she said.

Barker never missed a beat. "Glad we could finally hook up," he said, surprising Griffin with what sounded like a British accent even though Barker had lost a lot of it during ten years in Pennsylvania. "We'd love to have you come up and speak at our banquet. It's in three weeks."

Griffin couldn't help herself. She could laugh, she could cry, she could hang up. Or she could reward the kid for not taking no for an answer and go. She went.

"Jon was very old for twenty-two," she said. "He was a perfect host, made the entire day and night a pleasure. He also told me he was from Allentown. I was looking for help leading up to the Senior Open that summer, so I told him when he graduated if he was interested in coming and doing some work for us on the tournament, I'd be glad to have him."

Barker was very interested. "He showed up for his first day of work wearing a three-piece suit, carrying a brand-new briefcase," Griffin remembered. "It was very clear from the beginning that this was a very serious young man."

Barker worked for Griffin at both the Senior Open and the Women's Open that year. Once they were over, though, she had nothing for him. He landed a job waiting tables at a Jewish delicatessen in Allentown called Rascals.

Fortunately for Barker (and Griffin), Griffin's company's performance at the Senior Open had wowed David Fay. The event had generated three times as much revenue as any previous Senior Open, and Fay was amazed by the numbers.

"He called me in and said, 'How in the world did you do those numbers in the Lehigh Valley?'" Griffin remembered. "I told him we were able to do those numbers *because* we were in the Lehigh Valley. If we were in New York City, the Senior Open would be no big deal, but in the Lehigh Valley, it was a huge deal."

Even so, Fay was impressed. He offered Griffin a contract to work on marketing and corporate hospitality for future U.S. Opens. That meant Griffin needed to hire more people. She hired Barker, then promptly turned around and recommended him to Mike Butz when she heard the USGA was looking for someone relatively young to spend a lot of time working on Shinnecock leading up to the '95 Open.

"It was kind of amazing," Barker said. "I went from serving people corned beef sandwiches to helping prepare for a U.S. Open in a period of weeks. Some of it was overwhelming. But I was still working out of Mimi's office when I wasn't at Shinnecock, and she kept a pretty close eye on me."

Barker's work at Shinnecock was good enough that the USGA decided to start putting someone in place at each Open site at least two years out, starting with 1998. Barker was told he would be sent to San Francisco to the Olympic Club in the summer of 1996. Which left him with almost a year with nothing to do.

So he went back to working at the deli. From there, he went back on the USGA payroll in the spring, then to San Francisco. When that Open was over, Butz and Mike Davis called him in. The next two Opens were going to be "resort" Opens — Pinehurst and Pebble Beach. That meant the companies that ran the resorts would do most of the pretournament work. The next all–USGA Open would be at Tulsa in 2001. After that would come Bethpage.

"Your call," Butz said. "You can work either one."

Barker picked Bethpage. "It was pretty much a no-brainer," he said. "The kind of golf I play, besides being lousy, is going with my buddies to some public golf course, playing a few holes, and drinking some beer. This Open was going to be about that kind of golfer. I've lived in the northeast, I like New Yorkers, and I liked this challenge. I knew it was going to be an Open like no other Open."

If Barker had any doubts about that, they were put to rest the first day he arrived at Bethpage. Driving to the park, he spotted a water tower with large black lettering on it. The lettering read Welcome to Bethpage, Home of the 2002 United States Open.

The Open was almost four years away. The sign had been up for almost two years.

In late 1998, a small sign went up outside a cabin at the far end of the parking lot. It said: USGA Tournament Office. Jon Barker had arrived.

Barker's first mission once he had moved into his small workspace a couple of hundred yards from the Bethpage clubhouse was to start looking for volunteers.

When you talk to anyone who works in golf, they will tell you, almost as a mantra, "We couldn't do it without our volunteers."

This sounds like public relations pap. And it is. It also happens to be true. No golf tournament can be held without finding members of the public who are willing to give up their time to work as marshals on the golf course; as parking lot attendants; as locker room attendants; as sales people in the merchandise tent; or on the hospitality committee, whose job is to keep the players' families entertained throughout the week.

What is remarkable is that so many people in so many cities are willing to volunteer at golf tournaments. Not only are they not paid, they actually pay to work, because they have to buy their own volunteer uniforms. There are perks: admission to the golf tournament when they aren't working, preferred (though hardly premium) parking, and, perhaps, a couple of free box lunches. Most do it because they love golf and because they all fantasize about being given an assignment that will allow them to say hello to Tiger Woods or Davis Love or John Daly. For that matter, most would be thrilled to say hello to Paul Goydos or Mike Muehr. They can then return to work the next week and say, "Let me tell you about this guy I met, Paul Goydos, great guy. And he's played with Tiger on four or five occasions."

The first time Barker had worked at a U.S. Open, he had been told to find 2,500 volunteers. For 2002, Barker had to come up with almost 5,000. What's more, he didn't have a volunteer chairman. *He* was the volunteer chairman. He had also been given a directive from Fay to make sure golfers who used Bethpage and other public facilities in the area were given a major role as volunteers. At most golf tournaments, entire clubs are brought in as marshals: Each club will take a hole and divide up the duties for the week. That wasn't the way it was going to be at Bethpage. Six clubs that used Bethpage and other public golf facilities were to be found; six private clubs would be invited, and six groups that had no formal attachment to any one club, public or private, would be found. It would be that way for all the volunteer groups, a genuine melting pot of golfers — and in some cases nongolfers — from the New York area.

Barker also had to negotiate with local hotels. The USGA needed huge blocks of guaranteed rooms during the week of the U.S. Open for players and their families, for members of the executive board, for staff, for the media, and for corporate clients. Naturally, when hotels understand that a group *must* have rooms, they go the gouge route. (Try getting a hotel room in Augusta during Masters week for less than $200 — and these are your basic roadside motels that normally have signs outside reading Vacancy — $39 a Night WITH Color TV.) When Barker began talking to the Hiltons and Marriotts that were in the vicinity of the golf course, he was being quoted rates in the neighborhood of $500 a night. It was brutal.

And then there were the politicians. One of the more important decisions Barker had to make was which train station would be used as the drop-off and pickup point for those attending the Open. From the beginning, everyone had been in agreement that traffic and parking were going to be difficult regardless, but convincing people to take the train would make the logistics of each day a little bit easier.

The question was which Long Island Rail Road station to use: Bethpage or Farmingdale. The two were about equidistant from the park. The parking lot at Farmingdale, it turned out, was wider than the one at Bethpage. This would make it far easier to operate the larger shuttle buses that make wide turns. There was also more room to stage them so they would be ready for masses of passengers coming off the trains in the morning. Just as important, Farmingdale had an extra rail, meaning extra trains could be backed up and held ready to go if needed quickly.

"That would be especially important if we got into a situation with bad or dangerous weather," Barker said. "There are only so many places on a golf course for people to find cover. A lot of them are likely to leave in a hurry in a thunderstorm, which you actually want to encourage them to do. At Farmingdale, we could have extra trains ready to go, if need be. We couldn't do that at Bethpage."

Armed with all this information as provided by Barker, Davis and Butz decided it made sense to use Farmingdale. None of the USGA people were all that attuned to the rivalry between the neighboring towns or the longtime political tensions that simmered there. As soon as Barker began telling people that Farmingdale was going to be the train station used during the Open, he got a terse phone call from Castro's office.

"Stop telling people we're using Farmingdale," he was told.

"But why?"

"Because we said so."

Apparently, the state was getting heat from the politicos in Bethpage — both the locals and those in the state assembly — about the decision to go to Farmingdale. They were furious.

"The funny thing about it, when I came to understand it better, was that they all saw it as an economic issue," Barker said. "They somehow thought that if people came in and out of their train station that it would be good for business in the village. Well, I could have told them that wasn't likely. People who go to the U.S. Open want to get on the shuttle bus, go watch the golf, then get back on the shuttle bus, and go home. They aren't likely to linger once they're through watching golf, and they've probably all spent their money on food and souvenirs at the Open anyway. Of course, they didn't see it that way."

While train-gate was being sorted out, Barker got another call. This time he was told that if any member of the media called either with a question or with a request to come out to Bethpage, the call was to be routed to Castro's office. "Sure, no problem," Barker said.

And then ignored the request. "If it was a political question, absolutely, I'm glad to send them the call," he said. "But if someone calls and wants to see the golf course or wants to come out and see how the redesign looks, I'm not sending them to fight through the red tape up in Albany. We *want* publicity for the event. Almost all of it is going to be positive. Why make it harder for someone to come out and write nice things?

"What you begin to understand after a while is that you're dealing with different agendas. They're trying to get reelected. We're trying to put on a golf championship."

When Barker ran into Fay at Golf House during a visit there, Fay asked him how he was doing. Barker told him that, overall, things were okay, it was just that sometimes what the state wanted and what the USGA needed simply didn't jibe.

"Look, from now on, someone gives you a hard time about something, just stick their name on a billboard somewhere," Fay said. "That will make any politician happy."

Barker laughed. "Every day in this job," he said, "I learn something new."

7

A New World

DAVID FAY WAS sitting in his office, computer turned on as always, sending off e-mails, when the first urgent bulletin about a plane hitting the World Trade Center came across the computer screen. Like everyone else, his first thought was that it had to be some sort of private plane that had veered horribly off course. He continued working. A few minutes later came the news of the second plane. Now, like everyone else, Fay knew this was no accident. He shut off the computer and turned on a TV to learn more.

As the day unfolded, Fay actually had golf decisions to make. A number of qualifiers for the men's Mid-Amateur Championship (amateurs over the age of twenty-five) were being held in the New York area that morning. The USGA was getting phone calls asking what should be done. Under the circumstances, there was no choice but to pull everyone off the golf courses and reschedule the qualifiers. Later, Fay would learn that one of the earlier finishers was a New York City firefighter named Ken Eichele who had just finished playing when word of the attacks reached the golf course. He left immediately to try to get into the city to help with rescue efforts. As it turned out, the qualifier was rescheduled for a week later. By then, Eichele was still heavily involved in the rescue efforts at Ground Zero. The score he had posted — 72 — would have made the field on the day the qualifier was finally held. Fay wrote to Eichele and told him he was giving him an exemption into the Mid-Am — which was to be held in mid-October, and if the crush of events in New York made it impossible for him to play, the exemption would still be good in 2002.

"It was a no-brainer," Fay said.

The other golf decisions Fay had to make that day weren't quite that simple. Both the men's Senior Amateur Championship and the women's Senior Amateur were being held that week. The women were playing their quarterfinals on that Tuesday; the men had reached the round of 16. Fay sent word to his on-site officials to call the players together and give them the option of calling off the championship — which probably wouldn't be rescheduled so late in the year — or continuing to play.

"My gut feeling was that they would play," Fay said. "Not out of any disrespect but because there was no way any of them could possibly get home with the airports shut down, so all they would be doing was going back and sitting in hotel rooms and watching TV. But if anyone was uncomfortable, we certainly weren't going to make them play. As it turned out, they all felt as I thought they would: they were there, they couldn't get home, they might as well play."

When the first plane hit, Bob Nuzzo was crossing the Tappan Zee Bridge. He was en route to Stewart Air Force Base, Newburgh, where he was scheduled to fly with a photographer over Bethpage to take aerial photos that would be used in putting together the security plan for the 2002 Open. Nuzzo was forty, a just-promoted lieutenant in the New York State Police Department. Earlier in the summer, he had been asked by Colonel Greg Sittler, who was in charge of all uniformed police officers in the state, if he would like to head up the security detail for the Open.

"It made sense on several levels," Colonel Sittler said. "To begin with, Bob's from Long Island, so he knew the area and a lot of people in the area. Plus, he's very organized and very good with people. He had worked with me at Woodstock [the 1999 reprise of the famous 1969 upstate New York concert], and I had been very impressed by the way he dealt with all the logistics there."

Nuzzo had grown up in Massapequa Park, about three miles from Bethpage. He was the third of four children who were raised, in large part, by their mother after his father died when Bob was eight. "If I have a hero in this world," he said, "it's my mother."

As a kid, Nuzzo spent a good deal of time at Bethpage — in the winter, on a sled. He wasn't a golfer, but he knew the park well because the hills on the golf courses made for great sledding. He was a good student in high school and went to college at SUNY, majoring in political science. When he graduated, he wasn't sure what he wanted to do with his degree. "I liked politics," he said. "I still do. But there wasn't anything right there that I wanted to do at the time." Both his older brothers were state police troopers. Nuzzo decided to look into the job.

"I almost hesitate to say this, because it will sound corny," he said. "But to me, being a policeman always seemed like a good way to help people. That's what I wanted to do." Nuzzo moved quickly through the ranks to become a lieutenant, the only casualty along the way — as is so often the case among policemen — being his marriage. The breakup was the one reason Nuzzo hadn't immediately jumped at the offer to coordinate Open security. He knew that taking on the job would mean time away from his five-year-old son, Michael. He and his wife shared custody, and one of the reasons Nuzzo had asked to remain in Kingston, New York, was because it meant he saw his son on a regular basis. But the Bethpage offer was compelling. "In the end, it was a two-hour commute, and I knew I'd be able to get home to him quite a lot," Nuzzo said. "I thought I could make it work, and I really wanted to do the job."

Of course, he never imagined what the job would become. On one of his first days at Bethpage, he and Dave Catalano got into a golf cart and rode around the park. Nuzzo reminisced about how he and his buddies would "borrow" trays from the clubhouse cafeteria to use as sleds.

"When was that?" Catalano asked.

"About thirty years ago," Nuzzo said.

"I was probably the guy chasing you guys to get the trays back," Catalano said.

The two men hit it off right away. He didn't figure it out until later, but Nuzzo saw a lot of his dad in Catalano, even though his memories of his father aren't totally clear. "Honest, smart, tough, someone you could rely on," Nuzzo said. If there was any doubt about the two of them bonding, it was eliminated the first time Nuzzo walked into Catalano's office. On the wall was a copy of Rudyard Kipling's "If." Nuzzo had the same poem on his office wall.

The first month of the assignment had gone well. Mary Nuzzo still lived in Massapequa Park and was more than happy to have her son move into his old room.

Most of the meetings focused on issues of traffic and parking. All of that changed as Nuzzo crossed the Tappan Zee that September morning. Instinctively, he knew something was seriously wrong, because he could see smoke coming from Manhattan as he crossed the bridge. He quickly forgot about the plane ride he was supposed to take and headed toward Long Island to offer help at the state police barracks there.

He was trying to get details on the radio when he reached the Throgs Neck Bridge. That was when he heard the news of the second plane. Looking to his right, toward Manhattan, he could see smoke billowing into the air. The once-clear blue sky looked black. He headed straight for the state police barracks in Lake Success to offer help.

"I spent the rest of that day helping with traffic, getting emergency vehicles and fire vehicles through to Manhattan, and turning away everyone else," he said. "Of all the unforgettable moments that day, the one that still gives me a chill is helping to put up a sign which just said 'New York City Closed.' I don't think any of us ever dreamed a sign like that would ever go up."

For the next several weeks, the last thing on Nuzzo's mind — or virtually anyone else's — was a golf tournament. He worked sixteen-hour days in Manhattan, helping with the rescue and recovery efforts, knowing in the back of his mind that at some point he would get back to Bethpage. And he knew that when he returned, the tone and direction of his planning would be entirely different than before 9/11. As with everything else in the world, golf had been changed forever by that day. That would certainly include the first U.S. Open played at a public golf course — a wide-open, eas-ily accessible public golf course.

"Any planning we had done prior to 9/11 was irrelevant," Nuzzo said. "We were back to square one — with a long way to go and a short time to get there."

It was mid-October before Nuzzo or anyone else from the state of New York had a chance to give any real thought again to the U.S. Open. In the meantime, as scheduled, the USGA held its semi-annual Open-prep staff meetings at Golf House.

The meetings were chaired by Mike Davis and lasted two days. One was held in October — a review of the previous Open, fol-lowed by a look ahead to the next year's Open and some early dis-cussions of future Opens where sites had already been chosen. The spring meetings, held in March, were similar, except that they focused almost exclusively on that year's Open, which at that time was three months away. Every aspect of the Open was discussed, from corporate sales and logistics to where TV towers were going to be built to parking and traffic to media access to shuttle bus transportation to hotels to legal matters to security.

"In the past, when we talked about security, we might take, oh, twenty minutes on it," Davis said. "We would talk about the con-tract with the private security company and how many people they were planning to send us each day. We'd ask the ops [operations] guys if we were covered by enough police to direct traffic. Then we'd move on."

Not this time. Over the two days, there was more than six hours of conversation about security matters. And when the meetings were over, a conference call with Joe Corless, the PGA Tour's security consultant who also helped the USGA with Open security, took up another hour.

"It's gotten to the point," Davis told the assembled group, "where we can't take anything for granted. Everything we assumed in the past can't be assumed anymore. We've even had a request from the state to have a blimpless Open because they want the skies completely clear. No aircraft. Zero."

Davis wasn't planning on telling NBC it couldn't have a blimp. There were a lot of other issues now on the table that simply hadn't existed before, not the least of which was background checks. The state wanted every single person with any kind of credential that granted anything more than access to the grounds to be put through a background check. That would include staff, executive committee members, all vendors, media members, volunteers, and the people hired by the private security company.

"This is going to be a nightmare," said Romaney Berson, the USGA's lead attorney. "We're talking about close to ten thousand people."

Initially, the state had also insisted that, when those who were to be checked signed the consent form allowing the state to conduct the check, the form be notarized. Berson had put her foot down there. "There's no way we can get that done," she said. "People are going to be angry enough about having to sign the form in the first place. You tell them they have to go out to a notary and we'll have chaos. Complete chaos."

The issue of the notarized consent form would become symbolic of the state's relationship with the USGA staff — especially those in operations and in the legal department — over the next few months. It wasn't that there was a lack of mutual respect or even that each side didn't understand what the other side was trying to get done. It was just that both sides felt fiercely that *their* way was right. Which made for some intense battles. Berson walked into one of her colleague's offices one day during a conference call with Nuzzo and some of his staff just in time to hear someone on the other end of the phone refer to her as "the pit bull."

She was convinced it was Nuzzo who had made the comment — and took it as a compliment. Nuzzo insisted it wasn't him but wasn't at all surprised that Berson took it that way. "A very tough lady," he said. "And I *do* mean that as a compliment."

Berson hardly looked like your typical pit bull. She was tall and willowy, with stylishly cut black hair and a wardrobe most TV anchors would envy. She was also the classic detail-oriented (some might say anal) lawyer who planned what she would wear in a given week well ahead of time. Her résumé was intimidating: she had graduated from Duke in 1984 at the age of nineteen and gone from there to Harvard Law School. She had married another lawyer and they had two sons. Berson's office was decorated not with expensive art or, like many in the USGA, paintings of golf courses, but with her children's artwork and various Duke basketball artifacts. The only person in the world Berson was unlikely to ever question on any issue was Duke basketball coach Mike Krzyzewski.

In a sense, Berson was the perfect person to be in the eye of the newly created security storm because it was all about organization and attention to detail and a willingness to keep hammering away on something until it was exactly right. Her legal training had prepared her for that as did her persona. One of the people she had often worked with prior to 9/11 was Mark Carlson, since she had been trusted to start up the USGA's streaming video for online computers in 2001. Carlson, ever the protector of the USGA's TV partners, was often at odds with Berson about what the streaming video should or should not be doing.

"Romaney can be tough to work with," Carlson said once, "because she's so anal about every little thing." Added a laughing Mike Butz, "And thank God for that."

Never was that more true than in both the pre-Open planning meetings. After 9/11 there really wasn't an aspect of the Open that did not in some way relate to security. Every vendor, whether they would be putting up tents or serving food or delivering equipment or providing security, had to understand that background checks had to be done on all their personnel, that getting in and out of the golf course wasn't going to be easy regardless of their needs, and that the phrase "we did it this way in the past" had ceased to exist. Members of the media were not only going to have to deal with background checks — some objected on constitutional grounds — but with being patted down every day before they could go on the grounds. NBC and ESPN, generally given carte blanche because they paid the USGA big bucks, would have to understand that equipment would be checked before it was allowed on the grounds and that off-limits meant off-limits — not off-limits to everyone but TV.

"We all have to understand that we've never done an Open like the one we're getting ready to do," Butz explained to the forty assembled staffers in the first-floor conference room at Golf House where the meetings were held. "This was going to be different anyway because of the venue. Now, nothing is the way it used to be — for all of us."

The other huge headache for Berson and her staff was insurance. Because so many insurance companies were going to be doling out so much money in the wake of 9/11, rates for everything had skyrocketed. Event cancellation insurance had become almost impossible, especially since no company wanted to include any clause that would allow money to be collected in the event of a terrorist attack canceling the event.

"And if something does happen," Berson said, "we have to be sure to get a claim in *that day,* because at this point, if we give these people any excuse at all not to pay off on an accident or anything else that happens, believe me, they won't."

The two men who would have the most to deal with in the next nine months were the two men who, arguably, always had the most to deal with leading up to any Open: Steve Worthy and Frank Bussey.

Their job title was simple: operations. What they actually did was anything but simple. Virtually every single item related to putting on an Open went through operations at some point. Legal would process all the vendor contracts — operations did the negotiating. TV would decide how much space it needed, how many trailers, camera positions, announcer towers — operations had to make sure they were built and placed where they needed to be placed. Roping the golf course? Operations. Bicycle rack (a kind of fencing) around the grounds? Same thing. Temporary roads built for tournament week? You get the idea.

They were, to put it mildly, an odd pair. Worthy and Bussey were working their tenth Open together, each having been hired prior to the 1993 event when the USGA decided to take operations in-house rather than let the host club hire a different contractor at each venue.

"We really are like an old married couple," Bussey said one day, sitting in the operations trailer at Bethpage on a winter afternoon, watching as rain came down in sheets. "We fight all the time, then eventually we figure out what to do, and we get it done. But if people just sat and listened to us, they'd think we were going to kill each other."

Worthy was forty, Bussey, fifty-three. Worthy looks preppy, with wire-rimmed glasses, neatly trimmed blond hair, and an easy smile. The smile hides an intensity he rarely shows to outsiders, one that surfaces when something needs to be done and Worthy senses that it isn't getting done — or isn't getting done the way it should. Bussey's hair is graying and tends to zigzag in several directions toward the end of the day. He is soft-spoken and appears quite serious on first meeting but up close has a sly, off-the-wall sense of humor. Worthy reacts to almost any request, no matter how outrageous, by shrugging his shoulders and saying, "No problems." Bussey is a bit more melodramatic. He will throw his hands into the air, toss his head back, shriek in pain, and then bury his head on the table in disbelief. Then he will look up and say, "How soon do you need this done?"

Both grew up in the South, but neither sounds the least bit southern. Bussey's father ran hotels when he was a boy, and Frank spent a lot of time working part-time jobs for his dad in the summers. "The joke among the staff was, If you screw up, Frank's taking your job," he said.

He was a tennis player, good enough to get a scholarship to North Florida University. After graduation he worked at various tennis clubs and eventually started a business building tennis courts. Throughout most of the 1980s, he worked in operations for several tennis tournaments, including the Lipton Tournament when it first launched. But as he got older, he found himself seeking more and more work in golf operations.

"Why?" he asked rhetorically. "Simple. Tennis tournaments are played at night and they can be stopped by rain. Golf tournaments are never played at night and, barring lightning, play through the rain."

In other words, the hours were a lot better — at least during an event.

In 1992, Bussey was hired by the Pebble Beach Corporation to do the operations for that year's U.S. Open. Shortly before the championship, he heard that the USGA was planning to hire a full-time ops person beginning the next year.

"I was forty-one years old and still hadn't found exactly the right job," Bussey said. "I thought maybe this was the one."

He applied for the job only to learn the week before the Open that the USGA had hired a thirty-year-old kid named Steve Worthy who had been working on operations at the Memorial Tournament. Foiled again, Bussey thought. Worthy even showed up at the Open that year to meet some of the people he would be working with in the future. He never did make it by the operations trailer.

What an arrogant, aloof bastard, Bussey thought.

"Actually, I was embarrassed," Worthy said. "I knew the guy had wanted the job, and I didn't feel like walking in there and saying, Hi, I'm the guy who got the job you wanted."

Worthy started work that summer. Out of work, Bussey kept in touch with Mike Davis and Mike Butz, convinced that if they were going to actually run all the operations in-house, they were going to need more than one person. "I pounded on them," he said. "I kept saying, you want to put yourself in the hands of someone who has never run an Open with no help at all? Finally, in February, they caved."

Bussey was hired as the number two man in operations. Now, he and Worthy had no choice but to meet. Bussey walked into Worthy's office, and after brief salutations, they got down to business.

"Mike Butz is insisting that we give out one parking pass for every corporate ticket [at Baltusrol] we've sold," he said.

"That's the most ridiculous thing I've ever heard in my life," Bussey said.

"We bonded at that instant," Worthy remembered, laughing.

Worthy had grown up outside of Baton Rouge, Louisiana. His father, Sidney Worthy, had been a doctor, who occasionally chided Steve as he grew up about finding some direction in his life. Most of Steve's early direction was toward sports. He was a very good high school athlete, lettering in football, basketball, baseball, and track. He was a quarterback, though his most vivid memory is of his last game, in which he threw five interceptions.

"Three were returned for touchdowns," he said. "My offensive line didn't tackle very well."

He was a good enough basketball player to receive some interest from the lower levels of Division 1. Thinking that two years of maturity might get him to the point where he could get a D-1 scholarship, he went to a junior college in Mississippi. He played well enough there to make the state junior college all-star team and did get some attention from D-1 schools, but no one was knocking his door down.

"It was time to be realistic," he said. "I'd had fun, but now I needed to think about what I wanted to do after college."

He enrolled at LSU, where he had a lot of friends, and promptly forgot about the after-college thing. "At one point my father was convinced I was majoring in flag football," Worthy said. "He wasn't completely right. I played a lot of flag football, but I played intramural basketball, too."

All of that changed quite horribly early in 1985, Worthy's senior year. He got a call from his father telling him he had taken a fall, popping his shoulder out quite painfully, and was resting at home for a few days. Maybe, he suggested, Steve could come down and spend a day. "I hadn't been home for six weeks," Worthy said. "Which was a lot, since my parents lived less than an hour from school and we were very close. So I went home.

"Stayed Wednesday night, then Thursday and Friday, too. Dad and I just sat and talked a lot. It was great. He was enjoying it, so was I, which was why I stayed. Saturday, I went out and played golf with some buddies, came home, and sat down on the couch to watch the Cubs and Cardinals on TV. Dad fell asleep late in the game. When it was over, I went to wake him up . . ."

Sidney Worthy was forty-eight when he died. His son spent much of the next few months worrying about his mom but also thinking about what his dad had often said to him: "You're plenty bright enough, but you need to find some direction at some point in your life."

That time had now come. Worthy ended up applying to Ohio University's sports communications program, probably the best-known Masters program in the country for those who want to get into sports management. He got in and, while at Ohio U., worked at Muirfield Village — Jack Nicklaus's course — first on the 1987 Ryder Cup, then on the Memorial Tournament, first in public relations, then in operations. His initial contact with the USGA was in 1991 when Butz, Davis, and Meeks came to Muirfield to begin preparations for the 1992 U.S. Amateur, which was going to be held there.

Soon after that — on the golf course, naturally — they were sounding him out about moving to the USGA to be the first full-time operations person the organization had ever hired. "I was thirty, I was single, the travel sounded great, and it was the U.S. Open I was being asked to run," he said. "It wasn't hard to say yes."

It was at the '92 Open that Bussey first spotted him as the guy who had gotten his job. "If only I had known then what I know now," Worthy said, "I'd have marched right into his office and said, 'Yup, I'm the guy who got the job you wanted.' Of course, if Frank had known me, he would have had about twenty different come-backs ready for me."

The parking issue turned out to be just the first of a myriad of headaches at that year's Open. Butz ended up learning from his mistake, but that didn't make things any better that year. Nor did the choked access roads leading into the club, the brutally hot weather, the un-air-conditioned school buses used as shuttles, or the fact that players had a terrible time getting from their hotel to the golf course.

About a month before the Open, Worthy was in the office — a rarity — when the switchboard called upstairs to tell him someone wanted to see him.

"Does he have a name?" Worthy asked.

"Mr. Tee Man."

How do you turn someone called Mr. Tee Man away? It turned out the guy had an act. He dressed up like a giant golf tee and entertained golf fans at golf tournaments.

"Not at the U.S. Open," Worthy told him.

Mr. Tee Man wanted the issue taken to a higher authority.

The higher authority, as always seemed to be the case when everyone knew the answer would be no, was Mike Butz. This one was easy, unlike some of the noes he was forced to hand out: Mr. Tee Man was not welcome at Baltusrol. Worthy gave the news to the disappointed Tee and moved on to other headaches.

He had completely forgotten about his old friend by the time the Open began. On Friday afternoon, during a rare lull, he was driving his mother and sister out to the back nine so his sister could watch Fred Couples play a few holes. "Typical female," Worthy said. "All she wanted to do was go out and watch Fred."

Worthy was waiting for a group to hit tee shots at the 13th hole so he could drive across the fairway and get to where Couples's group was when he noticed a commotion behind the 14th green. To his amazement, he saw his old friend Mr. Tee Man entertaining the crowd there. "I almost went berserk," he said. "I started to go under the rope, but my mom pointed out that Billy Ray Brown was on the tee. I had to wait — steam coming out of my ears. When I finally got over there, he saw me coming and he actually turned around and *ducked* as if I might not recognize him. He had bought a ticket and walked in. I couldn't stop him from doing that, but I could stop him from doing his act.

"I took him to the front gate and told him if he came back dressed like a normal human being he was welcome to come back. Then I said to the security guards, 'How in the world did you let the guy in looking like that?' One of them said to me, 'There's nothing on our list of banned items about mascots.' He was right."

Actually, Bussey's version of the story is much more colorful. In it, Worthy actually chases Mr. Tee Man down the 14th fairway screaming at him. "Could have happened that way," Worthy will admit. "Except that my mother never would have forgiven me."

As Worthy and Bussey worked on parking passes, cell phone rules, and player transportation, Mimi Griffin turned to coddling the bigwigs. Corporate hospitality has become a huge part of what the USGA does at the Open, and in 2002 there would be more tents than ever before — seventy-eight in all, with prices ranging from the $175,000 for the twenty-six tents that had a view of the 18th hole to twenty-six that were located on the first hole of the Green Course — adjacent to number one on the Black — that went for $155,000 to twenty-six that cost $140,000. Corporations could also buy tables of ten for $40,000 inside the clubhouse or $30,000 in what was called the Champions Tent.

Other than security, corporate planning was the most time-consuming part of the meetings leading up to 2002. Griffin was extremely detail-oriented because she knew that any misstep would lead to serious screaming and yelling from clients shelling out a lot of money for one week of entertainment.

"They pay a lot, and they expect a lot," she said.

The downturn in the economy since early in 2001 had brought some attrition. About a dozen corporations that had initially signed up for tents at Bethpage had dropped out, but all but one of those spots had been filled by companies on the waiting list. Surprisingly, no one dropped out in the aftermath of 9/11. "I think we'll see the effects of the economy and 9/11 more next year," Griffin said. "We're already running into problems selling '03 [in Chicago] since the downturn. And we're seeing companies wanting to be a lot more low-key about their involvement. Some have told us they don't want their names on their tents."

By the time the Open was played, only one company would insist on anonymity, but Griffin could sense that many weren't all that eager to broadcast that they were spending six-figure money on entertaining clients at a golf tournament. What's more, the changes in security and the logistics of the massive undertaking put Griffin and her staff under tremendous pressure throughout the week.

On the Saturday before the Open, Griffin and Mike Butz rode around the golf course doing an informal site check of the various corporate venues. It was a perfect June afternoon, and everything appeared to be in place or almost in place for the invasion of fans that would come on Monday.

"Mike, I really believe we're going to be fine this week," Griffin said. "I think we're ready to deal with whatever comes, but I also think we're completely stretched to the limit. I think we should look at this as being as far as we're going to go with corporate hospitality."

Butz, a man of few words, nodded his head and smiled. "I hear you," he said.

While his staff was locked away in a conference room in New Jersey for most of two days wrestling with the details and headaches of trying to make the 2002 U.S. Open a reality, David Fay was in San Diego, planning the 2008 Open.

"Bethpage is in my rearview mirror," he said, joking but not joking. "I'm way down the road from 2002. The smart guys are in charge now. Something has to be decided at this point, it's in the hands of Meeksie and the Mikes."

Around Golf House, Mike Butz and Mike Davis are often thought of as a single entity: the Mikes.

The Mikes are remarkably similar in temperament, both low-key and unflappable, each with a dry sense of humor and a nonconfrontational manner that apparently works well in confrontational situations. Whether their similarities are the result of the fact that they grew up in the same hometown — Chambersburg, Pennsylvania — is open for debate, but there is no debating the fact that neither is likely to raise his voice in anger unless pushed very, very hard.

Meeksie — Tom Meeks — is another story. Butz is responsible for most of the pretournament negotiating and organizing, and Davis is in charge of almost everything that occurs outside the ropes at an Open. Meeks is primarily responsible for everything that occurs inside the ropes. It is his job to set up the golf course, a job that involves years of planning and multiple visits to each Open site. He will work with the course superintendent and Tim Moraghan on the width of the fairways, the length of the rough, the quality and texture of the sand in the bunkers, the speed of the greens, and, finally, the location of the holes.

Most people call hole locations "pin placements." Those who use that phrase around Meeks had better duck. "There are no pins on a golf course," he will say ferociously. "There are flagsticks, which are placed in the holes. If you want pins, go to a bowling alley."

Meeks is every bit as high-strung as the Mikes are low-key. He is sixty-one, short, with graying hair, glasses, and an ever-present smile. It can probably be argued that few people on earth enjoy what they do more than Tom Meeks. It can also be argued that few people on earth are imitated more than Meeks, whose high-pitched voice, emotional outbursts, and cackling laugh provide more fodder than anyone who is around him for more than fifteen minutes can resist. Early in 2001 when Chris Law, who ran the USGA members program for twelve years, left for a job in Boston, he was asked to give a brief speech at his going-away party. "I think my one claim to fame at the USGA," he said, "is that I'm the only person who has worked in this building who has never done an imitation of Tom Meeks." That sounded right.

Meeks is a midwesterner, born and raised in Lawrenceville, Illinois. His father, Joseph Meeks, and his grandfather both worked in the Texaco refinery in town, and Tom grew up wanting very much to not follow in their footsteps. His passion for golf was born when he began caddying at Lawrence County Country Club, a local nine-hole course. "My parents would always send me to a YMCA camp for two weeks in the summer," he recalled, "and I never had enough money to get all I wanted to eat at the canteen. My mom told me if I wanted extra money, I'd have to earn it. So I started caddying."

Meeks got seventy-five cents for nine holes, with a quarter tip bumping it to a dollar. "First time I worked, I was carrying for a guy named Mr. Muskie," he said. "I had an awful time. I couldn't figure out how to carry the bag. It kept slipping and sliding off my shoulder, and no matter what I did, it just hurt like crazy. I had no clue what I was doing. When we were done, I figured I'd be told never to come back. But Mr. Muskie handed me a dollar and said, 'Tom, you worked really hard, and I enjoyed being with you.' That inspired me. I decided I wanted to get good at this. If he hadn't been so nice, who knows if I'd have ever really gotten involved in golf."

By the time the summer was over, Meeks was competent enough to work doubles — two bags — for eighteen holes, pocketing four dollars in the process. He learned to play from the other caddies and was usually there from six-fifteen in the morning, when his grandfather dropped him off en route to the refinery, until dinnertime, when his mother called the pro shop and told them to send him home. The golf course became his home away from home.

A couple of years later, when he was in high school, his parents bought a membership in the club for $100 so he could play whenever he wanted instead of Mondays only, the day the caddies got to play.

Meeks was a good player, not a great one, a low handicapper —

"Been a zero," he said, "but it was kind of a funky zero" — who ended up going to Butler University, a couple of hours down the road in Indianapolis. He intended to become a pharmacist, having done some part-time work at the local drugstore, but changed his major to education once he got a whiff of all the science courses involved in getting a pharmacy degree. After graduation, he went to work in Indianapolis teaching and coaching, always staying involved in golf. He left teaching briefly, intending to become a CPA, but tired of that quickly and took a job as a golf cart salesman.

"That did not sit well with my parents at all," he said. "I remember my father saying, 'I didn't spend $10,000 sending you to college so you could sell golf carts for a living.' I told them just to be patient and let's see how this thing plays out."

It played out at a Christmas dance for the Indiana PGA in 1971. Meeks was married by then. He had met Suzy Cochrane one summer during college, and they had ended up teaching at the same high school a couple of years later. One day, sitting in the teachers' lounge smoking during an off-period, Suzy turned to him and said, "Why haven't you ever asked me out?"

"I told her that I sat in here and heard her talk about her social life and didn't want to get in line three weeks down the road," Meeks said. "She said, 'Why don't you try me and see what happens?' I said, 'Okay, how about Friday?' She said, 'It's a date.' It wasn't until years later that she told me if I'd said Saturday, she would have said no because she already had a date."

They were married in August 1965. Six years later, they were on the dance floor at the PGA Christmas dance when Mickey Walker, who was president of the Indiana Golf Association, mentioned to Meeks that the IGA and Indiana PGA were thinking of joining forces to hire an executive director and his name had come up.

"If you're interested," Walker said, "send us a résumé."

"No need," Meeks said, reaching into his jacket pocket. "I've got one right here."

Walker's jaw dropped. Meeks had heard about the job on the grapevine and decided to come to the dance prepared, just in case. He was hired a month later.

For Meeks, it was a dream job. He spent a lot of his time giving rules clinics, and during the warmer months he ran the major golf events in the state. He had been on the job for three years when he went in to meet with his bosses for his year-end review in 1973. They were very pleased with his work and offered him a $2,000 raise — to $18,000 a year.

Meeks was disappointed. "I thought I deserved more than that," he said. "I had young kids. I needed more than that."

That spring, Meeks had to write to P. J. Boatwright at the USGA about a rules issue. On a whim, at the end of the letter he wrote, "By the way, does the USGA ever add staff from outside and if so, how would one go about getting involved?"

The following winter, at a rules seminar outside San Diego, he met Boatwright, who was there to administer tests to rules officials. They played golf together one day, and on the last day of the seminar, Boatwright told Meeks that the USGA was thinking of adding what he called a public relations person.

Meeks shook his head. "I don't have any experience in public relations," he said sadly.

Boatwright shook *his* head. "I don't mean it that way," he said. "I mean someone who goes out and waves the flag for the USGA with members and the public, tells them what we're all about. That sort of thing."

"Now *that*," Meeks said, "I could do."

He flew to New Jersey a few weeks later to meet with Boatwright, Frank Hannigan, and the rest of the staff. On his last day there, Boatwright offered him the job — for $20,000 a year. Meeks was pretty certain he was going to say yes, but he wasn't ready to jump too quickly. "I'd really like to make $24,000," he told Boatwright. "And I have to talk this over with Suzy."

Boatwright smiled. He told Meeks he could probably get him $24,000 if that's what it took to get him. "Oh, there's one more thing," he said in his deep southern drawl. "If you go ahead and take the job, the executive committee would like you to fly down to the Masters for the week so they can get to know you better."

Meeks cackles retelling the story. "Ole P. J. knew what to say," he said. "Here I am, a midwestern boy who thought he'd never see the inside of the gates at Augusta, and he's telling me if I take this job that I'm kinda leaning toward taking anyway, the first thing I get to do is go to Augusta. I tell you [those three words being an oft-imitated Meeksism], if there was any doubt at all, it went right out the window when he told me that."

Meeks quickly established himself as an important and reliable figure within the USGA. He was tireless when it came to doing rules clinics around the country, to reaching out to regional branches of the organization, to putting together booklets and slide shows on what the USGA was and what it did for golf and golfers. It is probably fair to argue that Meeks is the (high-pitched) voice and face of the USGA to more golf people than anyone.

He was also responsible for bringing two key figures to the USGA. The first, in 1978, had been David Fay. "Just had a feeling about him," Meeks said years later. "He was smart and straightforward and he knew golf."

The second was Larry Adamson, to be administrator for all the championships. This was — and is — a critical job because it involves the monumental task of accepting and rejecting entries to all the USGA championships. It means dealing with a lot of angry people who can't understand why their entry was rejected or why they didn't get to play the golf course for qualifying that they requested.

Adamson was another midwesterner, another ex-teacher and ex–high school coach who Meeks had met during his days as a high school basketball referee. The two men had become friends when Adamson, who had just been assigned to coach his high school's golf team because he didn't have a last-period class, sought Meeks out for advice. Hired by Meeks in 1979, Adamson stayed at the USGA for twenty-three years, retiring in the fall of 2002.

"I'm pretty proud of some of the hires I've made here," Meeks said. "But I tell you, the most amazing thing to me about it all is the idea that an ex-caddy from little ole Lawrence County Country Club could end up getting to do the things, see the places, and meet the people I've met through the years. It's just been great. Every bit of it."

Well, not *every* bit of it.

Any criticism of an Open golf course setup or pace of play usually lands at Meeks's feet. In 1998, both those roles put him in the spotlight during the Open at San Francisco's Olympic Club.

It began on Friday at Olympic's notorious 18th green, a green with a severe slope back-to-front that made finding four workable hole locations difficult. After much debate, Meeks finally opted not to use three hole locations on the front of the green because he was afraid all that foot traffic could lead to a very spiky surface on Sunday. Concerned that a wayward spike mark might decide the U.S. Open, he finally opted to put the hole toward the back of the green for the second round.

Meeks knew the location was risky, that the slope, especially on a dry day, might make it difficult for putts to stop around the hole. Friday morning, he positioned himself near the 18th green to watch the first few groups come through. He could see that, even though the green had been heavily watered that morning, balls were rolling way past the hole. "I knew right then," he said later, "that I was a dead duck."

It didn't help that Payne Stewart, who was leading the tournament, had a putt come back almost to his feet late in the afternoon. Or that Tom Lehman, one of the most mild-mannered men on tour, went into a profanity-laced tirade that could be heard in most of the clubhouse after his three-putt finish. Meeks was pale that evening when he talked to reporters, taking all the blame even while Moraghan insisted he was as much to blame because he had encouraged Meeks to chance the location.

Two days later, Meeks had another encounter with Stewart and Lehman. They were Sunday's final group, and Meeks had to monitor their progress. Almost from the start, they had fallen behind the groups in front of them, and Meeks knew he had a problem. "If not for the Lee Janzen incident [Janzen hit a drive on the fifth hole that got stuck in a tree, causing a delay], I would have said something to them by the fourth hole," he said. "But because of what happened to Lee, they got back into position for a while."

By the 10th hole, they had fallen behind again, and Meeks began timing them, as the rules require when a group is out of position. On 12, his four-shot lead at the start of the day down to one (on Janzen), Stewart hit a perfect drive that had the misfortune to land in a spot where sand had been filled in to cover a divot. It was an awful break at a crucial moment.

Stewart toiled over his second shot at great length. He took one club out of the bag, talked to his caddy, Mike Hicks, then took out a different club. He chatted with Hicks some more and finally got over the ball and hit the shot, a nine-iron into a greenside bunker. He was standing there fuming when Meeks walked up.

"Payne, I'm sorry, I had to give you a bad time on that shot," Meeks said.

"Tom, those divots should not be filled with sand that way," Stewart answered, almost as if he hadn't heard what Meeks had said.

"That's another issue for another day," Meeks said.

At that point, Stewart understood why Meeks was out on the fairway. "You're giving me a bad time when I had to play from a sand trap in the middle of the fairway?" Stewart said. "Did you see that I had to change clubs?"

Meeks nodded. He had stopped his watch when Stewart changed clubs. Once he had chosen the nine-iron, he started his watch again — from zero. Stewart had forty seconds to hit his shot. He had taken eighty. "If he'd been under a minute I probably would have let it go, given the conditions and the moment," Meeks said later. "But at a minute and twenty I had no choice. You can't administer the rules when you feel like it. You do it or you don't."

Stewart, of course, didn't see it that way. When he went on to lose that day to Janzen by one shot, his single complaint was the bad time Meeks had given him. Meeks is not one to run and hide when criticized. He tracked Stewart down that fall and said he thought they should talk. They did, and while Stewart still didn't agree with what had happened, he did understand that there was no malice at all in Meeks and that Meeks had done what he felt he had to do.

Ironically, Meeks's most recent run-in with a player involved Janzen. On Friday morning of the 2001 Open at Southern Hills, players returned to the golf course to resume the first round after a massive thunderstorm had called off play Thursday afternoon. Before play began, the grounds crew had gone through the fairway with hoses to try to remove all the dew from the still-wet golf course.

Janzen had left the course the day before on the ninth fairway. When he got there the next morning, his ball was in a low spot that the hoses could not get to and was still covered in dew. Without giving it any thought, Janzen took a towel from his caddy and mopped the area, thinking, no doubt, that since the committee was attempting to remove all the dew from the golf course there was no reason for him not to finish the job before he actually began play again.

Unfortunately, he was wrong. Under the rules, no player can use an artificial device — in this case the towel — to improve his lie in any way. From across the fairway, rules official Jim Halliday, assigned to Janzen's group, saw Janzen mopping.

Halliday wasn't absolutely certain that Janzen had broken a rule. If he had, there was certainly nothing he could do about it at that moment. He said nothing to Janzen — which was a mistake. "In an ideal world, Jim would have walked over and said, 'Lee, I think we may have a problem here,' " Meeks said. "Then he could have called for a rover [one of the officials like Meeks roving the course in a golf cart] to either confirm that there was a problem or that there wasn't one."

Janzen completed the first round and then eighteen holes of the second round. Many groups did not finish the second round that day, so players returned to the golf course early Saturday, with the third round scheduled to begin as soon as the second round was complete and pairings could be made for the third round.

Meeks was sitting in the USGA rules trailer trying to work on third-round pairings and calculate the cut. He had a few groups left to finish when Halliday walked in, looking slightly pale. "Tom, something happened yesterday, and I've been thinking about it all night," he said. "I think you better read this."

He had written out exactly what he had seen Janzen do and what his response (or nonresponse) had been. Meeks felt sick to his stomach. Under any circumstances this was going to be awkward, since the rules official hadn't taken action after witnessing the incident. Meeks knew Halliday was experienced and dedicated, which made him feel worse about it all. He had made a mistake. The mistake involved a two-time U.S. Open champion.

Meeks immediately called Fred Ridley, the chairman of the championship committee, and Reed Mackenzie, the chairman of the rules committee, at their hotel. Both were trying to steal a little sleep before walking with the last two groups that afternoon. "I need you both back here right away," he told them. When they arrived, Meeks showed them Halliday's note.

Technically, Janzen had signed an incorrect scorecard after his first round, because his action called for a two-shot penalty. That meant automatic disqualification. But Mackenzie, Ridley, and Meeks were all of the opinion that since the rules official had witnessed what he had done and not informed him of the two-shot penalty, he was not responsible for signing for a wrong score. So, no disqualification, but the two-shot penalty had to be added to his score. Because Murphy's Law was clearly at work, the extra two shots moved Janzen from one shot safely under the cut line to one shot over the cut line — and out of the championship.

"I wish we'd had a choice," Meeks said. "But we didn't. The saddest part was that if Lee had called Jim over and said, 'Can I mop this up?' the correct answer would have been, 'No, you can't, but I can since I'm part of the committee.' Lee made a mistake. Jim made a mistake."

Meeks had to make the phone call to Janzen to tell him what had happened. Janzen was angry but said he understood — only he didn't. Shortly after the Open, he wrote a letter to Meeks and the

USGA saying he thought the situation had been mishandled and he had been treated unfairly. After receiving the letter, Meeks tried to track Janzen down on the phone. "I don't mind it when guys challenge us," he said. "They have a right to do it. I wanted to hear what he had to say."

Janzen sent word back to Meeks through Mike Shea, a PGA Tour rules official, that he had no interest in talking to Meeks about it anymore. Meeks was fine with that. At the Players Championship in the spring of 2002, he saw Janzen.

"Lee, you still mad at me?" he asked.

"Nah, I've put that behind me," Janzen answered. "We're okay."

But they weren't okay. A few weeks later, Meeks was in his customary place at Augusta, the scorers' tent, taking scores from players as they completed their rounds, something he has done for the last twenty years there. When Janzen came in the first day, he went through his card, signed it, and handed it to Meeks.

"My card okay?" he asked.

"Looks fine to me, Lee."

"So you aren't going to call me tomorrow and tell me I'm disqualified?"

A number of responses — none of them pleasant — ran through Meeks's mind. But he stifled them. "I've learned through a lot of years in a lot of scorers' tents that you just let players vent in there," he said. "I think I snapped back once, in 1987, when Tom Kite, who I consider a friend, came in after shooting 75 the first day and started going off about how poorly the golf course was set up. I said, 'Tom, you know that's not fair. You're blaming your bad play on the USGA.' He just kind of stormed off. The next day he came up to me and said he was sorry, that I was right. Still, I've learned to just let them go after a bad round."

Meeks let Lee Janzen go. But he wasn't happy to do so.

Most golfers know Tom Meeks and know his role with the USGA. Almost none of them have any idea who Mike Butz is. Which is fine with Butz, whose title is assistant executive director, meaning he is the number two man in the organization. All the details David Fay hates dealing with, Butz takes care of. Fay is the out-front guy, Butz the man behind the throne. Which is fine with him. He loves to work in the shadows. When the Golf Channel was putting together a thirty-minute documentary on the key people involved in putting on the Open, the producers kept trying to pin Butz down on a time when they could talk to him on camera. Butz kept telling them — honestly — that he was busy. After a while, though, he admitted he was ducking them.

"It's sort of a challenge," he said, laughing. "I'm pretty sure they don't need me, because they've talked to all the other guys, so I'm going to see how long I can go without actually talking to them."

While Fay and Meeks and even the low-key Mike-squared (Davis) all willingly spend time with NBC during Open week discussing the golf course and the logistics of the event and the weather and anything else the TV types want discussed, Butz is nowhere to be found around the TV compound. He's just as happy to be inside the off-limits-to-everyone weather center monitoring incoming storms with the weather interns hired for the week.

"I guess I'm my father's son that way," Butz said with a laugh. "He's always been a guy who was never big on calling attention to himself."

Stan Butz grew up in the small western Pennsylvania town of Crabtree. His father was a coal miner, and his mother died when he was in junior high school. He dropped out of school following the eighth grade to help out with his six siblings at home. At seventeen he became a Maytag washing machine salesman, a dream job since the automatic washing machine had just been invented. "He said it was a can't-miss deal," Mike Butz said. "People got one look at what the thing could do and bought it."

Like a lot of kids from western Pennsylvania, Stan Butz grew up playing football and baseball. He first heard about golf from a supervisor at Maytag. Curious, he went to a hardware store and bought a set of clubs. Making his sales rounds one day, he drove past Ligonier Country Club. Since he had some free time, he pulled off the road, walked into the pro shop, and asked where a beginner might go to learn something about golf.

"Well," said the pro, "you might just go out to the first tee and join up with those two guys getting ready to tee off."

"But I've never played," Stan Butz said.

"They won't mind."

So Stan Butz picked up his clubs, walked to the first tee, and introduced himself to the two men, explaining he'd never played before but the pro thought it might be okay if he tagged along with them. No problem, said the two men.

The first one introduced himself as Deacon Palmer. He had a young son at the time to whom he was just teaching the game. His name was Arnold. The second man was a friend of Deacon Palmer's from overseas who was visiting him. His name was Bobby Locke. Between 1949 and 1957, he would win the British Open four times.

So Stan Butz played his first nine holes of golf with Arnold Palmer's father and a future four-time British Open champion. And apparently did okay. "I think he just baseball-gripped it, swung away, and hit it pretty well," his son said.

Soon after taking up golf, Stan Butz was on a business trip. En route from Chicago to San Francisco, he had a rough ride. He had been out a little too late the night before, and the trip on the DC-3 didn't make him feel any better. An attractive young stewardess (they were still called stewardesses back then) helped him through the flight. When it was over and he was feeling better, he asked Betty Moss if he could have her phone number. It wasn't long after that they were married.

They eventually settled in Chambersburg, a town of about 18,000 a couple of hours east of Crabtree, in central Pennsylvania. Stan Butz opened a furniture and electronics shop, and his oldest son, Sam, became his partner when he grew up. Mike, born in 1956, was the third of the four children. By the time he was four, he was tagging along to Chambersburg Country Club most weekends with his father. Stan Butz had won the first of his eight club championships there in 1946 (he won the last in 1971 at the age of fifty-five), and all the Butz kids became golfers. "My sister [Cathy] might have had the most talent," Mike said. "But back then golf was sort of a guy's game, so she never really got caught up in it. The rest of us did."

Mike had thoughts of playing college golf but they ended fairly quickly when he got to Wake Forest in 1974. Wake was *the* college golf power in the country at the time and had players like Curtis Strange, Jay Haas, Scott Hoch, and Bob Byman, who would go on to win forty PGA Tour events among them, including Strange's two U.S. Opens. "I was about a three-handicap," Butz said. "There were guys who couldn't make the traveling squad who I couldn't even think about competing against. I think they had 125 guys try out for ten spots — backup spots — behind Curtis and Jay and Scott and all those other guys. Intramural golf at Wake was brutal. You could shoot even par in a match and get closed out on the 14th hole. I was way over my head."

In fact, it took Butz a while to adjust to college. Wake is a small school with little more than 3,000 students, but it seemed huge to him. On his first day on campus, he pulled in, driving a 1971 orange Datsun, and parked behind the Wake chapel. As he was getting out of the car, a man walked up to him with a smile on his face.

"First day on campus?" he said.

"How'd you know that?"

"Because anyone who has been here before knows if you park here for more than about five minutes, you get towed. What dorm are you looking for?"

"Kitchin."

"Get in your car and follow me."

As it turned out, Butz's savior was the janitor for the nearby administration building.

He learned his way around campus, recovered from an awful first semester academically, and graduated with a degree in business, moved to Atlanta, and got a job selling copiers for 3M — a little tougher sell in 1978 than washing machines had been in 1932. "But I did make the sale on my very first presentation," he said. "I

was giving my little speech when someone asked about the kind of
toner we used, because the liquid toner they had in their copier
was always spilling all over the carpet whenever they had to open
the machine. I said, 'Aha, we now have *dry* toner.' I opened the
machine to show it to them but forgot to turn off a fan inside the
machine. The fan blew the toner all over my brand-new three-
piece suit. I was black from head to toe. They felt so bad for me,
they bought the copier."

Knowing that particular sales pitch wouldn't work forever, Butz
took a job working for BASF, the German audio-video company,
and spent most of a year pitching Beta tapes to people in a market
dominated by VHS. "The BASF people kept saying VHS will die
out, we're sticking with Beta," Butz said. "That was 1979. I don't
think it's happened yet."

While he was wondering how to sell Beta in a VHS world, Butz
was visited by an old high school buddy, Steve Dodd, who was trying out with the Atlanta Braves. On a rainy Sunday afternoon, the
two of them were watching the conclusion of that week's golf tournament on TV when Dodd turned to Butz and said, "Do you ever
find yourself still dreaming the dream?"

Butz laughed, remembering how shocked he had been to find
that a three-handicap at Wake Forest and a quarter would get you
a cup of coffee. "Steve," he said, "the dream died about six years
ago."

Dodd was quiet for a moment. Then he said. "Well, did you ever
think that there are people out there who *run* golf tournaments?"

That comment got Butz's attention. "In fact, I had never given
that any thought," he said. For a week, Butz couldn't get Dodd's
line out of his head. Finally, he went to a library, pulled out a book
on sports organizations, and looked under golf. He knew about the
PGA Tour, and he also knew there was something called the PGA
of America, which was made up of club pros. He had never heard
of the USGA. When he got to the listing, he read past all the stuff
about being in charge of the rules and promoting and growing the
game of golf to the list of events it ran. One jumped out at him: the
United States Open Championship.

Now that, thought Butz, sounds cool.

He wrote three letters, one to the PGA of America, one to the PGA Tour, and one to the USGA. In each he described himself as a young businessman with a passion for golf who had been a decent player. He mentioned that he was a Wake Forest graduate, knowing the reputation of its golf program, without specifically pointing out that his college play had been limited to intramurals.

Remarkably, he got a phone call soon after from P. J. Boatwright. "What I didn't know, of course, was that three days before my letter arrived at Golf House, Mike Waldron, who was the regional affairs director, had left to take a job at the LPGA," Butz said. "His office was in Atlanta."

Boatwright asked Butz if he could fly up to New Jersey for an interview. Yes, he could. He flew up there — "I think I paid for the plane ticket," he remembered — met with Boatwright, and was offered Waldron's job. BASF was paying him $20,000 and providing him with a car. The USGA offered $17,000 and no car. Unlike Tom Meeks, Butz didn't negotiate. "It was less money and no car," he said. "But it was golf. It was the people who ran the U.S. Open. I was doing it."

He moved into a small office space in Marietta that was right behind Ed's Barbecue and began measuring courses, doing rules clinics (once he learned the rules), and helping out with USGA events in the Southeast. In the summer of 1980, having been on the job for a little more than three months, Butz got a call from David Fay, who was then enduring his second summer as tournament relations manager, meaning he was on the road from early May, when he went out to advance the Open, until September, when the last of the (then) seven USGA Championships was played. Fay was coming to Nashville to run the Women's Open and wanted the new regional affairs director to help him during the week. Butz was more than happy to oblige.

Nashville in August was predictably brutal. "I think the average temperature for the week was about 107," Butz remembered. On one sweltering afternoon, Butz and Fay were inside the clubhouse when a call came across the radio for Fay. The Tennessee State mounted police had just come through the USGA compound and their horses had left behind quite a few, well, remembrances. "We need some help figuring out just what to do," Butz heard someone saying to Fay through the radio.

The next sound Butz heard was Fay's radio shattering against a wall on the other side of the room. "Keep a close eye on what I'm doing the rest of the week," Fay said. "Because next year at this time, you might be the one doing it."

Butz didn't take the comment all that seriously, figuring it was 107-degree heat, twelve weeks on the road, and cleaning up after police horses talking. But sure enough, that October, he got a phone call asking if he was willing to move to New Jersey to succeed Fay. In essence, that meant he would be responsible for running the 1981 U.S. Open. "In one year I had gone from never having heard of the USGA to running the U.S. Open," Butz said. "The whole thing was slightly unreal."

He got through that first Open at Merion with considerable help from a woman named Nancy Jupp, who had been contracted by the various clubs through the years to run their end of each Open. But it wasn't easy. On Wednesday night, he left Merion shortly after ten P.M., nervous as a cat about whether everything was in place for play to begin. He was supposed to meet a friend who lived in Philadelphia for a late dinner. One block from the club, his car died. Butz left it sitting on a corner of Ardmore Avenue and ran — it was, naturally, raining — to a nearby gas station. He convinced someone there to tow the car to the station and get a mechanic to look at it the next morning. He then called his friend and told him what happened.

"I was staying in an apartment about thirty minutes from the club," Butz said. "There was no way to get back there and get back at five-thirty the next morning. Fortunately, my friend had a brother who lived right near the club. I ended up spending the night sleeping on the floor in the nursery with their two-month-old daughter."

Butz — who normally looks as if he just stepped off a shoot for *GQ* — returned to Merion the next day for the first day of his first

U.S. Open wearing the same mud-spattered clothes he had worn the day before. "To say I got some funny looks," he said, "would be a vast understatement."

For the next five summers, Butz directed all the USGA Championships. In 1985, on a sweltering August day, he was trying to put up a starter's tent in preparation for the U.S. Women's Open at Baltusrol. "One minute I was hammering something, the next minute I was looking up at everyone," he said. "Apparently, I just fainted."

They took him to the hospital and ran a battery of tests. The doctors finally came in to tell him that they had reached a comprehensive conclusion about his condition: He was really, really tired. After that, Frank Hannigan took steps to cut back his workload, but Butz, whose son, Spencer, had been born in 1984, with daughter Molly coming along four years later, was still on the road for most of the summer. Finally, after Fay took over in 1989, it was decided that he needed full-time assistance on all the championships, not some help on some championships.

That was when Mike I called Mike II.

Mike Davis is seven years younger than Butz and knew his younger brother Joe better than he knew Mike growing up in Chambersburg. "I played a fair amount of golf as a kid with Mr. Butz [Stan] because I was always hanging out at the club," he said. "I knew of Mike more than I actually knew him."

Davis's father, Bill, was a lawyer, a man whose nature was so non-confrontational that he often turned down cases if they involved litigation because he found verbal sparring in the courtroom distasteful. That characteristic clearly was handed down to his only son. Davis's definition of being seriously critical of someone often involves a solemn shake of the head and saying something like, "Gosh, you know, I think we goofed on that one."

Davis was a very good player as a teenager, winning the Pennsylvania Junior Amateur in high school, though he never did qualify for the U.S. Junior or the U.S. Amateur. "Been an alternate a bunch of times," he said. "But never got in."

He chose Georgia Southern for college, even though academically he could have gone a lot of other places. His reasoning was simple: Georgia Southern was a golf power. "It wasn't as if I thought I was absolutely going to be a pro or anything. I wasn't that foolish," he said. "But my priority was golf. My decision making was based on golf. I wanted to go somewhere I could play and find out how good I could get."

He found out quickly it wasn't going to be good enough — at least in terms of a career. "I took one look at Jodie Mudd and Gene Sauers [teammates who went on to win tournaments on the PGA Tour] and said, 'Whoa, this is a different level — one I'm not going to get to.'"

He played on the team for four years, always the solid guy in the middle of the lineup who would deliver a score around par. "I was never the guy who would shoot 67 or 77," he said. "Low 70s. Steady, a good guy to have around but nothing special."

His degree was in business, and like Butz, he landed in Atlanta after graduation, selling commercial real estate. In the course of sending out résumés as a college senior he decided to send one to Butz, who by then was established at the USGA. "I knew Mike was there, I knew he'd know my name at least, and I liked golf," he said. "I didn't expect anything to come of it. I got a very nice note from Mike saying he'd keep my résumé around in case something came up. I never dreamed he'd actually do it."

Butz did it. When it came time for him to look for someone who would eventually take his job, he thought of Davis. He knew he'd been a good player, had liked him the few times they met, and thought he might have the kind of even-keel personality needed for the job. The only issue was money.

"I was three years out of school, and things were going very well for me," Davis said. "I was with Coldwell Banker, and we were involved in some nice projects. Going to the USGA was going to mean a fairly serious pay cut."

It was his boss who made the decision for him, telling him if things didn't work out at the USGA he could come back. Davis came on board early in 1990 and traveled to Medinah with Butz that spring to begin preparing for the Open. That he was going to be involved in putting together a United States Open was almost an incomprehensible thrill for him.

"We get to Medinah, and Mike calls me in for my first assignment," Davis remembered. "All the magnetics from our leader boards — the numbers, the letters for players' names — are shipped from site to site every year. They had just arrived. Mike wanted me to go down and inventory them."

So Davis's first job at his first U.S. Open was to sit in the middle of a parking lot and stack letters and numbers, keeping a careful count and being sure not to mix the *t*'s with the *i*'s. It was a huge job, made no easier when one box turned out to be filled with carpenter ants. Welcome to the glamorous world of championship golf.

8

Getting Ready, Phase Two

ON A REMARKABLY warm late November day, Craig Currier and Dave Catalano stood outside the Bethpage clubhouse, blinking into the morning sun. Catalano had a cigarette in one hand, a Diet Coke in the other. Currier had his hands wrapped around a cup of coffee. Both had been on the grounds since dawn, but now, with the clock pushing seven they were checking their watches as if sunset would be closing in soon.

"He's late," Catalano declared at precisely seven.

"Good," said Currier. "Means I've got something to give him a hard time about."

It had been more than five years since the euphoric day in August 1996 when the formal announcement that the U.S. Open was coming to Bethpage had been made. Much had changed around the park since then. Rees Jones and his men had completed the redesign and the clubhouse had been completely rebuilt, redone by Carlyle on the Green to the tune of $8 million.

"It's too damn nice," David Fay said when he saw it. "It looks like an upscale country club. That's not what this is supposed to be."

Fay had similar complaints about the golf course. Given the money to hire a veritable army — he now had seventy people working on the five golf courses — and given money for new equipment, Currier had taken Jones's rebuilt golf course and made it pristine. The scruffy, beat-up muni that the USGA Twelve had played in 1995 was long gone. It had been replaced by a sparkling, beautifully manicured golf course, one that could compete with any country club when it came to conditioning.

"I wonder," Currier said, grinning his broad grin, "if Tim Moraghan still thinks this isn't going to be like Congressional."

During the five years that they had worked together, the Bethpage group and the USGA group had grown close, become friends. Which was why Currier was so much looking forward to Tom Meeks's arrival that morning. Meeks being late would be a good place to start the ribbing that would continue throughout the day.

At 7:07, Meeks pulled into the parking lot.

"What'd you do, sleep in?" Currier yelled before he had even climbed out of his car.

"I've been up since four-thirty," answered Meeks, who made the two-hour drive from Clinton that morning, leaving his house at five to beat the traffic into New York.

This was, by his unofficial count, Meeks's tenth trip to Bethpage since the Open had been awarded to the golf course. Normally, he would have had Moraghan with him, but Moraghan was away at a meeting of agronomists. No one from the USGA had spent more time at Bethpage than Moraghan, who, it can be argued, has the most thankless job at the USGA this side of Meeks.

As the tournament agronomist, Moraghan, who is forty-five, is charged with overseeing the work of the local superintendent at each USGA championship golf course. He is expected to make certain the course is in the best shape possible.

An agronomist is, simply put, a turf expert. In Moraghan's case, he was part turf guy, part superintendent, part architect. He worked with the architect, making suggestions on what grasses should be used on greens, tees, fairways, and roughs. This varied depending on weather. Certain grasses worked some places and not in others. He worked with all the local superintendents on basic maintenance, on decisions on length of rough, speed of greens (Meeks was also very involved in all this), and whether some trees should stay or go around the golf course. Technically, Moraghan had final say on almost nothing. But because everyone from Fay down respected his expertise both technically and in a golf sense, he was listened to more often than not.

If something is wrong with a golf course, Moraghan will hear about it. When the 18th green at Southern Hills looked like a potential disaster area during practice rounds in 2001 (balls were hitting on the center of the green and rolling off the green and all the way down a hill), Fay went straight to Moraghan and Meeks with one question: How the hell could this happen? The answer was lengthy and complicated and had to do with different sorts of grass and seeding, but the bottom line was Fay held them — not the local superintendent or the architect who had done the redesign of the golf course — responsible.

If a golf course was considered a success, however, if the players raved about its conditioning, all the credit went to the local superintendent and the architect. Already stories were being written singing the praises of Jones's redesign and Currier's work with the greens, the bunkers, and the fairways. Both deserved every bit of credit they were getting. But no one — repeat no one — ever mentioned Moraghan, who had worked with both men on the project from day one.

Moraghan would have loved more attention, but he understood that not getting credit came with the territory. "Everything I have in my life, I got because of golf," he said. "I have a job I love. I get to travel to great places and play great golf courses [like most at the USGA, he is a single-digit handicapper, usually playing to about a three], and I've met great people. I've gotten to be friends with a lot of the best players in the world and met a group of people I really enjoy. Heck, I met my wife because of golf [Karen Moraghan was the Open tournament director at Pebble Beach in '92], so how can I complain about any of it?"

Still, Moraghan wouldn't have minded if once, just once, during the Open awards ceremony somebody would say, "And thanks, too, to Tim Moraghan. . . ."

It wasn't likely to happen anytime soon.

Meeks was at Bethpage on that November day for one of his periodic course checks. The Black Course had closed for the winter a week earlier, and Currier and his staff had started working to repair the damage done by the 45,000 rounds of golf that had been played there since April.

The Black gets far less play than any of the other four courses at Bethpage. It is the only one of the courses that shuts down during the winter, and since golf carts aren't allowed, it takes longer for players to get around the golf course. What's more, some shy away from the course, taking the sign on the first tee seriously.

"People love to play the Red because it's also a Tillinghast design, it's tough, but not as tough as the Black, and you can play it in a cart," Catalano said. "The others are also cheaper than the Black, which for a lot of public course players is important."

The state had raised the greens fee for the Black from $25 on weekdays and $29 on weekends to $31 and $39 two years earlier, just prior to the time when, by contract with the USGA, it could not raise the greens fee until one year after the Open. Bernadette Castro had called Fay before the increase had gone into effect, not wanting him to think the state was doing an end run on the USGA before the contract kicked in.

Since it was such a nice day, Meeks and Currier, joined by Garrett Boddington along the way, decided to walk rather than ride.

Most of what he saw pleased Meeks. The fairways had been narrowed to Open-style widths, some of them no more than 26 yards across in the landing areas, most of them 28 to 30 yards. On each hole, Meeks took his special Bushnell binoculars and stood on one side of the fairway while Currier stood on the other side so he could get an exact reading. The only fairway Meeks thought a little bit wide was at number five, which was 28 yards across 180 yards from the green. "What do you think, Craig?" Meeks asked.

"I think we should tweak it in a little from the left side," Currier said.

"I agree," Meeks said, making a note.

Meeks was working off a sheet he had brought with suggested changes from his last visit. At each spot where he had asked for a change, he checked to see the results. Most were to his liking. He was especially happy with the new tee on the ninth hole, which had extended the hole by about 25 yards and made it almost impossible for a player to take a previously available shortcut down the left side. The parks department had actually swapped a piece of land with SUNY Farmingdale in order to have the room to move the tee back.

"We took a nothing hole here," Meeks summed up, "and made it into something good."

He and Currier made their way down the ninth fairway, only to have to swerve into the rough because of goose droppings. Currier shook his head in disgust.

"I hired a guy to deal with this," he said. "He's supposed to come out here early in the morning with four or five collies and chase the geese away. But he's been coming too early. He chases them away, and then they come back before the sun's up. I'm going to have to talk to him again."

Meeks and Currier finished checking the ninth green and walked to the 10th tee. "The front nine will play three strokes easier than the back," Currier predicted. "The guys who have to start on 10 are not going to be happy. Just look at this hole." He waved his hand in the direction of the fairway, which was out somewhere in the distance — after one carried a tee shot at least 230 yards over high grass, fescue, and rough.

Meeks shook his head. "We are definitely going to hear about that decision," he said.

The decision he was referring to was to start the Open from two tees. Traditionally, the major championships have always had every player start every round on the first tee and finish every round on the 18th green. For years, though, the PGA Tour has used what is called a two-tee start, having players tee off simultaneously from the first and 10th tees in two waves — one in the morning, the other in the afternoon. Using two tees usually does two things: It makes for a better pace of play because the afternoon wave starts with open holes in front instead of being backed up right away by players who have just teed off, and it makes the last tee time — and thus the finish — much earlier.

In 2001, the first threesome had teed off of number one at Southern Hills at six-thirty. The last group had gone off at three-twenty, meaning that even without a rain delay it would have been fighting darkness at the finish, since later rounds usually take at least five and a half hours the first two days at the Open. With a two-tee start, the first group wouldn't tee off until seven-fifteen — giving the grounds crew more time to get the course ready for play in the morning — and the last group would be off by 2:05.

"In other words, we save at least two hours before all is said and done," David Fay had said. "To me, it's pretty obvious that the time to do this has come. Talk tradition all you want, we've got to do what is best for the championship."

Others, however, did talk tradition. They talked about everyone playing the golf course in the same manner — one through 18 — as the architect meant it to be played. That argument was absolutely specious. For one thing, Open courses were often what are called combos, grabbing a hole here and there from an adjoining course on a thirty-six-hole layout to make the course tougher or fairer or easier to get around. When the Open was played at Congressional in 1964, the 17th hole of the golf course was played as the 18th because no one wanted the Open to end on a par-three. In 1997, Judy Bell, then the USGA president, decided to play Congressional's Blue Course as it was — ending the Open on that par-three.

"And we got killed for doing that," Fay said. "No matter what you do, you're going to hear complaints."

He was right about that. The day the USGA had announced the two-tee start, Meeks had gotten a phone call from Frank Hannigan, denouncing the USGA for caving in to the players. It was Hannigan's contention that the two-tee start was needed because players had been allowed through the years to slow their pace of play to a crawl. Hannigan thought the answer was to start warning them, timing them, and penalizing them rather than giving them two more hours of daylight to creep around. ("Ask Frank how many players he penalized for pace of play," Fay huffed.)

In fact, players *are* considerably slower today than they were twenty, thirty, or forty years ago, and nothing the USGA does is going to change that. "The first truly slow player was Ben Hogan," Fay said. "What he did was this: he said to the USGA and everyone else, 'This is how I play. If you want to penalize me for it, go ahead — if you dare.'"

No one dared. And after that, no one dared penalize Cary Middlecoff or Jack Nicklaus. Today, no one dares penalize Tiger Woods, who can be maniacally slow.

"These days everyone is slow," Fay said. "The last truly fast players in golf were [Tom] Watson, [Tom] Kite, and [Lanny] Wadkins. They were outnumbered. Now, all the young guys have these psychologists who tell them they have to visualize their shot before they get over the ball. Christ, go out and watch college golf or any amateur tournament or your club championship and you'll see all these guys visualizing their damn shots. It's maddening. But it's what they do. Should they play faster? Of course. But if we turn around and slap Tiger Woods with a two-shot penalty during the Open, we'll get killed for it. And Frank Hannigan and everyone else knows that. Two tees is common sense in today's world, especially with all the weather delays we get. For whatever reason, if you look back, there just weren't as many weather delays thirty years ago as there are now."

At a lot of golf courses, the 10th tee is virtually adjacent or at least close to the first tee. But Bethpage has what is called Scottish routing — the first nine holes go out and the second nine holes come back into the clubhouse, meaning that the 10th tee is as far from the clubhouse as any spot on the golf course.

With a two-tee start, the players starting on number 10 would have to be transported from the clubhouse to the 10th tee. Since they couldn't simply be carted through the hordes of people outside the ropes on the golf course and since they couldn't be taken inside the ropes with play going on, they would have to be taken in vans onto the roads surrounding the course and then back onto the golf course at number 10. This meant another major headache for Steve Worthy and Frank Bussey, who were told to find the quickest, most efficient route to get the players to the tee on time.

"Problem is," Currier said, "there is no quick way. No matter what route you take, it's going to take fifteen or twenty minutes to get out here."

That wasn't going to make players happy. Every golfer has a routine he goes through preround. Usually, it involves warming up on the range, making their way to the putting green, and walking on to the tee two or three minutes prior to their tee time. If it was going to take twenty minutes to get from the putting green to the tee, a lot of players were going to be concerned about stiffening up on the ride there.

That was one headache. The other headache was the routing itself. Worthy found a route that he calculated could cut the ride down to under ten minutes, especially since Round Swamp Road would be closed to traffic during the week of the championship. But there was a problem: The route went right through a Superfund site — a spot that had been designated by the federal government as environmentally dangerous because toxic materials had previously been used there. In this case, it was an old paint factory.

The Department of Environmental Control (DEC) was not inclined to cooperate, but eventually they offered a compromise: The players could be transported through the Superfund area if each time they rode through it, they signed waivers while in the van and handed them to a DEC employee as they approached the site.

Worthy had visions of players balking enroute to the 10th tee at signing or someone insisting on reading the waiver. Or, most likely, players simply not understanding what was involved and getting upset about being asked to learn what was involved five minutes before they teed off in the U.S. Open. He met with the DEC one last time to see if he could explain the uniqueness of the situation, pointing out that no one involved would spend any time on the site but would merely pass through it in a closed vehicle.

No go. It was the DEC's way or the highway. Worthy decided to find another route.

A lot of people, Meeks included, had thought of waiting until 2003, when the logistics of a two-tee start would set up much more easily at Olympia Fields outside of Chicago. Not Fay. "We did it at Pine Needles for the Women's Open and that was the same kind of deal, the 10th tee out in the middle of the golf course," he said. "We did it there, we can do it here."

Of course that had been a relatively quiet tournament with 15,000 spectators in a quiet corner of North Carolina, without all the headaches brought on by post-9/11 security measures. And there had been no superfund site involved. This would be in the post-9/11 world in the middle of Long Island with more than 42,000 spectators on the grounds. And a superfund site to deal with.

"Not a problem, " Worthy said, repeating his mantra. "We'll figure something out."

Currier was certainly right about one thing. Starting a round on the 10th hole — van rides aside — would not be easy. Where the front nine began with an average par-four, a short par-four, a middle iron par-three, and a birdieable par-five, the back began with a monster par-four, a deceptively hard par-four, and the longest par-four in history.

"You could have guys standing on the 13th tee at two or three over par, looking at the board, seeing guys playing the front nine who are already a couple under," Meeks said. "That could be discouraging." Of course a good start on those first three holes might give a player a boost, knowing he would reach the front side already warmed up and with his early jitters behind him.

The 10th was the toughest driving hole on the course because the carry to the fairway was so far. Some of the shorter hitters would have trouble reaching the fairway, especially in any kind of wind. If they did, they would still be looking at more than 200 yards to the green in many cases. The 12th was listed as 499 yards. "It's actually 501 from here," Meeks said, looking down at the tee marker. "But we'll play it under 500 so the players won't get on us for making a 500-yard par-four. We could play it all the way back up to 515. But we won't do that."

The next two holes — the par-five 13th and the par-three 14th — represented the only respite on the back nine. Currier was worried that the short 14th might be too easy. "Don't worry, Craig," Meeks said. "We'll tuck a couple of flags."

From 14 green, the players would walk down a hill and back across Round Swamp Road. Even without the Currier-Boddington tee — which would be covered by a bleacher, much to their chagrin — 15 would be as tough a par-four as you could find. The second shot was straight uphill to an elevated green, the only green on the course that worried Meeks in terms of hole locations.

Most of Bethpage's greens are relatively small and flat. The 15th, though, is a multitiered green where any ball that lands on the front will back off the green and down the hill leading to it. Any front-hole location would lead to Southern Hills 18th–type of scenes, with balls landing hole high and ending up 50 yards from the flag.

"We won't even go anyplace near the front," Meeks said, surveying the green. "That would be suicide."

The 16th was Meeks's favorite hole, a downhill tee shot to a deceptively difficult green. "Most underrated hole on the course," he said. The 17th was where a lot of people thought the tournament would be decided, a long par-three with a wide green, deep bunkers, and a natural amphitheater around the green that could create a wild scene in the final moments of the Open.

And then there was 18. No hole had been redone more in the redesign than 18 for the simple reason that everyone believed it was a weak closing hole, especially for the 72nd hole of a major championship. The tee had been moved, the bunkers had been moved closer to the fairway, and the rough around the green had been lengthened. "It is the one hole on the golf course that you must now describe as being a Rees Jones hole," Fay said. "Because he had to completely redo it. There was no choice."

Fay had one complaint when he saw the new hole. "Looks too nice," he said. "It has no muni feel at all." He had complained about this several times, but most notably at 18. Currier had let the rough grow a little bit more and had allowed grass to grow around the bunkers. "Scruff it up a little," he said.

It was true — what Meeks saw on that November day could hardly be described as scruffy. In the seven years since Fay's walk, the Black had gone from being the teenage girl with thick glasses and her hair tied in a bun to a drop-dead gorgeous young woman who dropped jaws at the class reunion.

"This place is ready," Meeks said, stomping into the clubhouse, his feet soaking wet, a satisfied smile on his face. "We could tee it up tomorrow and play if we wanted to."

9

Counting the Days

GOLF NEVER STOPS completely at Bethpage. While the Black Course shuts down for the winter, the other courses remain open. And, if the weather on a given day is above freezing, there are going to be golfers showing up to play.

During those months, a good deal of time is spent inside the clubhouse, which nowadays has the look and feel of an upscale country club rather than a downscale muni.

"I think a lot of the regulars preferred it more downscale than this," Jon Barker said one day during the lunch hour, looking around at an almost empty dining room. "In the old days, you grabbed a tray, went through the line, had lunch for five or six bucks, and you were done. Now, it takes longer and it's more expensive. The food is much better, but I'm not sure this is what they're looking for."

David Fay, whose favorite place to eat near Golf House is the local train station, agrees with those regulars. "It looks and feels like a country club," he said. "I'm not criticizing the work there or the money spent, it just wasn't what I had in mind."

For the purposes of the Open, though, the clubhouse was perfect. The new locker rooms provided the kind of atmosphere players were used to — new lockers with lots of space, comfortable carpeting — and the ballrooms at the far end of the building from where the restaurant was located would provide plenty of space for hospitality. There would be a hospitality room for guests of the state; a separate room for corporate table-holders, who would pay $40,000 for a ten-seat table inside the clubhouse; another room set aside for evening events; and then the restaurant itself, which would be used for USGA hospitality — members of the executive committee, past presidents, and their guests. The pro shop would be the player hospitality area. Every piece of merchandise would be moved out a month before the Open so the shop could be made over to fit the needs of players and their families.

In other words, every inch of the refurbished building would be needed and would be used during Open week.

"And when it's all over," Dave Catalano said, "it will be awfully quiet around here."

Months before the Open, Catalano and everyone working at Bethpage were beginning to wonder what would happen after June 16. "We've all been working on this for almost six years," he said one winter morning, sitting in a corner of the bar, the one room in the clubhouse where smoking was allowed. "Obviously, we have plenty to do on a daily basis in the park, but there's not a day that goes by where we aren't thinking about the Open or making decisions regarding the Open or doing something that is Open related. It's become a big part of our lives. I think not having it be part of our lives is going to be a big adjustment. I'll miss a lot of those people we've been working with."

Catalano would turn fifty-five on September ninth and would be fully vested with the state at that point. "In other words," he said, "I'll be making the same money working as I can make not working."

He was holding off any decisions on retirement until the Open was over. In fact, he had made a pact with Craig Currier that he would stay if Currier stayed. Because the golf course had received so much attention already, everyone expected Currier to be flooded with offers from ritzy clubs to go work for big money making their golf courses as pristine as the Black. Currier wasn't thinking in those terms.

"I'd like to stay," he said that same morning. "I'd like to think the state is still going to have reason to want to keep these golf courses in great shape when the Open is over and will spend the money to continue to have the staff and the equipment." He smiled. "For the last five years, I've had five golf courses to work on. That means there's always something to do. I've been helping to get one course ready for a U.S. Open, and the only guy I really have to deal with before I do anything is Dave.

"So now the Open's over and some club comes to me and says here's a lot of money to come work for them. Probably I have one golf course and some greens chairman who thinks he knows more about the golf course than I do. My big challenge every summer is making sure it looks great for the member-guest. Wow, how exciting. And then, after we do get it into great shape, they could turn around and say we don't need you anymore, and then what do I do?"

The answer to that worst-case scenario was probably move on to another ritzy club for more big bucks, maybe even a club that was getting ready to host a U.S. Open. The larger point was that Currier liked being where he was. Catalano was not only an ideal boss but almost a second father to him. His "members" were people he could relate to, sit down with in the morning for a cup of coffee.

"Dave, we're going to have so much work to do when this is over the snow will be flying before we even get a chance to breathe," he said. "And you're going to be right here with me when it does."

Catalano smiled. "Whatever you say, boss," he said.

There were still a lot of miles to be traveled before anyone could start worrying about post-Open blues. By early March, as the mild winter began to wind down, Jon Barker had plenty of company at the far end of the parking lot. He had moved from the small cabin that had served as his office for the better part of three years into a double-wide trailer that had two offices, a conference room, a reception area, and two large storage rooms. It felt like the Taj Mahal.

Frank Bussey had been on-site off and on throughout the fall and moved into the operations trailer — a smaller double-wide that was down the hill from Barker world — on a full-time basis in midwinter. Bussey had his hands full dealing with the contractors who needed to start laying down temporary roads and building the various tents that would turn Bethpage into a small city of about 65,000 people for one week. In 1998, at the end of the Open at Olympic, some of the locals who had worked with Bussey throughout the winter and spring had presented him with a wooden sign. It said: "Welcome to Busseyville. Mayor, Frank Bussey. Population, 1."

The population of his latest Busseyville was expanding on a daily basis as the weather slowly turned warmer. The worst weather of the winter came late. March was full of rain and wind and a couple of small snowstorms. It slowed things down considerably.

"You have to plan for some bad weather," he said. "Our only goal is to have everything up and ready on Sunday night at eight o'clock before Open week begins. We do that, I'm very happy."

This was Bussey's eleventh Open. Had he ever met that goal?

"Once," he said, "and that was an accident."

Up the hill from Busseyville, Barker's empire was expanding almost daily. In late 2000, he had been joined in Bethpage by Tricia Solow because there was just too much work for one person. At twenty-four, Solow was even younger than Barker, but like him acted as if she had been putting on major championships for about twenty years. On March first, two interns and a temporary assistant joined the staff.

Soon after that, two more trailers sprang up next to Barker's trailer. One was for Mimi Griffin and her corporate staff. The other was for Mary Lopuszynski and her merchandise staff. Lopuszynski's arrival in late March meant that Bussey's workload tripled. At least it felt that way. Lopuszynski's tent — which was referred to by one and all who worked for the USGA simply as Mary's tent — would be the largest on the grounds: 300 feet by 100 feet. It also had to be built to Lopuszynski's exact specs because she wanted to make certain every foot of available space was used to maximum efficiency. She was well aware of the fact that there would be more people at this U.S. Open than any other, and she was going to be very upset if her tent didn't do record business.

Lopuszynski's attention to detail — to use the polite term — was the subject of much kidding among USGA employees. In the weeks leading up to the championship, when Bussey would conduct morning meetings that involved all the on-site department heads, he would finish the meeting by going around the room and asking people what they needed. When he got to Lopuszynski he would look at her, pretend not to see her, and go on to the next person.

"He knows I'll get him sooner or later," Lopuszynski said, laughing. "I let him do it because it gives him the false impression that he can somehow escape. We never fight. We just have a special way of communicating."

Barker, who often had a ringside seat for the Lopuszynski-Bussey tête-à-têtes, always laughed when Bussey threw up his hands, screaming that there was no way to get the specs for that corner of the tent exactly as Lopuszynski was demanding and that no reasonable person would even think to ask for such a thing.

"And then, of course, he gives Mary exactly what she wants," Barker said. "We all do that, though. What's the saying? There's something about Mary.

Mary was thirty-eight, 5 feet 8, with dirty-blond hair, a friendly smile, and one deep, dark secret that she tried to keep strangers from learning: she was (is) an absolute, completely out-of-her-mind U2 groupie. She would travel anywhere, anytime to see the group perform, and according to informed sources, would scream, yell, dance, and act like a complete fool at any U2 concert she could get to. She claimed to have watched the entire 2002 Super

Bowl, not just the halftime show, which featured U2, but few people who knew her bought the story.

"Ask her the final score," someone suggested.

"Um, well, it was a great game," she answered when the question was raised.

What made the whole U2 thing so amusing to those who knew her was that it was so completely out of character. If you were to suggest that she grew fangs at night and slept in a coffin it would have been slightly more believable than the notion of her screaming her lungs out at a rock concert. This was someone who spent her days worrying for hours at a time about whether she had ordered enough U.S. Open–logo umbrellas or if there were enough cash registers to keep traffic flowing through her tent. The notion that she willingly spent evenings behaving like a lovesick sixteen-year-old was either jarring or hysterically funny. Or both.

"My one real fantasy is that Bono shows up at the Open, comes to the tent, and I give him a personal buying tour," she said one day while walking through her unfinished tent at Bethpage. "Then, of course, he invites me to sit onstage at his next concert while he performs, wearing our stuff."

And if Bono needed a stage built for that performance, Lopuszynski would no doubt call Bussey and demand he build it. In fifteen minutes.

And Bussey would get it done.

Lopuszynski had first worked for the USGA on a contract basis prior to the '95 Open at Shinnecock. She had grown up in the New York suburbs and started working in a pro shop in high school. She and her brother Mike had both worked for Jim McLean, the well-known teaching pro at Quaker Ridge Golf Club, which was right across the street from Winged Foot. Mike had gone on to become an excellent golfer, playing at Duke and then becoming a teaching pro himself. Mary went to Rollins, in Florida, and went home intending to work for McLean her first summer out of school and then find a job. At the end of the summer, McLean, whose teaching business was expanding, asked her to take over all of his pro shop and merchandising operations.

Soon after that, McLean began spending winters in Florida, at Doral Country Club in Miami, where he taught a number of pros — including Tom Kite — and a number of well-known golf people: Frank Hannigan and David Fay among them. It was Hannigan who first mentioned Lopuszynski to Mike Butz, and it was Butz who hired her when the USGA began to look seriously at taking its merchandising for the Open in-house.

Shinnecock was the first Open at which the USGA took the merchandising out of the hands of the club. For many years, the pros at the clubs ran the merchandising during the Open, and they often walked away with huge profits. In fact, there had been considerable unrest among the membership at the Olympic Club in 1987 because the pro ended up making more money from the Open than the club did.

As the USGA began moving more and more of its Open operations in-house, it made sense to eventually take over the merchandising, especially given the potential for great profit. Of course there was also danger, in that a poorly run operation could lose a lot of money. Once Lopuszynski was on board for '95 and had shown the USGA how much money there was to be made — the gross that first year was almost $8 million — there was no way they were going to let her leave, even though the contracts for four of the next five Opens — all but '98 — had already been written, with the host clubs or resorts holding the merchandising rights.

"Once '95 was over and Mary did what she did, it was pretty apparent we'd be foolish not to take the thing in-house on a permanent basis," Butz said. "I don't think any of us ever dreamed she would be able to do what she has done so quickly."

Lopuszynski spent '96 and '97 working on selling merchandise through the USGA catalog and to corporate customers while preparing for '98. She did the same sort of thing after '98 while preparing for 2001 and beyond. By the time the Open was held at Southern Hills in Tulsa in '01, she had her 300 by 100 tent and a gross exceeding $10 million — not including the more than $2 million in sales to corporate customers. For '02, Lopuszynski was hoping to go well over the $10 million mark.

"We're selling 17 percent more tickets," she said. "So I would hope our sales will go up 17 percent. We've ordered $10 million worth of product [retail], but we're ready to reorder right away if that becomes necessary."

Perhaps no one outside the legal staff was more affected by 9/11 than Lopuszynski and her staff. Every single truck or box coming into the park had to be security checked before it could be unloaded into the tent. Among the 4,850 volunteers, only the marshals (almost 1,800) were a larger group than the 1,067 folks assigned to Lopuszynski. What's more, no group of volunteers had more responsibility than Lopuszynski's. They would be manning forty-four cash registers and handling millions of dollars worth of merchandise, all the while trying to move potentially huge throngs through the tent, making sales, dealing with credit cards, and sometimes dealing with angry customers.

"Actually, if there's an angry customer, they're supposed to call me," Lopuszynski said. And if she couldn't solve the problem, there was only one thing left to do: call Bussey.

When the USGA staff gathered at Golf House in late March for their final pre-Open get-together, a lot had changed since the October meetings.

The questions about security remained an ongoing issue, one that would be changing constantly not only until the Open began but right until the moment it ended. "One thing is obvious," Mike Davis said. "We're going to have to make a lot of decisions on the fly. Some things that are going to look good on paper just aren't going to work in reality."

One example of that was the original plan to scan every credential of every person going to the range and the locker room. In reality, there was no way to stop and scan every player and caddy walking onto the range or every player walking into the locker room. There would, without doubt, be a riot.

When this came up during the March meetings, Steve Worthy said, "What you do is ask the volunteers to use common sense. If they see Tiger Woods coming or a player they recognize, they let them go. Otherwise, they get scanned."

That was actually a worse idea than scanning everyone, because there was going to come a moment, without question, when a volunteer recognized Davis Love but not Tom Kite. Or Phil Mickelson but not David Duval. Take your pick, it was going to happen. And the unrecognized player was going to throw a fit.

Eventually, scanning on the range and going up to the locker room were dropped.

The most important nonsecurity decision that had finally been made concerned parking. Pre 9/11, parking and traffic had been the single largest ongoing issue between the state and the USGA. Initially, the USGA had thought the best place to park most of the public was SUNY Farmingdale, which backed up to the golf course and had, in all, close to 14,000 parking spaces. This wasn't enough room for everyone but it would accommodate a majority of the public.

When the state police heard about that plan they came back and said no, that wouldn't work. The main road into and out of SUNY Farmingdale was Route 110, which ran north and south between the three major east-west highways on Long Island: the Southern State and Northern State parkways and the Long Island Expressway. Route 110 was choked with traffic in the mornings and evenings under normal circumstances. Adding a majority of the traffic coming to and from the Open would, in the opinion of the police, wreak havoc on traffic in the area.

Where, then, do we go, asked the USGA.

Jones Beach, came the reply.

Jones Beach? That was impossible. It was thirteen miles from Bethpage, thirteen miles that could easily take forty-five minutes or longer to travel by shuttle bus. There were ways to make the trip shorter: dedicated lanes just for the buses and temporary exits carved out strictly for the Open. But this was Long Island, with Long Island summer traffic. The police were insistent. They would make it work. Finally, the USGA, after making several practice runs on the route from Jones Beach to the golf course, said okay.

Then the state got involved. Bernadette Castro and her chief aide, Nancy Palumbo, were less than thrilled with the idea of clogging the Jones Beach lots with cars filled with people going to the golf tournament. There was lots of parking at Jones Beach — more than 20,000 spaces in all. But if it was a hot weekend, that might not be enough. And the traffic getting in and out of the park would be horrific. There was another problem: The parks department was planning at least one concert at Jones Beach during Open weekend. A second was a possibility.

Now it was the USGA's turn to be upset. No one had said anything about a concert. The idea of thousands of golf fans trying to exit the Jones Beach lots while thousands of concertgoers tried to enter them was a potential nightmare.

Round and round they went. Finally, early in the spring, a complicated compromise was reached. It went something like this:

- Jones Beach would be the primary parking lot for ticket holders, with dedicated bus lanes and extra exits off the highway near Bethpage.
- The state agreed to stage only one concert, and it would be on Friday, not on the weekend, when traffic would potentially be at its absolute worst. The USGA would make certain to give Tiger Woods an early tee time on Friday, knowing that a lot of fans would leave the golf course as soon as he was finished. That would mean at least some of the Jones Beach traffic would be cleared out hours before the concertgoers began arriving.
- SUNY Farmingdale would be used, but in a limited way, for some volunteers, for the TV people (since the school

backed up to the area next to the 10th hole where the TV compound would be), and for some corporate ticket holders. Most corporate ticket holders would park on the Green Course, on which the state had reluctantly agreed to have cars parked.

- The polo fields, located about a mile from the clubhouse, would be used for caddies, some officials, and anyone who didn't quite make the cut for the 225 spots available at the clubhouse, 150 of which were reserved for players.

The plan was complicated and full of risks. If rain wiped out the Green Course and the polo fields, Grumman's lots would be considered as a backup. No one was completely happy with the plan, but everyone seemed to understand that compromise was crucial. The USGA was far from convinced that the Jones Beach plan would work. And one other problem now cropped up. The state was now planning *two* concerts for the weekend, one on Friday and another one for either Thursday or Sunday.

Davis looked at Worthy as he finished explaining the new twist. "If you're joking, Steve, please smile now," he said.

There wasn't even a hint of a smile on Worthy's face. "The question," he said, "is how firm do we want to be on this?"

"The answer," said Davis, "is very firm."

Up until the 1970s, there weren't that many full-time caddies on tour. Most of the clubs that hosted tournaments insisted that players use the caddies from their clubs. As more money came into the game and players could afford full-time caddies, they began campaigning to be allowed to bring them with them wherever they played.

The last place to insist on players using local caddies was Augusta. By 1983, when the Masters finally dropped that rule, almost every player on tour had his own caddy. Player-caddy relationships were often as volatile as those between husbands and wives. Some players and caddies stayed together for years, others broke up in weeks, and others were on-again, off-again.

During the 1980s, clubs treated caddies as little more than indentured servants whose presence on their land was barely tolerated. They were strictly forbidden to set foot in any clubhouse and were fortunate if they were allowed to park with the general public. But caddying changed greatly when big money came into golf. Many caddies today are more educated than the players they work for. Almost any caddy who works for a successful player now flies from event to event, and almost all who work for a top-100 player make a good living. A handful are wealthy men whose annual income is well into six figures.

In recent years, they have become far more vocal, and most of the time, they are backed by the players. Most tournaments now have parking areas reserved for caddies. They are allowed in the clubhouses (at least to walk into the locker room with their player) and are provided with their own dining area at most tournaments.

Note the word *most*. In 2001, the USGA had issued caddies vouchers, allowing them to eat at the concession stands on the grounds. That had not gone over well. Caddies had no desire to stand on line in hot, steamy weather (when it wasn't raining) and then find a place among the masses to sit and eat. Particularly after a round, when they were hot and tired, they wanted a quiet place to sit down and eat, preferably one that was air-conditioned.

Davis knew the USGA had to do a better job at Bethpage than it had done at Southern Hills. Traditionally, the USGA has been looked on favorably by most caddies. It was Fay, in 1998, who decided the time had come to give caddies the option to wear shorts. Both the Tour and the PGA of America had balked at repeated requests by the caddies, who carry a forty-pound bag up and down hills for more than four hours a day, to not wear long pants in hot weather.

During the 1996 PGA, with the heat index well over 100 degrees for the opening round in August in Louisville, Kentucky, two caddies had shown up on the first tee in shorts. By the time they reached the second tee, PGA officials were waiting for them. They were given two options: Put on long pants immediately or surrender the bag. Both had known this was going to happen and had come prepared with long pants to change into. But they had made their point.

"They should wear shorts when it's hot," Fay said. "Heck, they should wear shorts whenever they want. That's tough work. They ought to be comfortable."

Fay, being Fay, actually had no problem with the idea of players wearing shorts. "If the weather's hot, why not?" he said. "If you're playing at your club in the summer and it's 100 degrees, would you want to wear long pants?"

Actually, most players were more traditional than Fay and thought they should wear long pants regardless of the heat. But the caddies were grateful for the change, and soon after, both the Tour and the PGA changed their rules. Nonetheless, the caddies felt the USGA had failed them in Tulsa and had told them so.

That's why, when Steve Worthy mentioned during the March meetings that caddies would be parking at the Bethpage Polo Fields, Davis quickly asked if there would be a shuttle just for them.

"No," Worthy said. "But there will be plenty of shuttles from there."

"No, not good enough," Davis said, cutting him off. "They want their own shuttle, and frankly, they should have it. They shouldn't be sitting squeezed in with people, and they shouldn't have to wait on a line to get back after they're done for the day."

Worthy didn't argue. "We'll get them their own shuttles, then," he said.

The USGA was planning to have a caddy trailer parked right next to the range. It would be air-conditioned, provide meals, have both a massage and a workout area. It would be the greatest caddy perk in golf history. Also for the first time, each caddy would be provided with one caddy guest badge to get on the grounds. Given that the players were given virtually unlimited badges, giving the caddies one didn't seem unreasonable.

Davis had turned down only one caddy request: comp tickets. "Not gonna happen," was his answer on that one.

In 1997, President Bill Clinton had attended the final day of the Open at Congressional. This, of course, was a nightmare for the USGA, especially since his decision to come was relatively last minute. The Secret Service had initially wanted a special grandstand built for the President next to the 18th hole. That would have been a logistical nightmare, since the area around the grandstand would have been off-limits to spectators, making it virtually impossible for anyone to get to or from the green. As a compromise, the USGA offered the 16th green. That was acceptable.

The President arrived, was taken to the 16th, and sat happily watching the golf. In the meantime, two death threats were received. The first one turned out to be from a bar, where someone had made a bet. The second one was turned over to the Secret Service.

"They didn't report back to us on what they found," Davis said, smiling.

Now, every day at the Open was going to be like that day at Congressional — times ten. It would be seven days on high alert, seven difficult days for spectators, who would be subjected to pat-downs and, undoubtedly, long lines to get through security and to get on buses going to and from the event.

Even after Romaney Berson had won her battle with Bob Nuzzo on the issue of having all the permission forms notarized, getting close to 10,000 people checked, verified, and cleared was a massive undertaking for everyone. Some people had not been cleared, most of them employees of various vendors who would be working on-site. So far only one had actually had a warrant out seeking his arrest. Jon Barker's staff had discovered that a volunteer who had been assigned to the transportation committee had three DUI's. He had been reassigned.

Some members of the media — and Frank Hannigan — had objected to the background checks, seeing them as a violation of their civil rights. Fay, a civil libertarian most of the time, didn't disagree. "When you are in a state of war, and that's what we're in right now, things change," he said. "Am I comfortable with it? No. Do I hope we don't have to go through this again next year? Yes. But do I understand the need this time, a few months after 9/11, thirty-five miles from Ground Zero? Absolutely."

So the checks went forward. And that wasn't all.

It was decided that all questions about security would be sent to two people: Nuzzo on the state side and Marty Parkes, the director of communications, on the USGA side. Of course once you got to Nuzzo or Parkes, other than being told about what could be carried into the championship, you weren't going to get very much information.

"I will say nothing in a very articulate way," Parkes said.

The USGA's experience with security may have been best explained by Mike Butz's response during his first Open in 1981 at Merion when someone telephoned in a bomb threat. "My first reaction was, I better get in a golf cart, go out there and find the thing," he said. "Then it occurred to me that there were state police on the grounds and maybe they could help."

Already, in preliminary meetings with the local police for the '03 Open outside of Chicago, Worthy had been told that one idea was to have snipers on the roof of the clubhouse.

Berson laughed when that one came up. "Maybe the best thing to do is only let the golfers on-site and no one else," she said.

"Make it a pay-per-view event," Worthy said.

Both were joking. But the joke wasn't all that funny, considering the work that lay ahead to get 42,500 people to and from Bethpage State Park for seven days in June.

As the meetings wrapped up, Butz shook his head at the immensity of it all. "We knew Bethpage was going to be the biggest, toughest Open to run we've ever had," he said. "But I don't think any of us ever dreamed it would be like this."

There were seventy-nine days left until the first ball went into the air. They were going to need every single one of them.

10

One Hundred and Three to One

ON MAY SIXTH, local qualifying for the 2002 U.S. Open Championship began. Locals, as they are called in the golf world, would be held in 105 locations across the country from Maine to Hawaii over a period of sixteen days. There was a total of 8,468 players entered in the Open. In all, seventy-five of them would be exempt into the championship and would not hit a ball in anger until June 13. The other 8,393 were left to compete for the remaining eighty-one spots.

In other words, the chances for those teeing it up in the locals were about 103-to-1.

And yet almost all of them showed up to play bright-eyed and absolutely convinced that they were going to succeed. In fact, most took the approach that Han Solo took maneuvering through the asteroid field in *The Empire Strikes Back* when he said, "Never tell me the odds."

From the locals, winners went to twelve sectional tournaments held in June. Everyone who had made the top 125 on the PGA Tour money list the previous year was exempt from local qualifying, and so were players who had written in about past exploits on tour and been granted a spot in the sectionals. This meant a total of 140 players were exempt into sectional play, leaving the rest to compete for the remaining 610 spots. Once the locals were complete, 750 players would head to the sectionals. If you made it this far, your odds had improved to close to 9-1.

Before the locals could actually begin, Larry Adamson and his staff had some work to do. Once all the entries were in, they had to go through them and make sure that each local site could accommodate all the golfers who had signed up to play there. Every year, there were some sites that were overbooked. When that occurred, Adamson and friends simply went on a first come, first served basis. In other words, when 197 players signed up for the qualifier in Pinehurst, North Carolina, and Ray Novicki, the assistant director of the Carolinas Golf Association, informed Adamson that no more than 132 players could get around the golf course before dark — figuring in extra time for the inevitable playoff — the last sixty-five players to enter and write site number 94 (Pinehurst) as the spot where they wanted to play their local would have to play someplace else.

"We try to make the alternate site as close to the first one as possible," Adamson said. "In other words, if someone enters Pinehurst, we aren't going to reassign him to play in California, if he has to be moved."

In 2002 qualifying, close to a thousand players did not receive their first choice of venue for the locals. Even though the entry blank states clearly in the box where one requests a qualifying site that some players may have to be transferred, a lot of people don't read it. When they receive notification from the USGA that they have been moved to another site — sometimes to another date, too — they are often unhappy. That was certainly the case with Sean Murphy.

Murphy was thirty-six, one of those players never quite good enough to have consistent success on the PGA Tour. He had been the player of the year on the Triple A Nike Tour in 1993, winning four times to earn exempt status the following year on the big tour.

But he hadn't been able to stay there in 1994 or in 1996, when he again earned exempt status. His career had slipped to the point where he was now struggling to regain exempt status on the Buy.com Tour (Buy.com having taken over what had been the Nike Tour).

Murphy was one of those players who had to be moved from the Pinehurst local. Like everyone else who had to be moved, he had received a letter from the USGA informing him of the change. The only problem was he wasn't home, he was on the road playing golf. He never found out about the change — which involved both venue and date — and simply showed up at Pinehurst ready to play. Seeing that his name wasn't on the list of starters, he called the USGA to find out what had gone wrong. It was then that he learned that his qualifier had already been played.

Murphy appealed for a reprieve. The appeal went to Tom Meeks, whose answer — regretfully — was no.

"I feel badly about it," Meeks said. "The guy made an innocent mistake, caused by the fact that he was on the road. But the entry form states clearly that this can happen, and it was up to him to make certain he got the venue he requested. If no one was checking his mail at home, he could have called the office and said, 'Did I get Pinehurst?' He would have been told no, here's where you're playing, and there wouldn't have been a problem."

Murphy listened politely when Meeks called him to tell him he had turned his appeal down. Can I appeal, he asked, to a higher power? Absolutely, Meeks said, I will explain the situation to Mike Butz, and if he sees it differently than me, I'll let you know. He did call Butz, from Bethpage on the spring morning that he walked the course with Davis, Moraghan, and Currier. When he explained what had happened to Butz, the reaction he got was predictable: We can't do it.

Murphy understood. "Sean, I feel awful about this, I really do," Meeks said. "But can I give you a piece of friendly advice for next year? Enter early."

❖   ❖   ❖

Wind is a golfer's worst enemy. Rain is uncomfortable but slows the greens, making it easier to stop shots close to the flag. Heat isn't any fun and may wear you out by the end of the day, but it doesn't affect your ability to strike the ball. The same is true of cold. As long as you can keep your hands warm enough to grip your club, you can play.

Wind is a different story. It makes every shot an adventure, and it wears you out because you can't let down mentally for even a second. Tee shots can soar sideways, putting becomes exceptionally challenging when the ball won't stand still. Nothing is easy in the wind.

But only lightning — not wind — stops a golf tournament. So on the morning of May 15, 150 players showed up on the eastern end of Long Island at Fox Hill Golf and Country Club to compete for ten spots in the sectionals. Most of the locals are treated the same by the USGA — the number of spots is based on the number of entrants. The only exception are the venues nearest Buy.com Tour stops — in this case one in Virginia and one the following week in North Carolina — where extra slots are allotted because of the strength of the field created by the presence of the players who are one step away from the PGA Tour.

The locals are golf's truest melting pot. Every kind of player with any talent for the game at all shows up in the locals. There are old pros — Joe Moresco, seventy, a retired club pro was entered at Fox Hill — and teenage amateurs who see Open qualifying as their first step toward the PGA Tour promised land. There are former stars hoping for one last shot and Buy.commers looking for their first. There are minitour pros and club pros and outstanding amateurs and amateurs whose greatest thrill will simply be saying they played in a qualifier. There are fakes who don't belong — and are likely to get a "prove you can play" letter when all is said and done — and very good players who choke like crazy and get the same letter.

For many players in the locals, just reaching the sectional would be a huge achievement. "I'd just like to play thirty-six holes at that level and see how I could do," said Jamie Friedman, one of fifty amateurs signed up to play at Fox Hill. "Anything after that would be gravy."

Darrell Kestner, the pro at the Deepdale Golf Club, had qualified for seven Opens. He had also qualified for the PGA Championship nine times. At forty-eight, he was two years away from
being eligible for the Senior Open, but he badly wanted to make
the 2002 Open because of the venue. He had set the course record
for the Black playing in the Assistant Pro Championship in 1986,
shooting 65 on his way to winning the event.

"I love the changes to the golf course and seeing it in the condition it's in now," he said. "I've heard some of the USGA guys saying
the scores are going to be low because the greens aren't tough
enough. Ha! They couldn't be more wrong. There's a lot more
slope in those greens than people know. Just wait."

For Kestner, an eighth Open, especially this Open, would probably mean more than any of the others. "For someone like me, getting into the Open anytime is about the biggest feather I can put in
my cap," he said. "It validates what you do at your club and
reminds people that you can still play a little. Getting to play in an
Open or in the PGA is a nice reward, but it's one you have to earn.
This one, though, I think I want more than any other."

Kestner had played overseas briefly, joining the South African
Tour in 1983 and 1984. He had hooked up with Rick Hartmann
there, another American trying to make a go of it away from home.
They had stayed friends even after Kestner came home and Hartmann continued on to play successfully for a number of years on
the European Tour. While there, he had qualified for several
British Opens, but it wasn't until he came home and became the
pro at a ritzy Hamptons club — a job he got with Kestner's help —
that Hartmann had qualified for the U.S. Open. He had now done
it twice — and had made the cut at Pebble Beach in 2000 — and,
like Kestner, badly wanted to play at Bethpage.

Kestner and Hartmann had more at stake than just a spot in the
sectional: whenever they played in an event together, they bet a
hundred dollars on who would shoot the lower score. "It can be a
bloodbath," Kestner said, trying to look grim.

The morning was something of a bloodbath for everyone. The
winds blew scores way up, and when the morning players had

finished, no one had broken par (72) or even matched it. When Kirk Oguri, a minitour player who lived on Long Island in the summer and Florida in the winter, posted a 73, a number of people were congratulating him on being the medalist.

"I could care less about that," Oguri said. "I just hope the wind keeps up in the afternoon and I make the top ten. That's what we're all here for."

About an hour after Oguri finished, someone did beat him: Mark Brown, a thirty-five-year-old club pro from nearby Tam O'Shanter, posted a remarkable 71. As the morning turned to afternoon, no one else had come close to breaking par.

Oguri was twenty-eight, a young player still hoping to make a breakthrough somewhere, sometime. He had never made it to a sectional. As he stood outside the tiny cafeteria on the bottom floor of the clubhouse that had become the unofficial hangout for players who had finished (survived?) their rounds, he reluctantly accepted congratulations from other players who had staggered home with much higher scores. "Still a lot of day left out there," he said quietly.

His words were echoed a few minutes later by the second player to post a 73: Raymond Floyd Jr. Floyd's score turned a few more heads than Oguri's simply because of the name attached to the number. Floyd was the oldest son of Raymond Floyd, the 1986 Open champion who had won four major titles, twenty-two PGA Tour events in all, and was a member of the World Golf Hall of Fame. A tough legacy to follow, to put it mildly. Floyd, who was twenty-seven and a successful equities trader on Wall Street, appeared completely at peace with his famous name.

"I've had enough time to get used to it," he said, laughing, sitting in the cafeteria sipping a soda. "My brother and I were lucky in that Dad never once acted as if we *had* to play. He made it clear the opportunity was there if we wanted it, and he'd help us all he could, but he never pushed us."

Ray Jr. still had vivid memories of his father's victory at Shinnecock, even though he and his brother Robert, who is sixteen months younger than he, hadn't been there to see it. "The deal was, if he was close after Friday, we'd stay," he remembered. "If he wasn't, we were leaving for a sleep-away camp in Virginia. Well, he shot 75 the first day and was way back. Then he shot 68 on Friday to move into the pack, but he was still a ways behind. So off we went.

"The camp where we were, there was one TV set in the whole place, in the director's office. Sunday afternoon, we were outside doing something when he came and got us. He said maybe we needed to come inside and watch. There were three holes left, and we walked in just as Dad birdied 16. Watching the finish was very emotional. I was twelve, but I understood what it meant to him. Then, when they interviewed him afterward, he started talking about his dad [it was, of course, Father's Day] and about his own kids and . . ." He paused. "Needless to say, it was something I've never forgotten."

Ray Jr. ended up going to Wake Forest, his brother to North Carolina, also an excellent golf school. In 1995, he played with his father in the PGA Tour's father-son event and "made everything all week. I remember Dad saying, 'This should tell you that it's there if you want it.'" He decided to give it a try after college. He played in a few Nike Tour events in the summer of 1998, then went to Q-School. "Made it through first stage," he said. "Finished dead last at second stage."

He wandered to South Africa but wasn't terribly happy. When a family friend suggested that he might have what it took to make it on Wall Street, Ray Jr. decided to see if he was right. He had done some work at the stock exchange during college. Unlike his father, who radiates intensity when he walks into a room, Raymond Jr. is easygoing and friendly, traits that go a lot further on Wall Street than on the golf tour. He decided to go in that direction. He had not looked back.

"I know I made the right decision," he said. "I'm happy doing what I'm doing. I love living in New York, and I'm enjoying golf when I play now far more than when every putt mattered in terms of my future. I admire Robert for hanging in [Robert is still playing minitours] because there will always be a part of you that wonders, could I? Robert's a battler. In '96, if he had beaten Steve Scott in the semis of the U.S. Amateur, he and Dad would have been the first father and son ever to play in the Masters together. [Both Amateur finalists qualify for the Masters.] He lost three and two, and I know that just crushed him because he wanted that so much.

"But he hasn't given up. He's got the game if he can ever get things going in the right direction. It would be fun if we could both make it to Bethpage."

Robert Floyd had already made it through his local down in Florida. As the afternoon wore on, Ray Jr.'s situation had gone from comfortable to nerve-racking to precarious. He had made the thirty-minute drive to his parents' house in Southampton after the round, hoping he could take the rest of the day off. His father was there and asked how he had done. He had been a little bit upset with himself coming in because of two late bogeys but realized that he had played well in the conditions. "Dad, I did everything I could do out there," he answered.

His father smiled. "Good, then no matter what happens you should feel good about the day."

In the middle of the afternoon, Ray Jr. had called the clubhouse to see how the afternoon scores were looking. The news wasn't encouraging. The winds hadn't died, but they had abated. What's more, the stronger half of the field had gone out in the afternoon.

Hartmann had shot 72. Kestner had won the $100 by shooting 71. Marc Turnesa, a minitour player from Florida whose dad was a club pro in Rockville Center — and his caddy for the day — had shot 70. In all, by the end of the afternoon, there were eight players who had managed 72 or better, led by P. J. Cowan, who was the medalist at 69.

"That might be the best round of my life," Cowan said, looking drained as he accepted congratulations that he knew would not have to be withdrawn later. He already had the paperwork for the sectional in hand, along with a beer and a cigarette. "I've shot 59 twice [once on the Nike Tour], but I swear I didn't play any better in those rounds than I did today. It was that tough out there."

Of all the players in the local, Cowan might have been the one most motivated to make this Open. "I can't take no for an answer when it comes to the Black," he said. "I know this could be my chance. If I can get there, I honestly believe I can be a threat. There's not going to be anyone in that field who will know the golf course like I do."

Cowan was thirty-four, one of those players who were good enough to dominate on the local level but never quite good enough to make a dent with the big boys on the PGA Tour. He'd had moments of success at the Triple-A level and ample success in the New York area but had never cracked the big time. His confidence when it came to the Black was understandable. He had been playing the golf course since the age of ten, when his father dragged him there early in the morning to wait on line so he could play a course he hated.

"It was too tough for me back then," he said. "It wasn't till I got older and started to get good that I appreciated it. By the time I was a teenager, I loved it. All the great courses we have on Long Island, I always liked it the best. I think it's the prettiest, hardest, best course I've ever seen."

Cowan estimated he had played the Black more than a thousand times in his life. He had won the New York State Open there three times in four years and was convinced that if he could get to the first tee of the Open, he could be a factor on the 72nd green. "I can be a contender," he said, doing his best Brando. "The hardest part for me is getting there. That's why I'm so happy I played well today under these conditions. Now I've got to get through thirty-six holes [in the sectional] and then see what happens."

Cowan had never played in the Open. In 1995, he had been the first alternate at Shinnecock and had spent the entire day on Thursday sitting next to the first tee, clubs and caddy in tow, hoping word would come that someone had withdrawn. Everyone showed up.

He took a swallow of his beer. "But I'll start worrying about that tomorrow. Right now I want to sit down and get warm."

He was certainly entitled.

The eight players who had managed 72 or better could relax and pick up their paperwork for the local from Gene Westmoreland, the Metropolitan Golf Association official who was running the qualifier. All Open qualifiers are run by local officials from that area although at the sectionals there are USGA people looking over their shoulders. At the locals, the locals are on their own.

Four players had shot 73: Floyd and Oguri in the morning, Jamie Friedman and Bob Longo in the afternoon. Two pros, Oguri and Longo; two amateurs. Longo was fifty-two, a longtime club pro who had made it to the sectional ten times but never to the Open. Floyd had made it to the sectional a year ago and had a feel for the Open the others couldn't possibly have because of his family background. Friedman was thirty-seven and found himself on the verge of achieving one of his lifelong golf dreams.

Two of the four players would go to the sectional. The other two would go home and spend at least a year what-iffing about the one shot they had given away that they couldn't afford to give away.

It was seven o'clock by the time the last group finished. Oguri, who had been in the first group of the day, had finished his round almost eight hours earlier. Floyd had waited close to six hours. But they were all out there in the chill of early evening, the winds still whipping. They would play the par-five 10th hole, the idea being that a birdie hole was likely to get the playoff over with more quickly. They drew tee positions from Westmoreland, he wished them all luck, and about a hundred spectators crowded around to watch.

There may be nothing quite like the tension of playoffs like these. Of course, when players reach playoffs in a sectional, the pressure is especially intense because the winners will actually play in the Open. As recently as 1996, a player who had survived a playoff in a sectional — Steve Jones — had gone on to win the Open.

But the pressure in a local playoff is just as real, maybe even more so. By sectionals, the odds of making the Open are much more reasonable, and the players have the comfort of having at least advanced to within striking range. But to be so close at locals, when the odds were stacked so high against you, and to blow it reminds you not just what could have been but what will most likely never be.

Three of the four players found the 10th fairway. Floyd was not one of them. His wife of eight months, Cheryl, was caddying for him, carrying a lightweight Sunday bag with a Wake Forest logo on it, and she watched him hit his drive, as the players like to say, left of left. "Could have caught a fish with that hook," he said, keeping his sense of humor.

While the other three players marched to their balls, Westmoreland and a couple of officials drove ahead to try to track down Floyd's ball. They found it down a hill in the adjoining fairway. Westmoreland turned as Floyd walked up, pointed in the direction of the ball, and said, "It's all the way down the hill."

"Good down the hill or bad down the hill?" Floyd asked. In other words, do I have a shot?

He did, sort of, a tough angle over a number of trees. He managed to hook the ball around the trees, but the ball continued to sail left — it had no choice — took one hop off the cart path next to the green, and bounced way over.

But Floyd wasn't dead yet. None of the other three players managed to hit the green, even downwind. Oguri found the back bunker, Friedman the right. Longo hit the best shot, coming up just short and left of the green. Next, Floyd hit a gorgeous wedge shot from an impossible lie that he somehow managed to stop on the green, leaving him 18 feet for birdie. Oguri's bunker shot spun eight feet past the hole. Friedman hit the best shot of the playoff, stopping his bunker shot inside three feet. Longo, putting, was five feet short.

That left them all with birdie putts, albeit of different lengths. Floyd's slid right. For one instant he showed frustration, swiping his putter through the air before tapping in for what he suspected was a fatal five. Oguri then gave him a ray of hope by missing, too. But Longo and Friedman were each dead center. Just like that, it was over. Longo was in his eleventh sectional, Friedman his first. Floyd and Oguri were the Brooklyn Dodgers: Wait till next year.

The toughest thing about losing a playoff is having to make your way back to the clubhouse, the sun setting, feeling as if you have wasted an entire day. Even so, Floyd still had a smile on his face as he and Cheryl walked back in. "What the heck," he said. "For a weekend golfer, I had a pretty good day."

Once upon a time, local qualifers were thirty-six holes, just like the sectionals. But ten years ago, the USGA realized that trying to get the golfers through thirty-six holes in one day was virtually impossible. As it was, getting sectionals, in which everyone is a proven player, done before dark had become a major challenge.

Even the eighteen-hole format ran into occasional problems. Most were caused by weather. Just about any delay meant that finishing in one day would be nearly impossible, especially if there was a playoff — and almost all locals end in a playoff. If they didn't, spectators would demand their money back — if they had paid any money.

In 2002, one local ran into a problem perhaps unlike any other: a hole location delay. It happened at River Bend in Great Falls, Virginia (a suburb of Washington, D.C.), at a local in which eighty-seven players, almost none with any playing experience beyond local golf, were trying for six sectional spots. With only eighty-seven players, this should have been one of the easier locals to get through for everyone involved.

It didn't turn out quite that way.

The trouble began (as the police like to say) when the morning dawned unseasonably cold and windy. The start of play had to be delayed thirty minutes because there was frost on the greens when the first group was scheduled to tee off.

No big deal. If the rest of the day went off without further delay, the last group would still finish well before five o'clock.

That wasn't what happened.

The second hole at River Bend is a 445-yard par-four, the toughest hole on the course. The drive is downhill into a valley, the second shot uphill to a green guarded by water and several bunkers. The day before the qualifier, as is customary, the officials running the local from the Washington Metropolitan Golf Association had gone out to set hole locations. At number two, they had selected a spot back, right on the green. What they had apparently failed to notice was that the location was right on a ridge, one so steep it made Tom Meeks's hole location at Olympic's 18th in 1998 look flat as a table.

"It probably wasn't a good choice," Bob Brenly, the WMGA official in charge of the event said later. "But we didn't realize the greens were going to be so fast."

The people at River Bend insisted no one had said anything to them about green speed. As it was, Dick Taske, who had set up the golf course, averted further disaster when he noticed early in the morning that the flag at number nine was also sitting on a ridge and changed the location. His intentions were good. But as Tom Meeks would tell him, pick a bad spot on one hole and you aren't going to have people patting you on the back about the seventeen good ones.

What made the location at number two so disastrous was that it brought play to an absolute standstill at the start of everyone's round. By midmorning, groups coming off of number one found as many as three groups waiting on the second tee, because players were forced to wait forever in the fairway while those ahead of them almost comically tried to coax their ball into the hole up ahead on the green.

"The only thing the hole lacks is a nice big windmill," said Bobby Feinstein, who had been club champion at River Bend a few years earlier and was playing in his first-ever Open qualifier. "A lot of guys walked off that green and could have gone right to the parking lot, because their day was over."

Ben Brundred III, a standout amateur player who had won the club championship at two-time Open site Congressional on multiple occasions, reached the second green in two. He walked off with a nine en route to shooting 86. Throughout the day, players watched putts stop above the hole for a second and then start rolling — stopping anywhere from 10 to 20 feet below the hole. For the day, the stroke average on the hole was an unbelievable 5.8. A grand total of eleven players made par. They probably should have been granted instant exemptions into the Open.

Indeed, the entire day could have used a windmill. One player, Jay Woodson, was disqualified for illegally practicing on the golf course before his round began. Woodson accidentally mistook a bunker near the club's chipping green as part of the practice area. It turned out to be part of the 11th hole. He never made it to the first tee.

The final group didn't make it in until seven o'clock. Even without the second green debacle, the golf course had played tough for a group that for the most part were not accustomed to a U.S. Open–type of setup, even a U.S. Open qualifier–type of setup. Only one player, Robert Stock, a club pro from Charlottesville, managed to shoot 70 — even par, since the short par-five first had been played as a par-four.

"The key to my round was one-putting at number two," he said, with a smile. "Honestly, the ball went in the hole backward. I putted it by, and it rolled back in. If it misses, it might still be going."

Unless it hit the windmill.

For Stock, like everyone else who got through, reaching the sectional was a big deal. Reaching the Open would be gravy. The exception among the six who made it might have been Pat Tallent, a forty-eight-year-old amateur who had twice been one shot away from making the Open. Tallent had played college basketball at Kentucky once upon a time before transferring to George Washington to play for his older brother Bob, then the coach there. Tallent had made enough money to semiretire and work almost full time on his golf. He was looking forward to turning fifty, although he insisted he was not seriously considering taking a shot at the Senior Tour.

"I kind of like my lifestyle," he said, smiling. "The Senior Tour's a lot of work and a lot of pressure. I like the kind of golf I play now. It'd be nice, though, to make the Open once. Just once."

Tallent shot 72, which put him in a five-way playoff for the last three spots. He survived the playoff with a superb up-and-down from a bunker at the par-three 10th. That three matched Brendon Post and Jason Pool and left Fred Widicus and Todd Demsey, who made fours, making the long, sad walk back to the clubhouse.

The biggest cheer of the day came at 7:35 P.M. when Pool's par putt tumbled into the hole, clinching his spot. Pool was the current club champion at River Bend, and most of the 150 spectators for the playoff were club members thrilled to see one of their own make it to the next level.

For some, making it through a local is nothing more than a necessary step toward a goal still thirty-six holes away. For Jason Pool it was an accomplishment worthy of celebration. He and his family went to dinner and toasted with champagne when the long, long day was finally over.

As it turns out, one doesn't have to actually win the U.S. Open to earn a champagne toast. After surviving the windmill hole and a playoff, no one deserved a raised glass more than Jason Pool.

As is always the case, a number of stories, ranging from worth noting to remarkable, emerged from the locals. Andy Bean had once been a real live star on tour. He had won eleven times and had finished in the top four on the money list four different times. But he hadn't been an exempt player (top 125 on the money list) since 1991, and that meant he had to go back to play a local. This would probably be his last one, since he would turn fifty the next year. He was now thirty-six holes away from playing in an Open for the first time since 1991.

Bobby Clampett had last played in the Open in 2000. He had first played in the Open in 1978 as an eighteen-year-old college phenom and had been low amateur. A year later at Inverness he missed the cut and was asked if he would like to stick around for the weekend to act as a playing marker. On the PGA Tour, if the number of players who make the cut is an odd number, the first player on the golf course for the last two rounds usually plays alone unless he requests that someone play along with him. At the majors, a playing marker is always assigned, often a distinguished amateur. (At the Masters, the playing marker for many years has been Danny Yates, a past U.S. Amateur champion whose father and uncle are longtime club members.) Clampett accepted the offer and was assigned to play with David Edwards, then a young pro who had made the cut on the number. Clampett quickly went from playing marker to class clown. He hit shots off his knees, tried trick shots, did anything he could to draw attention to himself. After a couple of warnings, P. J. Boatwright had seen enough and ordered him off the golf course.

That turned out to be the most noise Clampett ever made in an Open. He turned pro amid much fanfare a year later and had success early in his career. He won a tournament in 1982 while only twenty-two and that same year led the British Open by six shots after thirty-six holes before fading. His career never took off as expected. He was fourteenth on the money list in 1981, seventeenth in 1982, and never cracked the top sixty again. He was last exempt (116th) in 1991. In 1995, he had retired to do TV for CBS and to work on his successful golf course design business.

But he always tried to qualify for the Open. By 2000, he was back playing locals and missed the sectional by a shot. He was an alternate, but being an alternate to a sectional means little unless you are first alternate — Clampett wasn't — since very few people drop out. The week prior to the sectional, Clampett worked at the Kemper Open outside of Washington, D.C., for CBS. Since his sectional was being played the next day a few miles away at Woodmont Country Club, Clampett showed up that morning just in case.

Sure enough, there was a dropout and no other alternates in sight. Clampett jumped on the golf course, played superbly, and qualified for the Open, held that year at Pebble Beach, which had practically been his home course as a kid growing up in California. He shot 68 the first day and was in fourth place. He ended up thirty-seventh, living proof to all the dreamers that fighting through a local was worthwhile.

Clampett had made it through his local in 2002, but again there was a story behind it. He had been in Houston on business the day before he was supposed to play and had a mechanical problem with the private plane he flies, trying to get out that night. He had called Tom Meeks to ask if there was any way he could switch the date and venue of his qualifier, since he was stuck in Houston. Absolutely no way, Meeks told him. Clampett hiked from the private plane area of the airport to the commercial area and found there was one flight left that night that could get him home to Raleigh so he could play the next morning. He got on that flight, made it through the next day, and then went about figuring out how to get his plane home.

One set of twins had qualified: Eric and Aaron (no relation to Tom) Meeks. Eric was the 1988 U.S. Amateur champion, now playing on the Buy.com Tour; Aaron had played overseas for years. Mario Tiziani, who was the brother-in-law of Steve Stricker, a three-time winner on tour, had made it to the sectional, too. So had George Zahringer, the same George Zahringer who had first put the idea of taking the Open to the Black Course into David Fay's head. The youngest player to make it through was sixteen-year-old Derek Tolan, a high school sophomore from Denver, Colorado. Gary Nicklaus, son of Jack, was an alternate. So was someone named Michael Jack Schmidt, the same Mike Schmidt who had hit 548 career home runs as a Hall of Fame third baseman with the Philadelphia Phillies.

One story, though, stood out from all the others, even though it involved a player who had absolutely no chance to make it to the Open. The player was Jeff Julian, a forty-year-old who had spent most of his pro career a step away from the bright lights of the PGA Tour. Twice, Julian had made it through Q-School and had gotten on tour, in 1996 and 2001.

During that second stint, he began to feel tired, began to get the shakes on the golf course, something that had never happened to him before. He underwent a battery of tests and, in the fall, was given the worst possible news. He had ALS, Lou Gehrig's disease. ALS is, to put it bluntly, a death sentence. Most people don't live two years after being diagnosed. Julian understood all that. He also knew that he wanted to do what he loved doing most for as long as he possibly could: play golf. He told PGA Tour officials in the fall that he was concerned about playing in Pro-Ams because he was starting to slur his words and he didn't want people to get the wrong idea about why.

But he kept playing. He lost his playing privileges at the end of the year but was given a number of sponsor exemptions early in 2002. He hadn't made a cut but hadn't played poorly, either. A lot of times his problem was that he tired badly near the end of rounds. He just didn't have the stamina to walk eighteen holes a lot of days, especially if it was hot.

He had played in a local in St. Louis and had finished tied for second, shooting 70. There was absolutely no way he was going to be able to walk thirty-six holes in a sectional, especially in June when the weather was probably going to be hot. There were suggestions that he should ask the USGA for a cart. Given the Casey Martin decision a year earlier in which the Supreme Court had ruled that a disabled golfer had the right to play in a golf cart, Julian probably would have been given a cart if he had asked.

But he didn't ask. He was a believer that walking is a part of competing in golf, regardless of any court ruling. He would show up at the sectionals and walk as far as he could and play as long as he could. He made it through eighteen holes of his sectional on a blindingly hot day in St. Louis before he was forced to quit. Prior to the sectional, David Fay had thought for a fleeting moment about offering him an exemption into the Open but had quickly put it aside. The precedent would be a bad one, and, he suspected, it would call attention to Julian in a way that would have made him uncomfortable.

In all, though, it wouldn't have been a bad thing to do. The USGA has the flexibility to increase the size of the field by up to three golfers if it wants to — it had done so in 1994 when Arnold Palmer, Ben Crenshaw, and Seve Ballesteros had all been given exemptions — so giving Julian a spot would not have taken anyone else's spot away. And, unlike most players, Julian almost certainly would not get another crack at the Open in a year.

Julian didn't make it to Bethpage. But his performance in the local and in the sectional were absolute proof that a player doesn't have to win the Open to be a hero. In this case, he didn't even have to make it to the first tee.

11

Thirty-six Holes to the Promised Land

THERE ARE MANY different ways to earn an exemption straight into the U.S. Open, seventeen of them to be exact. They range from winning the Open — which makes you exempt for ten years — to making the top two on the Australasian PGA Tour money list. In between are things like winning one of the other three majors, which gives you a five-year exemption; finishing in the top fifteen in the previous Open; winning the U.S. Amateur or the U.S. Senior Open; finishing in the top thirty on the PGA Tour money list; and being in the top fifty in the world rankings. Some players just make one of the lists; some make many.

The world rankings list for the 2002 Open was finalized on May 27. With the rankings in place, there were seventy-four exempt players. One, Hale Irwin, was a category 13 exemptee: "Special exemptions selected by the USGA executive committee." Irwin, a three-time Open champion, had been awarded his exemption during the USGA's annual meeting in January, part of an unofficial tradition that called for Open champions to be given what amounted to a one-year extension on their ten-year exemption if they were still active players. Irwin had been given one of those exemptions in 1990, eleven years after his second Open victory, and he had taken full advantage, winning the golf tournament, becoming the oldest man in history (forty-five) to do so. He had qualified for the Open on his own in 2001 by winning the Senior Open the year before, so 2002 counted as his extension year.

David Fay looked over the exempt list, then looked over the money lists from around the world and world rankings. He wanted to be sure there wasn't anyone who was nonexempt who deserved to be exempt. One name jumped out at him: Nick Faldo. Faldo had never won the Open, finishing second to Curtis Strange in 1988 in a playoff, but he had won six major titles. At forty-four, he wasn't the player he had once been, but he was still competitive. In fact, just that weekend he had finished fourth in the Volvo Masters, the biggest nonmajor event on the European Tour.

Fay sat down and sent an e-mail to Reed Mackenzie, the president of the USGA, and to Fred Ridley, the chairman of the championship committee. He made the case for giving Faldo a special exemption by noting that, besides Faldo, only one active player other than Tiger Woods had won more than two majors (Nick Price). Fay also noted Faldo's performance over the weekend and his eighth-place finish at the Masters as proof that he could still play. His last sentence may have been the clincher: "And just think, it will give Frank Hannigan one more thing about the USGA to complain about."

Ever since leaving the USGA, Hannigan had become notorious for ripping special exemptions. "They should only be given out when the system fails," he said, "when someone who deserves to be in falls through the cracks, like [Ben] Hogan in 1966. It isn't supposed to be a nostalgia thing, and that's what they use it for more often than not."

Hogan had received the USGA's first special exemption in 1966 when the Open returned to the Olympic Club, the site of his historic 1955 playoff loss to club pro Jack Fleck. Hogan hadn't played in an Open since 1961. He had finished twelfth in '61, but back then only the top ten were exempt into the next year's Open. At forty-nine, having never completely recovered from the injuries he suffered in the car accident that almost killed him in 1949, Hogan simply didn't think he could play thirty-six holes in a qualifier. So he sat out the next four years. But at the Masters in 1966, he shot 30 on the back nine on Saturday en route to a 66 and a fifth-place finish. That ended any doubts about whether he should receive an exemption.

"That was the right thing to do," Hannigan said. "The problem was, we opened Pandora's box."

Not exactly. It was eleven years before the USGA gave another exemption. In 1977, it gave two — to Tommy Bolt, bringing him back to Southern Hills where he won in 1958, and to sixty-six-year-old Sam Snead. "That's when they got into the nostalgia business," Hannigan said. "When I took over [in 1983], Jim Hand [then the president] and I agreed we just weren't going to do it." That was why Palmer ended up playing in qualifiers seven times. In the '80s, there just weren't any exemptions to be had, even for him.

Fay changed that almost as soon as he succeeded Hannigan, giving Irwin the exemption that led to his win in 1990. Hannigan tolerated the Irwin assist, but the three in 1994 — Arnold Palmer, Ben Crenshaw, and Seve Ballesteros — drove him crazy.

Palmer's exemption was strictly nostalgia. He was sixty-four and had grown up near Oakmont, that year's site. He had also lost a playoff there to Jack Nicklaus in 1962 and had last seriously contended in an Open there in 1973. Ballesteros got his exemption largely because he screamed and yelled that he deserved one and because the one time he had made a serious run at an Open had been in 1983, also at Oakmont. Crenshaw got his after winning a tournament and because the USGA didn't want to look as if it was bowing to Ballesteros's whining. So it invited both Crenshaw and Ballesteros on the grounds that both were playing well that spring.

Nostalgic or not, Palmer's exemption that year produced one of the most memorable moments in the history of the Open, Palmer's tearful walk up the 18th hole on Friday. "Never should have happened," Hannigan said. "He was noncompetitive. So Doc [Giffin] had a good cry. That means it was okay?"

Doc Giffin is Palmer's longtime aide-de-camp and close friend, and if he cried when Palmer came up the 18th that day he was far from alone. Hannigan, right far more often than he is wrong, was wrong. Palmer belonged at Oakmont in '94.

And Jack Nicklaus belonged at Olympic, Pinehurst, and Pebble Beach in '98, '99, and '00. Those exemptions could also be considered nostalgic, though Nicklaus had finished sixth in the Masters in 1998. Some would make the case that Nicklaus and Palmer should be allowed to play the Open forever. Not Hannigan.

"It's a lot of crap," he said. "Nicklaus and Palmer were a huge part of golf, I get that. But Hale Irwin at the age of fifty-seven? Why? Faldo? When was the last time he won a golf tournament? [1996.] These days, with the top fifty getting in, people don't slip through the cracks unless they've been injured. There's just no reason to do it."

In his e-mail to Mackenzie and Ridley, Fay pointed out that he had been right when his gut had told him Irwin was still a good enough player to compete in 1990, and he felt the same way about Faldo. Mackenzie and Ridley agreed. Faldo, who had signed up to play the qualifier at Woodmont on June third, was granted a Get Out of Sectionals card and advanced straight to Bethpage.

That left eighty-one qualifying spots for the 772 players who had reached the twelve sectionals. Two of them — the so-called PGA Tour sectionals — would have fifty-seven of the available eighty-one spots. The other ten sectionals would divide up the remaining twenty-four spots. The Tour sectionals were being played at Woodmont, one day after the nearby Kemper Open, and on two courses in Purchase, New York, a couple of miles from Westchester Country Club, where the next week's tour stop would be.

A lot of players sign up for the so-called tour sectionals because of the extra spots, figuring that even though there is more competition, the odds are better. At Woodmont, the odds were slightly better than 6-to-1; at Purchase just under 7-to-1. The odds were no better than 15-to-1 at any other site and as high as 25-to-1 at Old Memorial in Tampa, Florida.

Even so, that was where Greg Norman went to qualify. Norman had been the number one player in the world for most of the pre-Tiger half of the 1990s. He had been, without question, the best-known and wealthiest golfer in the world in those years. He was an excellent player and a brilliant self-promoter, making the most of his almost-white blond hair and the Great White Shark nickname hung on him early in his career to make himself as successful — perhaps more successful — in business as he had been in golf.

His Achilles' heel was closing the deal in major championships. He had won twice — the 1986 and 1993 British Opens — but was far more famous for losing majors than winning them. In 1986, he had won the fifty-four hole slam, leading all four majors after three rounds but only winning one of them. He had the unenviable distinction of having lost each of the four majors in a playoff. Occasionally, he had been very unlucky — Larry Mize's miraculous chip at the '87 Masters comes to mind — but on other occasions he had done himself in. People remember Bob Tway holing out from a bunker to beat Norman at the 1986 PGA; often they forget that Norman shot 40 on the back nine to blow a four-shot lead that day. He had shot an amazing 63 during the last round of the British Open at Troon in 1989 to get into a playoff with Mark Calcavecchia and Wayne Grady, then started the four-hole playoff birdie-birdie only to finish bogey-X, hitting a bunker shot out of bounds on the 18th hole, wiping out twenty holes of fabulous golf.

But his most memorable collapse had come in 1996 at Augusta, the tournament he readily admitted he wanted most to win. He had led by six shots after three rounds only to shoot an appalling 78 on the last day, allowing Faldo to storm past him to a five-stroke win. His handling of that defeat made him more popular than ever, but he had never completely overcome the enormity of what had slipped away from him. He had been the number one player in the world in 1995. He won twice in 1997 but hadn't won since then and had seriously contended in a major only once — the 1999 Masters, when he was in contention late on Sunday only to finish third behind José María Olazabal and Davis Love III.

Norman was now forty-seven, still a crowd favorite, but almost a forgotten man on tour. He played infrequently. He had played so few times in 2001 that he hadn't qualified for tour membership in '02 and was playing on sponsor exemptions — and in the Tiger-dominated world of the twenty-first century was an afterthought at the majors. He had been given an exemption into the Masters earlier in the year, no doubt in tribute to his near-misses there (six top-three finishes) but had missed the cut and faced the very real possibility that he might not return to the Masters. He had played in eighteen Opens, twice finishing second — the lost playoff in 1984 to Fuzzy Zoeller and a loss late on Sunday to Corey Pavin in 1995 — but hadn't made a cut there since 1996. Now, if he wanted to play, he would have to qualify.

"I don't have any problem with that," he said. "In '92, when I had my slump, I wasn't exempt, and I tried to qualify for Pebble and missed by two shots. Sometimes in golf you have to take your medicine. This is the U.S. Open, and we should all want to play. I hope by going and playing it will send a message to other players that if you aren't exempt, you shut up and go play."

What a lot of people didn't understand about Norman was that one of his role models in golf was Arnold Palmer, who had taken him under his wing when he first came to the United States to live in the early 1980s, during Hannigan's USGA reign. Eight different times, Palmer had slogged through sectional qualifying, trying to play in the Open, making it just once.

"If Arnold can play in a sectional, anyone can," Norman said. "It shows a certain kind of commitment to the game. I want to play in the Open, particularly this one. I've heard so much about Bethpage, I really want to see it and play it and compete on it. But if I'm going to do that, I have to earn it."

There would be eighty-seven players competing for four spots at Old Memorial. It would be a long, hot day. Was Norman looking forward to the challenge? He smiled. "Hell, no," he said. "But it's something I have to go and do."

As soon as he saw the list of entries for the qualifier at Woodmont, Tom Meeks knew he had a problem. There were 204 players entered. That was too many. Getting all of them around thirty-six holes before dark, even on one of the longest days of the year, would be extremely difficult. Getting everyone in *and* conducting a playoff would almost certainly be impossible.

"I already told the guys down there to figure on the playoff being Tuesday morning," Meeks said. "And I know when I get there, I'm going to hear about this from guys."

Actually the USGA and Middle Atlantic Golf Association, which would run the qualifier, were already hearing about it. "It's absolutely brutal," said Peter Jacobsen, a longtime tour member. "You're looking at six-hour rounds out there. If they get hot weather, forget it. They'll never finish."

Jacobsen, who had undergone hip surgery a year before, had decided not to put his body through the thirty-six-hole walk or his emotions through the potential twelve-hour grind and had withdrawn. Everyone else would play, but most were dreading it. "We'll just get them around as fast as we can," said Mike Cumberpatch, who would be in charge of the qualifier. "Our goal will be to finish before dark."

The first tee time would be at seven A.M. There were thirty-four Bethpage spots available. The field was just about as strong as some PGA Tour events. It included four past major champions: Jerry Pate and Scott Simpson, who had won the Open in 1976 and 1987 respectively, along with Mize, Norman's nemesis at the '87 Masters, and Fred Couples, the '92 Masters champion. Sectionals can be humbling: none of the four qualified. Pate appeared to have the best chance after a 66 in the morning, but he skied to a 74 in the afternoon. "I just couldn't get out of my own way," he said. "It's pretty discouraging."

Couples had a different problem. He simply couldn't get motivated to play as hard as he had to in order to contend. He had
remarried in 1998, had adopted his wife's two children, and had
become, essentially, a part-time tour player. He had finished out of
the top 125 on the money list for the first time in twenty-one years
on tour in 2001. That didn't affect his status on tour — he was
exempt through 2006 because of his 1996 victory at the Players
Championship — but, at forty-two, it was tough to get himself
psyched up to play, especially thirty-six holes at a brutal pace on
what was an almost empty golf course. Couples was used to big
crowds, not knots of a dozen spectators. But while he wanted to
play in the Open, he just couldn't get his emotions geared up to do
what he had to do to qualify.

The USGA and the players had caught one good break: the
weather. It was perfect, the kind of day that made you almost *want*
to play thirty-six holes of golf. Woodmont has two courses, the par-
72 North and the par-71 South. Since the South is 500 yards
shorter than the North, it was easy to get deceived just looking at
scores after eighteen holes. A score of 70 on the North was proba
bly just as good as a 67 or 68 on the South. Those who didn't score
well on the North knew they had a chance to get back into contention in the afternoon on the South. A poor round on the South
in the morning probably meant your chances of qualifying were
between slim and none.

"In the end, it always comes out the same," said Loren Roberts.
"You need to shoot five or six under for the two rounds. Every year
they've ever had a qualifer here (sixteen times), that's the way it
comes out." Roberts wasn't far wrong. One year, when the wind
had blown all day, the number had been 142 — one under par.
Most years, though, it was between four under and seven under.

Perhaps no one in the field wanted to get to Bethpage more
than Roberts. He was forty-seven, a late bloomer as a pro who
hadn't won for the first time on tour until he was thirty-eight, and
had gone on to become a very good player. He had almost won the
Open in '94 at Oakmont, missing a four-foot putt on the 18th

green Sunday that would have given him the victory; instead, he lost in a playoff the next day to Ernie Els. He had been one of a very small handful of players who had made the effort to go and play Bethpage the previous fall, and he had been blown away by it. "Tough to believe it's a public course," he said. "I've heard about what it was like before they put all the money into it, but now it's just unbelievable. I think a lot of the guys are going to be shocked by it."

"There's a reason why most pros haven't seen the golf course," Lee Janzen had joked during the Masters. "We aren't the kind of guys who are going to sleep in our cars to get a tee time." And when someone asked Scott McCarron what he knew about Bethpage, he smiled and said, "Beth Page? I dated her in high school. Great kisser."

The day was a whirlwind for most of the players. They raced around eighteen holes as quickly as possible, had about thirty minutes to go inside for a hamburger, then reported for their afternoon tee times. The morning rounds had backed up enough that the USGA decided to push back some of the later starting times by a half hour for the simple reason that not pushing them back would mean players had to report directly to the tee with no break for their afternoon round.

Overall, the day ran as smoothly as could be hoped. There were backups. On some holes, players had to wait forty minutes to get off the tee. "I was rolling along feeling great, then we had to wait forty minutes on the 10th hole in the afternoon," said Brent Geiberger, a four-year tour veteran who was the son of 1966 PGA champion Al Geiberger. "I got stiff and tight and made three straight bogeys. I thought I was finished. Then I got lucky at 18 and holed a 38-yard bunker shot for a birdie. Maybe that will get me in. If it doesn't, I'll remember those three bogeys."

That's the killer part of qualifiers. One bad shot, one missed putt, and you can go home with nothing to show for twelve hours of work. No one gets paid at a qualifier. There are three rewards: a USGA medal to the low scorer; a similar medal to the low amateur;

and, most important, a spot in the U.S. Open. Missing by one shot is worse than missing by ten, because you will what-if yourself forever.

As dusk began closing in, players came off the golf course, their faces creased with exhaustion and tension. A scoreboard had been set up near the putting green with all 204 names on it and their scores next to the names. At the far end of the board, a makeshift leader board had been put up, with the lowest scores listed. People gathered in small groups at that end, pointing as scores went up, speculating on what the qualifying number would be. The consensus was that Roberts was going to be right: the playoff would either be at five-under 138 or six-under 137.

But he would not be in it. Roberts trudged in shortly before dark at two under, a sad look on his face. Even without looking at the scoreboard, he knew he wouldn't be playing in the Open.

One player who was nowhere near the scoreboard was Charles Howell III. He stood almost at the other end of the clubhouse, arms folded, not even looking in the direction of the scoreboard. "I'm not going near that thing," he said. "Looking at it will just make me even more nervous than I am already."

Howell was in the 137 group. He had made a remarkable afternoon comeback on the South course, shooting 64 after a morning round of 73 on the North. Howell was tired. He had played five straight weeks, trying to hang on to a spot in the world's top fifty. That would have made him exempt and kept him out of the qualifier. He had finished fifty-third. "I guarantee you these things ain't no fun," he said, his drawl coming straight out of Augusta, Georgia, his hometown as a kid. "I was trying as hard as I could to avoid this. But I couldn't, so here I am."

Howell was one of the tour's young phenoms. He wouldn't turn twenty-three until the week after the Open, and he had made $1.5 million in 2001 as an unofficial tour member, forced to play on sponsor exemptions at the start of the year because he had failed to make it through Q-School. He was rail thin, outgoing, and friendly and hit the ball about as long as anyone in the game. He was young and wealthy, newly married, and had everything going for him in life.

But as the sun set on a gorgeous June evening, he couldn't stand still, waiting for the last groups to finish. "At least I birdied the last hole," he said. "I had a 25-footer, and I told myself, make this and you'll get in. I made it. Now I'll see if I was telling myself the truth."

His agent walked by. "Hey, agent," Howell called. "How do I look?"

"You're in," he said.

"Yeah, right," Howell said, still refusing to venture near the scoreboard.

It was becoming clear that 137 was probably going to at least be in a playoff. Of course, since the playoff wasn't going to be until the morning, no one wanted to be part of it. The 137s were hoping that somehow the parade of scorecards coming in at that number or better would stop before there were thirty-five of them.

None of the six who had made it through the River Bend qualifier seriously contended. Robert Stock, who had been the medalist, never could get loose after working all weekend and shot 151. Pat Tallent was at 147. Jason Pool shot 143 and felt good about the day because he had been paired with tour veteran Willie Wood and played solidly. He finished third among the amateurs in the field. Pool was delighted when George McNeill, his college teammate at Florida State who had flown up from Florida to play because of the extra qualifying spots available, came in at 136. McNeill was a minitour player, and making it into the Open for the first time was a big deal. He beat long odds by qualifying. Of the thirty-four who survived Woodmont, thirty had PGA Tour playing privileges. Two — Steve Haskins and Lucas Glover — were on the Buy.com Tour. The nontour qualifiers were McNeill and Jerry Haas, who had once played on tour and was now the golf coach at Wake Forest.

Getting in was also a big deal for Steve Pate, not because it was his first Open — he had played in thirteen previous Opens — but because he had to overcome a vicious case of the gout to survive the thirty-six-hole trek. "I've been taking Indocin for several days, and I was taking Tylenol 3 with codeine all day today," he said. "I was okay in the morning, but midway through the afternoon my foot started screaming at me. The last few holes were really tough."

Pate had dealt with bad karma throughout his seventeen years on tour. In 1991, he had made his first Ryder Cup team only to injure a hip when the car he was riding in to the official banquet on Wednesday night got plowed into. Five years later, he broke a wrist in another car accident and missed most of a year. He had made the Ryder Cup team again in 1999 but had struggled with his game in 2001 and dropped to 151st on the money list. "I was supposed to play the Kemper last week," he said. "First time in a while I've gotten in, and then this gout came on and I couldn't walk for about four days. I played a little bit out here in a cart Sunday and decided to try it today. I'm amazed I got through it."

Pate was one of the tour's characters, a bright, genuinely funny person whose temper had earned him the nickname Volcano early in his career. He had mellowed considerably with injuries and maturity but could still get pretty wired on occasion. He managed to shoot 136 and couldn't wait to get his paperwork and go home so he could get off his aching foot.

There were at least two people in more pain than Pate by nightfall. One was Bubba Dickerson, the 2001 U.S. Amateur champion. That victory had made Dickerson exempt for the 2002 Masters, U.S. Open, and British Open. But after playing in the Masters, Dickerson had decided it was time to turn pro even though doing so meant giving up his automatic spot in the two Opens. As a result, he was at Woodmont. He shot 72–68 for 140. He stared at the scoreboard for a while, figured out he had no chance, and headed for the exit.

"No regrets," he insisted. "I made my decision knowing this could happen. I just didn't play good enough."

Mike Muehr had played well enough — for thirty-three holes. He was eight under par with three holes to go. Muehr was thirty, in his second year on tour. He had struggled most of the year, mostly because he couldn't stop thinking about making the cut on Friday. "Instead of just playing and thinking about putting together four good rounds, I catch myself thinking, am I inside the cut number, what's the cut going to be," he said. "As soon as I do that, I go south."

Muehr was willing to try almost anything to get into the Open after missing yet another cut at the Kemper. Tommy Mensing, a buddy of his who was a Maryland graduate, had offered to caddy for him. He suggested that Muehr use his Maryland golf bag for good luck, considering that Maryland had recently won the NCAA basketball tournament. Muehr is a Duke graduate, and the thought of carrying a bag with a red turtle on it was appalling to him. But he was willing to try anything. He put his clubs in the Maryland bag.

The turtle was doing great until he reached the 16th hole on the North course, late in the day. Try as he might not to think about the number, Muehr knew he was probably just inside it. "No big numbers," he told himself. "Just make easy pars."

Boom. He bogeyed 16 and double-bogeyed 17. He turned in his scorecard and stood staring at the board, looking more crestfallen each time another number under 138 went up. By now, it was late, and everyone was counting. The number of players at 137 or better — led by Australian Peter Lonard who had shot a remarkable 15-under-par 128 — crept over thirty. Charles Howell still wasn't looking.

The last groups came in. Olin Browne, who had grown up in the D.C. area and had finished fifth when the Open was played at Congressional in 1997, was comfortably in at 135. "The only way to look at these things is the way I look at Pro-Ams," he said. "If you tell yourself you're miserable, then you're miserable. But if you look at it as an opportunity, then you can do yourself some good. I played pretty well under a lot of pressure today. Should give me confidence.

"I hear guys talk about how tough this is. Sure, it's a long day. But look at what we're doing, we're playing *golf*. How tough can that be?"

Shortly before nine o'clock, Michael Cumberpatch made an announcement. "There are thirty-three players at 137 or better who have qualified for the U.S. Open. There are twelve players tied for the thirty-fourth spot at 138. We will conduct a twelve-for-one playoff tomorrow morning, beginning at the eighth hole on the North course."

One spot, twelve players, and they had to come back tomorrow to try to beat those odds. Mike Muehr was sick to his stomach.

"You know what the most amazing thing is?" Tom Meeks said. "Twelve for one, and I can guarantee you every one of them will show up. A chance to play in the Open is a chance to play in the Open, no matter how small the chance may be."

Howell walked to the parking lot, a tired smile on his face. He had finally walked over to the scoreboard to pick up his paperwork, still not looking at the scores, almost as if he was afraid if he did, something would change. "I just hope," he said, "I don't have to go through that again anytime soon."

He spoke for just about everyone.

Muehr had trouble sleeping that night. He kept replaying the 16th and 17th holes in his mind. He thought about sleeping through his six o'clock alarm and just letting the playoff go on without him. "In the end, I was up anyway," he said. "I knew I'd be miserable if I didn't go out and give it a shot. And, I told myself, *someone* is going to get the spot."

As Meeks had predicted, all twelve players who had qualified to play off were on the eighth tee at eight A.M. They were divided into three foursomes, told to play one hole, and then wait until everyone had finished. There were six birdies on the first hole. Those six players — Muehr among them — advanced to the ninth hole. "The birdie at eight really helped, to say the least," Muehr said. "It helped put the night before behind me, and when we walked to the ninth tee it occurred to me that my chances to get in had just doubled."

The ninth hole on the North course is a difficult par-four. None of the six players still alive — Muehr, Erik Compton, Cameron Beckman, past Amateur champion Hank Kuehne, David Peoples, and Jeff Gove — could birdie it. All made par. Rather than go down the par-five 10th, they all went back to the eighth one more time.

Kuehne, one of the longest drivers of the golf ball on the planet, landed his drive no more than 10 yards short of the green. But his chip came up 12 feet short of the flagstick.

Muehr hit a wonderful second shot, a nine-iron that stopped about five feet from the hole. After everyone else had missed their birdie attempts, he stood over his putt, knowing that if he made it he was in the Open. He would never have to think about his finish the night before again. "Talk about flushing some demons," he said.

"Knock this in, and let's go to the fucking Open," Mensing said to him.

The putt rolled straight in, and the other five players heartily congratulated him. Disappointed as they were, they all knew about Muehr's finish the night before. No golfer wishes that sort of nightmare on another golfer.

"I was so tired I almost couldn't get my arms in the air to celebrate," Muehr said. "Even so, I felt as if I'd moved about a thousand-pound weight off my back. It was a great feeling."

While Muehr was celebrating his Tuesday turnaround, the other tour qualifier was being held in Westchester at Brae Burn and Century country clubs, which happen to be adjacent to each other. There weren't quite as many players on hand — 153 players playing for twenty-two spots. There also weren't as many tour pros, since almost everyone who had played in the Kemper Open had chosen to play at Woodmont.

Still, there were five more past major champions in this qualifier: two-time Open champion Curtis Strange, who talked about
golf (on ABC) more these days than he played it; 1982 Masters
champion Craig Stadler, and three PGA champions: Bob Tway
(1986); Wayne Grady (1990), and Steve Elkington (1995).

The two golf courses proved tougher than the Woodmont
courses, in part because of serious poa annua (a kind of weed) problems on the greens at Brae Burn. "I went into the day thinking
even par would probably get in," P. J. Cowan said. "When I saw the
greens at Brae Burn, I figured it would three or four over."

His original estimate proved closer to correct. The playoff came
at one-over-par 144. Unfortunately, Cowan was nowhere close to
that number. He could do no better than 74 in the morning at Century, then skied to 76 on the greens at Brae Burn. It was a sad way
to end a quest he had been convinced would land him at Bethpage.
"You know, after the morning I really felt pretty good," he said. "I
was a couple over, but I thought a couple under in the afternoon
would get me in. Then I saw those greens, and I knew I was in
trouble. This one is tough to take. I had my heart set on the Black.
It's just something I'm going to have to live with." Just as at Fox
Hill, he had a beer in hand as he spoke. This time, though, it was
not a celebratory drink.

As is always the case at sectionals, there were players who didn't
come close to the number who were still able to walk away with
smiles on their faces. Jamie Friedman shot 77–78 but was thrilled
to have been there. George Zahringer shot — his words — "a
smooth 80" in the morning, ending his hopes, but was proud of
himself for hanging in and shooting 71 in the afternoon. After all, a
lot of players who put up a number that starts with an eight disappear before the start of the second round at sectionals.

The major champions had better luck at Purchase than at Woodmont: Neither Strange nor Elkington came close to qualifying, but
Stadler and Tway made it through with shots to spare. Grady survived the playoff. It would be Grady's first Open since 1996.

The happiest man in the field may have been Bill Rosenblum, a thirty-three-year-old assistant pro at the Orchards Golf Club in Hadley, Massachusetts. Rosenblum had never made it through a local. Playing at Taconic Golf Club, he had shot 32 on the front nine and looked like a lock to make it through. But the pressure got to him on the back nine, and he staggered home with a 39 — one shot outside the number it took to qualify. He then lost a playoff for the first alternate spot.

Thinking he had nothing to lose, Rosenblum drove to Manhattan the day before the sectional and spent the night with a friend. He showed up at the golf course shortly before seven A.M. to register as an alternate who was actually on-site. He was told a few minutes later that he was the highest-ranked alternate who had shown up, and if anyone dropped out, he was in. "I had figured not a lot of guys would show as alternates," he said. "But I was surprised when I was at the top of the list. For someone like me, just playing in a sectional would be a huge deal. I mean, you look at the list and you realize you could be paired with Jesper [Parnevik] or [Fred] Couples or someone like that."

Twice, it looked as if Rosenblum's dream was going to come true. First, David Frost wasn't on the tee as his tee time approached. Rosenblum was told to report to the tee only to have Frost show up with about a minute to spare. Soon after that, Wayne Grady was missing. Again, Rosenblum was told to report to the tee. Again, he never got a ball in the air; Grady arrived just before he was supposed to be introduced.

There was one last chance. No one had seen Jim Thorpe, the fifty-three-year-old Senior Tour star who had requested and received an exemption out of the locals. Once again, Rosenblum reported to the tee, fully expecting Thorpe to arrive just as Frost and Grady had. But he didn't, and Rosenblum was paired with Mike Sposa, a third-year tour pro who would be thirty-three the next day, and Ken Bakst, the 1997 Mid-Amateur champ. Not exactly Jesper and Couples, but Rosenblum could not have cared less. He was two under par after five holes but couldn't keep it going. He ended up shooting 163 and still made the drive home with a smile on his face.

So did Rick Karbowski, a building supply salesman from Worcester who had made it through at Taconic in spite of being unable to practice for ten days prior to the local because he had been hit in the back of the head by a beer bottle while waiting in line to go to the bathroom in a bar. Apparently the bottle wielder thought Karbowski had cut in front of him in line and cracked him over the head. Karbowski shot 152, missing the qualifying number by eight shots, but felt pretty good about having made it as far as he had.

The award for best effort had to go to Larry Stubblefield. Once, he had been a promising young professional. In 1972, he was the medalist at the Tour Qualifying School and that same year he had qualified for his first and only Open. But his pro career never took off, and Stubblefield got his amateur status back after several years. He then turned pro again and got a club job at Oahu Country Club in Hawaii. He was first alternate in his local there and was somewhat surprised to get a call just before Memorial Day from Larry Adamson telling him that his local had the first alternate spot at Purchase. Did he want to come play?

"I talked it over with my wife," he said, "and we figured why not? I mean, everything is a long hop from Hawaii."

Stubblefield shot 167, far from what it took to advance. Two weeks later, he successfully qualified for the Senior Open, which would be held in Baltimore. Another long hop, but what the heck.

As with Woodmont, most of the qualifiers in Purchase were tour players. Tom Byrum, a longtime tour player, was the medalist at 138, followed by two players who had been serious contenders to win majors. One was Jeff Maggert, who had been part of the four-way back-nine battle at Congressional in 1997. He also had four other top five finishes in majors, including a pair of thirds in the PGA. The other was Jean Van de Velde, the quirky Frenchman who would be known for the rest of his life for throwing away the 1999 British Open by going for broke with a three-shot lead on the 18th hole and making a triple-bogey seven that led to losing in a playoff to Paul Lawrie.

Van de Velde was one of the brightest, most entertaining men in golf. He loved nothing more than sitting around with American players and telling them flat out that Tiger Woods wasn't *nearly* as famous as Ronaldo, the Brazilian soccer player. "There are millions, billions of people who have never heard of Tiger who worship Ronaldo," he would insist as the American players screamed that he was crazy. He would no doubt spend time in the clubhouse at Bethpage telling people why the ongoing World Cup was millions of times more important than any U.S. Open.

Others who qualified included Jay Haas — matching brother Jerry who had made it at Woodmont — and Jim McGovern, one of a handful of players who had been turned down for a requested exemption from the local. McGovern was thirty-seven and had won the Houston Open in 1993. He had not been exempt since 1996 on tour but did have a knack for qualifying for the Open; this would be his tenth. Eight of the ten times he had gotten in the hard way, by qualifying.

Rick Hartmann lost another hundred dollars to Darrell Kestner, though unlike at Fox Hill, where both men had left happy, only Kestner could enjoy the end of the day. He shot 143, which proved to be the number that avoided playing off and advanced him to his eighth Open. Hartmann could do no better than 150. He would still go to Bethpage, but only to cheer for his friend.

Along with Kestner, seventeen other players were at 143 or better, leaving four spots and seven golfers at 144. At 7:25 on an unseasonably cool night, the first three 144s who had finished — Per-Ulrik Johansson, Harrison Frazar, and Grady — stood on the first tee, ready to go. The last group of the day, which included one player, Richard Massey, with a chance to get into the playoff, was on the 18th green. About a hundred spectators, most of them club members with a beer or a drink in hand, stood on the tee.

Johansson, knowing a cell-phone toting crowd when he saw one, took control of the situation. "Okay, everyone, *please* turn off your cell phones," he said. "This is important to us."

One hundred hands, or so it seemed, reached into pockets to turn off cell phones. A minute later, the early-bird three convinced one of Gene Westmoreland's lieutenants to let them tee off even though the other four players (Massey had made it) weren't on the tee yet. Light was going to grow short soon. Westmoreland gave the order to let them tee off.

They were down the fairway on the par-four 10th hole by the time Massey, John Maginnes, Richard Parker, and Jim Carter were ready to go. The early three all made routine pars, then waited for the late four.

The late four were all over the golf course. None hit the green in regulation. All had par putts, ranging from Maginnes at 18 feet to Carter at eight feet. In order, Maginnes, Parker, and Massey missed. Johansson immediately began high-fiving Frazar and Grady because they were all in, regardless of what Carter did. Carter calmly sank his eight-footer for par to gain the fourth and final spot.

That left Maginnes, Parker, and Massey to trudge to the par-five 11th to play off for the two alternate spots. Maginnes actually had to make about a three and a half footer for bogey just to remain in contention to be an alternate. When he made the putt he wasn't sure whether that was good news or bad news. Most players believe alternate spots to be worth almost as much as a bag of golf tees, but they play off for them knowing that most years at least one alternate does get into the Open. Massey bogeyed the 11th to drop out, while Maginnes and Parker made pars. The sun was now beginning to set rapidly.

"Hey, Mag," Parker said as they walked to the 12th tee. "Does this mean anything at all?"

"I've got absolutely no idea," Maginnes said.

On the 12th hole, a short (357 yards) par-four, Maginnes stuffed a nine-iron to about three feet. After Parker missed from 20 feet, Maginnes made his putt to secure the first alternate slot. He did not celebrate. On the long walk into the clubhouse, Jeff Hall, who was representing the USGA at the site, gave him what USGA officials call "the alternate speech": Make sure we know how to contact you at all times; if someone from this qualifier drops out, you're in; if an exempt player drops out there is a list at USGA headquarters of the twelve sectionals, and we go down the list from one to twelve. He didn't know where Purchase was on the list.

Maginnes was thirty-three, an easygoing guy from eastern North Carolina who had bounced between the PGA Tour and the Buy.com/Nike Tour for about ten years. He was about as unassuming as anyone who had ever played on tour. One year, filling out a bio form for the tour, he had listed beer, tobacco, and women as his favorite outside interests. He had tried giving up beer and dipping for a while but found that his golf suffered. So he was back to drinking beer and dipping — and playing better golf. Now he listened in silence until Hall finished. "This has been one great week," he said finally. "Yesterday, I missed four-spotting [getting one of four qualifying spots] for Westchester in a playoff, and now I'm first alternate here. Tomorrow, I get to drive eight hours to Toronto [to play in a Buy.com event]. The only good news is before I leave I get to play over at Winged Foot."

Hall knew there was nothing he could say as consolation. "Nice birdie on the 12th wasn't going to cheer him up," he said later.

It was close to nine o'clock by the time the small cadre that had trudged to the 12th made it to the clubhouse. It was dark outside. Everyone but Hall, who had to call in the results to the USGA and to Jon Barker's office, headed for the parking lot.

The Open field was now set. Almost.

Fred Ridley, head of the USGA's championship committee. *Photograph by Kelly Campbell*

Jon Barker, the first man on site. *Photograph by Kelly Campbell*

Mimi Griffin, the USGA's corporate guru. *Photograph by Kelly Campbell*

Mike Butz: Mike the First. *Photograph courtesy of the USGA.*

Reed Mackenzie,
president of the USGA.
*Photograph by Kelly
Campbell*

David Fay: He had a dream. *Photograph by Kelly Campbell*

Steve Worthy: "That's not a problem." *Photograph by Kelly Campbell*

Tim Moraghan: Always working behind the scenes. *Photograph by Kelly Campbell*

Tom Meeks: "There are no pins out there." *Photograph by Kelly Campbell*

Mike Davis: Mike the Second. *Photograph by Kelly Campbell*

Superintendent Craig Currier: He never sweated— until Sunday night. *Photograph by Kelly Campbell*

Frank Bussey: "That can't possibly be done . . . Mary." *Photograph by Kelly Campbell*

Mary Lopuszynski: Note the ever-present cell-phone cord in her ear. *Photograph by Kelly Campbell*

Dave Catalano, the man in charge. *Photograph by Kelly Campbell*

Legendary course designer A. W. Tillinghast. *Courtesy The Tillinghast Association*

Rees Jones, "the Open Doctor." *Courtesy Rees Jones, Inc.*

Paul Goydos, the Open's leadoff hitter. *Photograph by Kelly Campbell*

Mark O'Meara, one of Tiger's few confidants. *Photograph by Kelly Campbell*

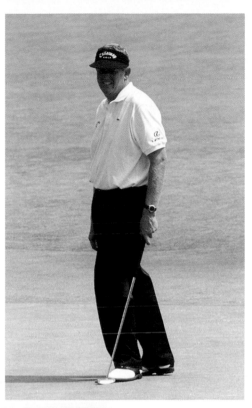

Colin Montgomerie, the golfer American fans love to hate. *Photograph by Kelly Campbell*

Stepped-up security was part of what made the 2002 Open unlike any other before it. *Photograph by Kelly Campbell*

Tiger Woods.
*Photograph by
Kelly Campbell*

Jerry Haas, golf
coach at Wake
Forest, and his
brother Jay.
*Photograph by
Kelly Campbell*

Sergio García. *Photograph by Kelly Campbell*

David Duval: A lost Open, a lost year. *Photograph by Kelly Campbell*

Davis Love III: His RV didn't get stuck on Sunday. *Photograph by Kelly Campbell*

Tiger Woods with Mark O'Meara.
Photograph by Kelly Campbell

Nick Faldo:
He got the
"Hannigan"
exemption.
Photograph by Kelly Campbell

Phil Mickelson: Still a couple of shots shy of Tiger. *Fred Vuich/Golf Magazine Picture Collection*

Tiger Woods with the 2002 U.S. Open trophy. *Fred Vuich/Golf Magazine Picture Collection*

12

On to Bethpage

ONCE HE HAD the names of the twenty-two qualifiers from Purchase, Jeff Hall called the championship office in Bethpage. Jon Barker and his staff would be receiving phone calls starting early the next morning from all the qualifiers, looking for housing, directions, how to get their courtesy cars, and perhaps most important, what kind of credentials they would need to get to the golf course. Starting Friday — this was Tuesday night — access to the clubhouse and the golf course was going to be severely limited.

Hall reached Mike Antolini, one of Jon Barker's interns, at about ten-thirty. Everyone in Barker's office had been working almost around-the-clock since Memorial Day, and Antolini was expecting Hall's call. Hall went down the list of qualifiers. When he finished there was a pause at the other end.

"Mike, you got everyone?" he asked.

"Jeff, you only gave me twenty-two names," Antolini said.

"That's because there were twenty-two qualifiers."

"According to what I've got here, there are supposed to be twenty-three out of Purchase."

Hall was baffled. Gene Westmoreland, who had run the qualifier for the MGA, had clearly written twenty-two on the scoreboard, on all the information packets, on anything that walked. He had been doing qualifiers for years and was about as reliable as any local official the USGA worked with.

"Let me call you right back," Hall told Antolini.

He hung up and called Larry Adamson at home. In addition to putting all the entries together, Adamson was responsible for letting the officials at all the qualifiers, local and sectional, know how many spots they were playing for. When Hall told Adamson what was going on, Adamson didn't have his paperwork in front of him.

"I think it is twenty-three, if my memory is right," he told Hall. "I'm pretty sure we added one there."

Sectionals often receive an extra spot after their original allotment because when Adamson doles out slots in May he does so after calculating the maximum number of exemptions there may be. Then, if the number of exempt players turns out to be fewer than that, he adds spots.

In 2002, six sectionals had been given added spots after the original allocation. The two exempt spots held for the leading money winners on the European Tour didn't have to be used because both players were also in the world's top fifty. The same had been true for four spots on the PGA Tour's top ten list for '02 that had closed on May 26. Adamson had sent memos to six of the qualifiers — Woodmont, Purchase, Tampa, Cincinnati, St. Louis, and Atlanta — informing the officials there that they had been given an extra spot.

He wasn't a hundred percent certain sitting at home that Purchase had gone from twenty-two to twenty-three, but that sounded right to him.

"Tell the folks in Bethpage I'll call them first thing in the morning and let them know for sure," he said. "In the meantime, if we are one short, who is the first alternate?"

"John Maginnes."

"Got a number for him?"

Hall remembered what Maginnes had said about playing at Winged Foot in the morning. "I don't have a number, but I think I know where he'll be." He told Adamson about the outing at

Winged Foot, and Adamson told him he'd track him down if, in fact, he was in the Open.

Hall hung up feeling a little queasy about what had happened. "When you think you've lost a playoff and you're just playing for an alternate's spot, your mindset changes in most cases," he said. "I felt badly that all three guys had thought they were playing for an alternate's spot when, in fact, they might have been playing those last two holes to get into the Open."

Adamson was in his office at five-thirty the next morning to make sure all was ready for Meeks when he arrived at eight A.M. to start doing the pairings. The first thing he did was look at his list to see how many qualifiers were supposed to come out of Purchase. He had been right: the number was twenty-three. He called Barker's office to tell them that, in fact, the right number was twenty-three and to add Maginnes to their list. Then he set about trying to track down Maginnes at Winged Foot.

He called the pro shop there, told the people who he was, and said that Maginnes needed to call him when he arrived that day to play. "Tell him it's important and it's about the U.S. Open," Adamson said.

When Maginnes called back a couple of hours later, Adamson caught himself smiling. For once he was getting to give someone pleasant news. "Mr. Maginnes, I think I've got good news for you," he said.

"The Open?" Maginnes answered.

"Yes, the Open," Adamson answered. "There were twenty-three spots at your qualifier, not twenty-two. You're in."

Maginnes was clearly a bit stunned. "Are you sure?" he asked Adamson.

Adamson laughed. "Yes, I'm quite sure," he said.

He heard Maginnes turning away from the phone, shouting to his caddy and playing partners. "Guys, guess what, I'm in the Open," he said, the glee in his voice apparent.

Now, finally, the Bethpage field was truly set.

❖   ❖   ❖

There were, of course, seventy-five players who hadn't needed to bother with qualifying. As championship week drew closer, some of them had started calling about getting on the Black. As far as anyone could tell, the only players in the field who had played it in the past were Len Mattiace, who was exempt, and Brad Lardon, who had qualified at Woodmont. Both had lived on Long Island as kids and had played the course with their dads.

In mid-May, Jim Furyk had come out to play. He had called Barker's office, and Tricia Solow arranged for him to play on a Monday when the golf course was closed. It was a cold, windy day, and Craig Currier spent some time with him on the course to get his feedback. Furyk was impressed. At day's end he had shot 74 — four over par — and when word spread that one of the world's top ten players had been unable to do any better than four over par, there was glee among the regulars in the Bethpage clubhouse.

"They shouldn't get too excited," Currier said. "We probably aren't going to have too many days during the Open as tough as that one. The wind was really blowing."

Perhaps. But 74 was 74, and everyone had smiles on their faces. The Black may not have passed its first real test, but it had, at the very least, gotten an A on a pop quiz. Soon other players who were exempt began calling about getting on the golf course: Matt Gogel, Michael Allen. Davis Love III and Billy Andrade called about coming out the week of the Westchester Classic, which was the tour stop prior to the Open, played about fifty miles from Bethpage. Solow was more than happy to make arrangements for all who called. She told them Mondays were best prior to the course closing on May 27, and any day after that was fine. All the players had to do was let her know they were coming.

On the morning of May 22, Solow took a call that she knew wasn't going to be quite that simple. It came from Kathy Battaglia, who said she worked for the ETW Corporation. Her boss was hoping to come and play the Black on May 27. Solow swallowed hard. ETW stood, she knew, for Eldrick Tiger Woods. Everyone had wondered all spring when he might show up to play the golf course. Now Ms. Battaglia was explaining to Solow that Mr. Woods would be playing the final round of the Memorial Tournament on May 26 in Columbus, Ohio, was hoping to fly in to Bethpage early the next morning, play the golf course, and then go to an afternoon outing in Toronto.

That, Solow explained, was going to be a problem. May 27 was Memorial Day, the last day the Black would be open to the public before the Open. The place would be swarming with golfers and, worse still for Woods, local media, recording the final day of play. It would be much better, Solow explained, if Woods could come the following day. The golf course would be closed, and it would be much easier to get him in and out under the radar screen.

Battaglia called back a little while later to say the twenty-eighth would be fine.

As soon as Solow hung up the phone with Battaglia she told Barker what was going on. Woods wanted to fly in from Toronto on Tuesday morning. Mark O'Meara, his pal, confidant, and older-brother figure, was going to fly in from Orlando to meet him. Their planes would land at Republic Airport, the small strip used by private aircraft that was located 1.8 miles from the park.

Barker knew two things were critical to make the visit come off without a hitch: keeping it a secret and having an airtight plan from touchdown to takeoff in terms of security. The last thing anyone wanted was a crowd, whether it be fans who just wanted to observe or media who might want to talk. He contacted Dave Catalano, Craig Currier, Steve Worthy, Bob Nuzzo, and Nuzzo's deputy, Dave Candaleria. Just to make sure the state parks people felt in the loop, Catalano let Nancy Palumbo, Castro's top assistant and his boss, know what was up. Then the group convened in Barker's office on the evening of May 26 to map out a plan.

Nuzzo would have troopers on hand but would not tell them beforehand exactly what they were being brought to Bethpage for. They would learn their exact assignment that morning. Barker suggested the idea of having Woods and O'Meara begin their round on the third tee. "We don't want them anywhere near the clubhouse before they tee off," he said. "People will see them and the word will spread. This way, by the time they get near the clubhouse [playing the 18th hole] they'll only have two holes left to play."

Everyone agreed that was the way to go. Have the players change into their golf shoes at the airport, then drive them down Round Swamp Road and up the hill behind the first green to the area near the third tee where Currier's maintenance barn was. Currier was assigned to come up with two members of his staff to act as caddies. As with the police, they were not to be told their assignment for the day.

Barker sent an e-mail to Mike Butz and Mike Davis filling them in on the plan.

On the evening of the twenty-seventh, after the Black had formally been shut down, Currier found Pete Cash, Garrett Boddington's deputy on the Black Course crew, and told him he needed him to be at the barn at eight o'clock the next morning and that he wasn't to worry about his normal on-course duties that day. He told him to bring Dave Dailey, a twenty-year-old Irishman who had joined the staff the previous fall. "I chose Pete because he's smart and experienced and I knew I could trust him to handle the thing well," Currier said. "I knew Davey had caddied in Ireland, and if my memory was right, he might have caddied for Tiger when Tiger played at Waterville a couple of years earlier." (Dailey had indeed been working at Waterville when Woods had been there, but hadn't caddied for him.)

Cash told Currier he would be there with Dailey at eight o'clock sharp. "What's the deal?" he asked.

"It's a big deal," Currier said. "Just make sure you guys wear nice clothes. You guys are going to have the loop [caddying is referred to in golf circles as looping] of your lives. But don't ask me any more questions about it."

Cash tracked Dailey down and told him what Currier had said.

"I'll bet I know who it is," Dailey said. "It's Michael Jordan."

Cash, who already suspected it was Woods, shook his head. "Nah, I don't think so, Davey," he said. "I'm not even sure they'd let him on right now."

He was more right about that than he knew. Earlier in the month, someone from Jordan's office had contacted Catalano to say that MJ wanted to play the Black sometime before the Open. Catalano was tempted to give the guy the phone number for the public's tee time computer but resisted. Instead, he politely told him that at that point the only special accommodations that were being made were for players in the Open. There had been one exception made to that rule: Rees Jones was bringing former New York City mayor Rudy Giuliani out to play one day. But that was it.

On the morning of the twenty-eighth, Barker, Solow, and Nuzzo, who was in an unmarked police car, drove to Republic to meet Woods and O'Meara. Their planes landed within minutes of each other. O'Meara was alone, Woods with his girlfriend, Elin Nordegren. Barker explained the plan to have them tee off at number three to avoid being spotted and suggested they change their shoes before getting into the car for the short drive to the golf course.

Woods rolled his eyes and glared at O'Meara. "This always happens whenever I go anywhere with you," he said. "It's always all this special security just because you're in town."

Everyone cracked up. The three visitors piled into Solow's car. The golf bags were loaded into the van Barker was driving, and the three-car caravan, led by Nuzzo, took off. They pulled up to the area behind Currier's maintenance shed, where Cash, Dailey, and state trooper Mark Lynch were waiting. Cash and Dailey caught their breath.

"Told you it wasn't Jordan," Cash said as they sprinted down the hill to where the cars were.

When Barker opened the back of the van, Cash saw that O'Meara's bag was closer to the door. He grabbed it. "I've got you, Mr. O'Meara," he said.

"Smart," O'Meara said. "You know who the big tipper in the group is."

"Actually, I just wanted Davey to have Tiger," Cash said later. "I knew what it would mean to him."

Dailey was wearing his Waterville shirt, and Woods asked him if he had worked there. "I did," he said. "I even got your autograph there."

Woods just smiled.

Since Nordegren didn't have any desire to walk eighteen holes on a muddy golf course, she left with Solow, who asked her what she wanted to do to kill the three hours. Shop? Eat? "Is there a bookstore anywhere nearby?" Nordegren asked. Solow took her to Barnes & Noble and left her there, reading John Grisham's *The Testament* in the reading area.

In the meantime, Woods and O'Meara and their caddies made their way to the third tee, where both players hit two balls since they'd had no warm-up and teeing off on a par-three under the circumstances was hardly ideal. After that, they moved at a brisk pace.

"It wasn't until the fourth fairway that we kind of got our legs under us," Cash said. "We were walking ahead to the green, and I turned to Davey and said, 'My God, that's Tiger and O'Meara right behind us!'"

Woods and O'Meara bantered with each other, made a series of wagers, and asked questions about distances, sight lines, and the rough. "You can bet these greens will be rolling a lot faster when we get back here in two weeks," Woods said at one point — accurately.

By the time they reached the difficult 12th hole, it was raining. As they came off the 14th green, Catalano was waiting for them. His house is located almost adjacent to the 14th green. "Why don't you guys come inside and dry off?" he said.

Woods and O'Meara accepted the offer — sort of. "They said they didn't want to come in the house and track mud all over," Catalano said. "I wouldn't have minded. But they decided to just stand in the garage and wait for the rain to lighten up a little."

While they waited, Cash made conversation with Woods. "It must be great to travel around the world and see all the great places you get to see," he said.

Woods stared out at the rain and answered quietly. "You want to know what I see?" he said. "I see a lot of great golf courses, expensive hotels, and airports. That's it."

That didn't sound all bad to Cash — especially the part about the golf courses — but it occurred to him that being Tiger Woods probably wasn't as easy as it looked.

The rain let up and they continued. By the time they reached the 18th green, word had spread around the clubhouse about who was out on the Black. A knot of spectators had gathered. Clifton Brown of the *New York Times* was also there. He had gotten a tip the night before telling him that Woods and O'Meara were coming. Like everyone else, he watched them play 18 and then walk to the first tee. Nuzzo had stationed several troopers by the first tee to make sure Woods and O'Meara wouldn't be interrupted by autograph seekers or anyone with a notebook or camera. The two men hit their tee shots, headed down the fairway, and that was the last anyone at Bethpage saw of them that day.

Except for the maintenance crew. They were all waiting behind the second green when the round was finished. Solow, Nordegren, Barker, and Nuzzo were back in the same place where they had dropped the golfers off a little more than three hours earlier. O'Meara and Woods thanked Cash and Dailey and tipped them $100 apiece.

Cash and Dailey returned to the maintenance barn to a hero's welcome. "Celebrities for a day," Cash said.

"The greatest golf experience of my life," Dailey added.

As they drove off, Woods and O'Meara were thinking more about food than golf. They asked Solow to stop at a Wendy's drive-through, where Woods ordered for everyone in a fake high-pitched voice. He then asked Solow if she needed gas when he spotted an Exxon station that was giving away stuffed tigers with a fill-up.

The planes took off shortly after noon, and everyone breathed a sigh of relief. The visit had come off without a hitch. Woods went back home to Florida to spend a few days spearfishing. (O'Meara, one of the few people in the world who can get away with teasing Woods, told him he liked to spearfish "because it takes you back to your roots." Woods's justifiable response is not printable in a family book.) O'Meara flew to Washington to play in the Kemper Open, where he spent the next few days telling his fellow pros that the Black would "give all of us all we want."

The following day on his web site, Woods called the golf course "the toughest par-70 I've ever played in my life."

That description spread around the clubhouse quickly. Furyk's 74 was one thing, but now the Great One himself was talking about how difficult their golf course was going to be. Still, Craig Currier wasn't jumping for joy . . . yet. "Next year at this time he'll probably be saying that Olympia Fields (the Open's '03 site) is the toughest course he's ever seen," he said, laughing. "He told me he liked it although he wasn't crazy about the ninth hole, the angle off the tee or something."

Currier was far more concerned with something Mark Lye had said. Lye, who had played the tour for a dozen years, was now a commentator for Golf Channel. He had walked the course soon after Woods and O'Meara had played and had told Currier there were places where he thought the rough was too easy. That distressed Currier. He and Boddington and the USGA had been going around and around on the thickness of the rough. Meeks and Davis wanted it no more than three-and-a-half inches in length. They wanted players to have a chance to get a shot onto the green if they found the first cut of rough.

"The days of pitch-out rough at the Open are gone," Meeks said.

Pitch-out rough is rough so thick that when a player lands in it his only option is to pitch out onto the fairway. It is, for all intents and purposes, a one-stroke penalty. P. J. Boatwright had been a believer in pitch-out rough. During his tenure, Hannigan had tried to get the rough toned down so players could gamble to get the ball on the green. That was more or less the way the Open had been set up in recent years. Currier wanted to be sure the golf course wasn't going to end up like a lot of PGA Tour events where finding the rough meant nothing more than having a little difficulty getting your ball to stop on the green. When Lye told him he thought the rough was a bit thin in places, he semipanicked.

Of course, everyone was a little bit on edge at this stage. The closing of the golf course, the arrival of Woods and O'Meara and others, the very striking presence of all the corporate tents now up along the first and 18th fairways, the fact that more and more people were arriving on a daily basis made the reality that the pop quizzes were just about over and final exams were about to begin.

"It's a little bit like living in a row house in London and being told Queen Elizabeth is coming over to tea," Rabbi Marc Gellman said as the days dwindled. "You don't want to go to all the work to get your house ready for her and then when the day comes look down and realize you've served the tea to her in a Hooters mug."

And with the arrival of the players less than two weeks away, any opinion about the golf course by anyone connected to golf in any way, shape, or form was taken as some kind of word passed down from heaven or up from hell. Lye's comment had everyone worried again. Maybe the players were just being polite about how tough the course was. Furyk's 74 *had* been on a bad weather day. When Lye arrived for the Open and heard about how seriously his remarks had been taken, he felt bad.

"I showed Craig a couple spots, maybe three, where I thought it was a bit thin," he said. "That was it. I didn't mean for anyone to think I thought the golf course was easy. I guess everyone's a little bit sensitive around here about the golf course."

He shook his head. "Someone shoots 10 under here, there are going to be a lot of long faces in this clubhouse, I guess."

He guessed right. Absolutely right.

13

Jeff Sluman?

AT NINE A.M. on the morning of June fifth, Tom Meeks sat in the third-floor conference room of USGA headquarters with 156 three inch by five inch index cards piled in front of him. On each card was the name of a player who had qualified for the 2002 U.S. Open. It was now Meeks's job to decide who would play with whom when the championship began in eight days.

Traditionally, it had been the job of the executive director to make the pairings. P. J. Boatwright had done it, Frank Hannigan had done it, and David Fay had done it. "Frank always said that the best way to do the pairings was take all the cards, throw them down a flight of steps, then pick them up three at a time," Meeks said, cackling at the thought. "He's right about one thing, that *would* be the fairest way to do it."

Fair has very little to do with golf pairings. On the PGA Tour there is a caste system, largely controlled by television, that has been in place for years. Players are divided into three categories — players who have won a tournament during the past three years (along with past greats like Jack Nicklaus or Tom Watson when they play in an event); players in the top 125 on the money list; and finally, nonexempt players, qualifiers, and players who get in on sponsor exemptions. The best tee times — midmorning, midafter-noon — go to the glamour guys. The worst — late, later, and latest — go to the nonexempt. These nonexempts are commonly referred to as the dog groups, because they are playing when the greens are already chewed up and, often, when the golf course has been deserted by most fans.

The tee times of the stars are usually divided up to ensure that there are always name players on the course when TV is on the air. For example, if Tiger Woods and David Duval are playing "late-early," as the players call it (afternoon on Thursday, morning on Friday), then Phil Mickelson and Ernie Els will almost certainly play "early-late."

The Open tee times are structured much the same way, the dif-ference being that TV is on the air virtually nonstop the first two days — ESPN signs on at eleven A.M. eastern time and signs off at seven P.M. eastern. But the key portion of the day in terms of tee times is the three P.M. to five-thirty P.M. window when NBC is on the air. There was no question that the most important player in the field — by far — was Woods. The USGA had already talked to NBC well in advance about wanting Woods to play late-early in order to get him off the golf course as early as possible on Friday because of the concert at Jones Beach that night. NBC was fine with this because it had an NBA playoff game the night before and was planning to promo the Open at halftime.

"We want to be able to say in the promo, 'And during our tele-cast tomorrow, you will see Tiger Woods,' " Tommy Roy explained.

NBC had, in fact, made requests involving six players. In addi-tion to wanting Woods on Thursday afternoon, it wanted Retief Goosen, the defending champion, it wanted John Daly — still a draw — and it wanted Greg Norman, who had successfully slogged through the thirty-six holes in Tampa and been the medal-ist there in the qualifier. On Friday afternoon, NBC wanted Mick-elson and Sergio García.

Meeks was well aware of NBC's requests. Before sitting down to work he had consulted with Fay about the one pairing that is normally automatic: the defending champion (Goosen), the reigning British Open champion (Duval), and the U.S. Amateur champion. Since Bubba Dickerson, the Amateur champion, wasn't in the field because he had failed to qualify after giving up his automatic spot by turning pro, Meeks suggested to Fay that David Toms, who had won the PGA Championship in 2001, be put into the Amateur spot. Fay agreed that was the right thing to do.

Since he couldn't just throw the cards down the steps and pick them up, Hannigan had injected humor into his pairings whenever he could. He had started an annual tradition of pairing three players together who were generally disliked. The trio became known to most in the golf world as the prick pairing. He also started putting together the three best players he could find who had never won a major. He would frequently give known late-night denizens the first tee time of the morning.

Hannigan also took requests. Most players preferred not to play with Arnold Palmer because of the circuslike atmosphere outside the ropes created by his "army." Jim Colbert, though, loved the noise and enthusiasm. It pumped him up and he felt he played better. Whenever he saw Hannigan somewhere, Colbert would tell him to keep him in mind when he was putting together Palmer's Open threesome. Hannigan complied.

"If you've got someone who wants a pairing most players don't want and it doesn't give the other guy some kind of advantage, why not do it?" Hannigan said. "It's different, for example, if [Mark] O'Meara says, 'Put me with Tiger,' because you can make the case that Tiger's more comfortable playing with O'Meara. Arnold could have cared less who he played with."

The pairing that Hannigan was most proud of was the 1980 group at Baltusrol in which he put Isao Aoki, a complete unknown at the time, with Jack Nicklaus. Hannigan had seen Aoki play at the British Open the year before and loved his game. "I wanted the world to see this guy," he said. "I knew putting him with Nicklaus, people would pay attention to him. I never dreamed it would turn out the way it did."

Nicklaus and Aoki ended up playing together all four days because they were first and second at the end of play on both Friday and Saturday. And, as it turned out, on Sunday. Hannigan remembers Nicklaus making his birdie putt on 18 on Sunday to clinch both the Open and the Open scoring record. Aoki still had a six-foot birdie putt that appeared meaningless — he would be second whether he made it or not. But Nicklaus frantically waved his arms at the crowd to be quiet because he knew that *Golf Magazine* had offered a $50,000 bonus to everyone who broke the existing scoring record of 275. Aoki made the putt and earned the bonus. "One of Nicklaus's greatest moments, and I think the only ones who understood why were me and [*Golf* editor] George Peper," Hannigan said.

Fay had gone even further than Hannigan when it came to off-the-wall pairings. He kept alive both the prick pairing and the best-player-never-to-have-won-a-major group and would look for amusing or even serious reasons to pair players. At Olympic in 1998, he paired Tom Lehman, Bernhard Langer, and Steve Jones. Why? All were avowed born-again Christians. "We're the God squad pairing," said Andy Martinez, Lehman's longtime caddy. And when the Open returned to a site, Fay would look up the pairings from the last time it had been there and reunite those in the field who had played together the previous time.

In 1999, Fay turned the whole job over to Meeks. "Too many people knew about all my little games," Fay said. "It was time to retire before I did something *really* crazy." Fay had decided once and for all he was going too far when he had put three women together at the Women's Open because he knew all three of them were in therapy. "That was over the top," he said.

Meeks was far more systematic than either Fay or Hannigan. When he sat down at the conference table he had divided the three-by-five cards into seven separate stacks. Three contained the names of American players, categorized as marquee, A, and B. The marquee stack had names like Woods and Mickelson and Duval and Love. The A group had players who had won tournaments but were not stars. The B group consisted of — with a few exceptions — players who had come through qualifying. He had three additional stacks divided the same way for foreign (or, in USGA terminology, international) players. And he had the names of the five amateurs in the field in a separate pile.

Doing the pairings in 2002 was different than in past years because of the USGA's decision to go to a two-tee start. Instead of simply starting at six-thirty A.M. and putting fifty-two threesomes on the golf course beginning at the first tee, Meeks had to work with four groups of thirteen tee-times. The morning groups would begin at seven-fifteen and continue until nine-fifteen. There would then be a three-hour break, and the afternoon groups would start at twelve-fifteen and end at two-fifteen.

"My only regret is that we didn't do this sooner," Fay said. "We're probably giving ourselves at least an extra ninety minutes of playing time — which we know we desperately need."

"It's another example of giving in to the players," insisted Hannigan, who wrote a scathing piece in *Golf World* magazine when the two-tee start was announced. "Instead of just enforcing the slow-play rules, they're telling them to take their sweet time."

On this morning, Meeks's only concern was coming up with fifty-two threesomes that would make four men happy. Those people were Fay, Tommy Roy, Fred Ridley — the chairman of the championship committee — and Mark Carlson, who would check them to see if they worked for foreign TV rights holders.

Knowing there would undoubtedly be changes to his original work, Meeks wrote in pencil. The first group he filled in was the defending champions threesome: Goosen, Duval, and Toms. Next, Meeks had to pick the players who would play with Woods. Because Meeks believes in putting at least one foreign player in each group — he could not do it with every group since there were only forty foreign players in the field — he first searched through his international marquee pile. He pulled out Darren Clarke.

"He beat Tiger in the world match play a couple years ago," he said. "That means playing with Tiger won't bother him as much as it might some other players, with the crowds and everything going on around the group."

He put Clarke's card with Woods, then began searching through the stack of American A's. He pulled out three cards: Chris DiMarco, Scott McCarron, and Kenny Perry, each a solid top-thirty type of player who had won on tour. He decided on DiMarco for a similar reason that he had decided on Clarke: He had played with Woods in the third round of the 2001 Masters and had held up well under the pressure. He had considered McCarron because he knew he was friendly with Woods, and Perry for his easygoing nature.

"I try to be careful picking guys to play with Tiger," Meeks said. "Obviously, on the weekend, the chips fall and there aren't any options. But Thursday-Friday, you try to put people with him who are less likely to be affected by all the hoopla surrounding him."

Meeks slotted Woods-Clarke-DiMarco at a relatively late time — 1:35 — to ensure that they would still be playing the four tough finishing holes on the back nine when NBC came on the air. One other group required careful selection in Meeks's mind: Mickelson's, which would be slotted early-late. Meeks pulled K. J. Choi from the international pile for two reasons: Choi had just won at New Orleans a few weeks earlier, his first PGA Tour victory. Meeks had watched him play and had been impressed not only by his golf, but his pace. "He's fast," he said. "I need at least one fast player with Phil because he's kind of deliberate."

So Choi went with Mickelson. From the American A pile, Meeks then pulled Jeff Sluman. Sluman had something Mickelson craved: a major title. He had won the PGA in 1988 and had gone on to carve out a very solid (seven victories) career on tour. He had finished second to Tom Kite at the Open in 1992 and had finished fourth that year at the Masters. What's more, he, too, was a fast player. It was a perfect pairing as far as Meeks was concerned.

Once he had placed that threesome in the draw at 7:55/1:05, Meeks began working much faster. He pulled a half-dozen American marquee cards and a half-dozen internationals. McCarron, whose card was already out, was paired with Norman — "I didn't give him a tiger so I'll give him a shark" — and with Meeks's old pal, Lee Janzen, a two-time U.S. Open champion as the marquee American. "That's a good group there," he commented. He went on to put Nick Faldo with John Daly, another slow player (Faldo)–fast player (Daly) pairing.

Each time he came up with a pairing, Meeks wrote the names in on a different section of the draw. He put Shingo Katayama, the young Japanese player who had finished fourth in the PGA in 2001, with Billy Andrade and Davis Love. "Now, that's a nice-guy group," he said. "Plus Andrade [Wake Forest] and Love [North Carolina] can tell Shingo all about ACC basketball."

He matched Colin Montgomerie, the Scotsman who had so often been mistreated by American crowds, with Mark O'Meara and Craig Stadler. "I'm giving him Stadler because he's real fast and Monty's not and Mark because he's such a good guy to play with. Monty deserves to play with someone pleasant."

He began mixing in B's after the first fifteen threesomes had been placed in the middle of the field. He put together a group that consisted of Americans Woody Austin and Pat Perez along with Per-Ulrik Johansson. All three were known for their tempers — Austin had once knocked himself silly with his putter after missing a putt — and the other two were also quite volatile. "What do you know," Meeks said. "I made a hothead group."

He paired 1995 Open champion Corey Pavin with fifty-seven-year-old Hale Irwin and David Frost, a veteran South African. "None of them are very long," he said. "This way they can be comfortable not having some of those kids bombing it 50 yards past them off the tee."

As luck would have it, the cards for Paul Lawrie and Jean Van de Velde came up one right after the other. It had been Lawrie who had won the 1999 British Open in a playoff after Van De Velde triple-bogeyed the 18th hole to blow a three-shot lead, one of the greatest collapses in the history of golf. Meeks looked at the two cards for a moment, shook his head, and said, "No, can't do that.

Not fair." Chances are Hannigan or Fay would have done it in an instant and thrown in Justin Leonard — the third participant in the playoff — for good measure.

When it came time to decide who would be in the first group to tee off — of course there would be two of them, one off number one and one off number 10 — Meeks trolled through the list of B's carefully. The group going off number one would symbolically begin the Open, and there had always been a certain honor attached to being the first player to put a ball into the air. Meeks was aware of the fact that Paul Goydos, a ten-year tour veteran who had won once in his career (Bay Hill, 1996), had grown up playing at a municipal course in southern California and had been a substitute schoolteacher in the inner city before making it on tour. He seemed like the perfect player to hit the first shot in the first Open ever played at a municipal facility.

Goydos was written into slot number one. After him came Mike Muehr, the survivor of the twelve-for-one playoff at Woodmont; slot number two a bonus for that achievement. The third slot went to Jerry Haas, the Wake Forest golf coach and brother of Jay Haas, in large part because Meeks liked Jay so much. The group going off first on number 10 consisted of two players who had been connected in tour lore for years: Steve "Volcano" Pate and Dudley "Minivolcano" Hart. Like the man who inspired his nickname, Hart was not wound nearly as tight now as he had been earlier in his career, but Meeks threw in mild-mannered Paul Stankowski just in case.

From there he worked quickly. Shortly after eleven A.M. his cell phone rang. It was Tommy Roy. Seeing the number come up on his caller ID, Meeks picked up and said, "Not done yet, Tommy."

"I know," Roy said. "I just wondered where you had put Goosen's group."

Meeks looked through his sheets. "He's at 8:05 Thursday," he said. "Early-late."

"Can you switch him, make him late-early?" Roy asked. "We'd like to have him Thursday afternoon."

"You want him *and* Tiger Thursday afternoon?"

"Yes," Roy said. "And Daly and Norman. Where are they?"

Meeks looked again. Norman was at 12:55 Thursday, no problem. But Daly was at 8:25.

"Can you switch them?" Roy asked.

"Sure," Meeks said. "I just need to flip a couple groups. It isn't a problem."

Roy asked if Mickelson and García were in the afternoon Friday. They were. García had been paired with Americans Joe Durant and Rocco Mediate. Meeks told Roy he would fax him the complete pairings as soon as he finished and hung up.

He took out his eraser — "That's why I work in pencil," he said — and moved Goosen-Duval-Toms from 8:05 to 1:35 on Thursday, flipping them with Andrade, Love, and Katayama. He then took Daly-Faldo and Stuart Appleby and moved them from 8:25 to 1:15 and shifted the group that had been there — Tom Lehman, Steve Stricker, and Padraig Harrington to 8:25. Then he went back to completing the remaining ten groups. The last group penciled in was Ken Duke, Scott Perel, and Brad Lardon, one of the two players in the field who had grown up playing the golf course. Duke, player number 156, was penciled in at 11:22. Meeks leaned back from his chair and said, "That's the end of round one."

Meeks headed out to lunch, taking his phone and pairings with him. He was halfway through his first Diet Pepsi at the restaurant when the phone rang. It was Roy. He had one more request and a comment. The request was fairly simple: In flipping Goosen to an afternoon time, Meeks had put him directly opposite Woods at 1:35. Roy wanted to show both players being introduced and hitting their opening shots live. It would be impossible if they were going off simultaneously. Meeks moved the Goosen group to 1:25, the third tee time assigned the defending champion.

What Roy said next surprised Meeks. "I think your Mickelson group is a little bit weak," he said.

Meeks looked at the sheet where he had written K. J. Choi and Jeff Sluman in with Mickelson at 7:55 on Thursday. "Well, you know Choi just won a tournament here a few weeks ago," he said.

"I know," Roy said. "I'm not saying he isn't a good player. But I'd just like to see someone else who is more of a name in there in either slot."

"You know Jeff Sluman's a major champion," Meeks said.

"And a great guy," Roy replied. "Just take a look at it, okay?"

"I'll give it some thought, Tommy," Meeks said.

He really had no intention of giving it any further thought because he wanted two fast players with Mickelson and he thought Sluman was just the right kind of name to pair with Mickelson. But a few minutes later the phone rang again. It was Fred Ridley. He thought the pairings looked great. He just had one comment. "Can't you find a little better name to put with Mickelson?"

Meeks stared at his phone as if he'd seen a ghost. "You been talking to Tommy Roy?" he asked, more rhetorically than seriously.

No, Ridley said, he hadn't been talking to Roy. He just thought Mickelson's group looked a little bit weak. Meeks felt outnumbered. Plus, Ridley technically had the authority to order him to change the pairing if he so desired. He knew Ridley wouldn't do that, but he also knew how to take a hint. He looked through the pairings. "What if I put Lee Janzen in that group and put Sluman with Norman and McCarron?" he said.

"Perfect," Ridley answered. "I think that's stronger."

Mark Carlson checked in a few minutes later. The pairings, he reported, were absolutely perfect for Japanese TV.

"That's great, Hammer," Meeks said, cackling, "because I never gave Japanese TV a second thought. No wonder I got it just right."

Fay was the last to check in, and he didn't bother with the cell phone. He just left Meeks a message saying the pairings looked fine to him. Apparently, the thought of Phil Mickelson playing with Jeff Sluman didn't bother him. Of course, he was playing golf that day on Fishers Island, a tiny enclave off the east coast of Long Island that might be the home of the most scenic golf course in the country. Few things were likely to bother Fay while on Fishers Island.

Meeks made the changes he had discussed at lunch with Ridley and Roy, then looked through all fifty-two pairings one last time before having them copied for internal distribution. They would be released the next day. "Now," he said finally, "if we could just figure a way to get all these guys around the golf course in about four and a half hours, life would be pretty close to perfect."

That wasn't going to happen. Not at the U.S. Open. And not at the Black Course.

14

Countdown

AS THE START of the Open drew nearer and nearer, the conference room inside the trailer that housed the championship office became more and more cluttered. Boxes were everywhere, maps were laid out across the table in the middle of the room, and folders and files seemed to accumulate there each and every day.

Hanging over the conference table was a small sign that the interns had put up in early May. It said Days Left. Underneath it were pieces of paper, each with a number on it, counting down to zero. At the end of each day, someone would remove one more piece of paper.

As the paper dwindled, the work mounted. Large chunks of time were devoted to volunteer training, work that was time consuming, often frustrating, and absolutely essential. For this Open there would be 4,850 volunteers who were divided into thirty-two separate committees. The largest group would be the marshals — just under 2,000 of them — followed by the slightly more than 1,000 assigned to the merchandise tent. Some committees were relatively tiny: twenty-two in player hospitality, thirty-five in admissions. All of them had to be trained, taught how to do jobs they had never done before and, in most cases, would never do again.

Each volunteer had gone through a background check. Once cleared, they were sent a date for their training session. If they couldn't make it, they either had to arrange an alternate date, assuming there was more than one for their committee, or drop out. No one got to volunteer without being trained. In fact, it was at the training sessions that credentials were handed out.

The USGA had become stricter about volunteer credentials after Shinnecock II, in 1995. That year, members of one local golf club had volunteered to work on a committee and then had failed to show up. It turned out they had been unable to secure tickets and had figured out that volunteers were given credentials for the entire week. With the new scanning system in place, it was now much easier to crack down on volunteer no-shows. "If you don't show up and don't call your chairman with a good reason why you haven't shown up, your credential will be turned off," Jon Barker said at every training session.

It fell to Barker to run most of the training sessions. He split the marshal sessions with Roger Harvie, who had been the USGA's guru of marshals for sixteen years. Each committee was walked through the specifics of their job by a supervisor of some kind: Mary Lopuszynski in merchandising, Craig Smith in the media tent, Mimi Griffin in corporate. Sometimes the committee chairs, volunteers themselves, talked specifics. The constant was Barker, who had his volunteer talk down to such a science that his interns had taken to imitating some of his pet phrases.

"You are now a part of our volunteer family, and that means you are a very important part of this championship. . . . Without you, we can't conduct this championship. . . . When you are in your volunteer uniform you are a walking information booth to most members of the public. . . . This is *your* credential, *your* parking pass, no one else's. . . . Show up with a cell phone and you are done, no questions asked, period. . . . When you are not working, come and watch this championship. It is the greatest championship in the world."

At these sessions Barker was part carnival barker, part Knute

Rockne ("Let's volunteer one for the Gipper!"), part teacher, part cheerleader, and part taskmaster. He would begin by telling the volunteers at length how much their participation in the event was appreciated and needed. Then, gently but firmly, he would run down the lengthy list of do nots: Do not ask players for autographs; do not ask them for pictures; do not come into the clubhouse at any time unless your job requires you to that day; do not go into the volunteer tent on days you are not working; do not (men) wear shorts unless you hear on NBC the night before (NBC *only*) that the temperature will reach 90 degrees; do not wear your uniform when you are not working.

Then would come the pep talk portion of the program. "This is going to be one of the greatest U.S. Opens ever played, and you are an important part of it." He would go on to describe the volunteer tent, which was located near the 15th hole (a fact that would become an issue during tournament week), as if it were a cross between the Four Seasons and the Ritz Carlton. The highlight, though, was his description of the volunteer lunch. Almost since the day he had first arrived, Barker and everyone else at the USGA had spent a good deal of time at B. K. Sweeney's, a Bethpage restaurant and watering hole frequented by a lot of the Bethpage golfers. "Going to Sweeney's with Jon is a little bit like walking into Cheers with Norm," Mike Davis had said once.

Sweeney's was going to supply the volunteer lunches. "We are going to give you a *choice* of sandwiches," Barker would say. "We are going to give you an *apple*. We are going to give you *chips*. And we are going to give you several different choices of soft drink!"

The food at Sweeney's was excellent. This, however, was a box lunch. By the time he was through, everyone in the room was convinced that they were going to be eating at Le Cirque every day.

Barker would then go through, in great detail, specifics on how to get to the golf course, where to park (different depending on your assignment), where to go to eat, what to do in case of any medical emergency — "Get on a walkie-talkie and give your location to the medical committee *first*, don't waste time with other details, get them moving toward you, then start filling in with other details" — and how to handle someone with a cell phone. The cell-phone issue had become a huge one, especially with all the post 9/11 security concerns, because explosives could theoretically be hidden inside them. The policy was zero tolerance. But the USGA didn't want volunteers confronting spectators.

"Here's what we want you to do," Barker said. "Tell the person that if someone from security or the USGA sees you with that phone, they're going to get thrown out. Advise them to disconnect the battery, put it in their pocket, and keep it there the rest of the day. That way they will see you as being on their side rather than being confrontational. If they ignore you, then find someone in authority and point them out. But don't play cop. Let the cops do that."

Barker would always end on an up note. "You only are being asked to work four days during the course of the week," he said. "Come out and watch the other three days. Enjoy yourselves, enjoy being a part of this great championship." Barker, like any good USGA staffer, would never, ever utter the word *tournament* in reference to the Open. Short of referring to one of Tom Meeks's flagsticks as a pin, calling the Open a tournament and not a championship was absolute heresy in USGA-speak.

During the training session for the player hospitality committee, one volunteer asked if golfers were like rock stars. "How do you mean?" Barker asked.

"Well, a lot of rock stars don't like having people actually look at their faces. Are some of the golfers like that?"

Barker laughed. "No, they're really not. Don't be intimidated. Most of these guys will be doing things with you — registering, picking up family tickets, signing up for practice times — that they do every single week. They're used to it. Most of them will be quite friendly."

The two largest committees, marshals and merchandise, had to have several sessions scheduled. Lopuszynski didn't like to have more than about 150 people at any one session because she liked to give them each some time learning to work the cash registers.

Since there were only forty-four registers, having more than 150 at any one time became unwieldy.

One of Lopuszynski's training sessions was interrupted when a small electrical fire was discovered in some of the wiring just outside the tent. A member of the maintenance crew walked in just as Barker was describing the Sweeney's apple and pulled Lopuszynski aside. Lopuszynski then interrupted Barker's description of the chips to pull him into the conversation. A moment later, Barker returned and said, "Okay, folks, we're going to evacuate the tent now. No need to rush, just walk to the back doors."

Needless to say, this made everyone nervous. They had been lectured at length already about the security concerns. Now, an evacuation, and tournament week hadn't even begun yet.

It only took about fifteen minutes to get the fire out. Barker and Lopuszynski brought everyone back inside and told them what had happened. "If that's the worst thing that happens all week, we'll all be thrilled," Barker said. Lopuszynski claimed to have never been nervous. "Everything in here is insured at retail," she said, smiling.

Not all the questions raised by volunteers were as easily answered as the rock star question. Some of the men were genuinely upset that women were allowed to wear shorts and they were not, unless it was 90 degrees outside. "Can we wear a kilt?" one man asked.

"As long as it's khaki, yes," Barker answered.

One man in the merchandising session complained long and loud about the cell-phone ban. "You ask us to volunteer our time and then we can't even bring our cell phones in," he said. "I don't think that's fair."

As it turned out, he didn't have to worry about that problem. As the session was ending, Lopuszynski, who had intended to take him aside and try to quietly explain that the cell-phone ban had been ordered by the state for security reasons, noticed him pocketing several ball markers that were to be on sale for two dollars each once the tent opened. When she pulled him aside, instead of talking about cell phones, she said very quietly, "You know the ball markers are two dollars each."

"What? What are you talking about?"

"I saw you pocket them," Lopuszynski said. "Why don't you just give them back to me, and we'll just take your name off the volunteer list."

The man hesitated, then pulled two ball markers from his pocket and handed them over. Lopuszynski was convinced he had a couple more in his pocket but wasn't about to get into a wrestling match over them.

"It wasn't so much the idea that he was stealing eight or ten dollars worth of stuff," she said. "It was the fact that he came in, made such a big issue of the cell phones, and then tried to walk off with stuff that isn't even worth stealing. Most of our volunteers are great, they really are. This guy just kind of made me feel sick."

Shoplifting is always a problem in the tent. Even though security appears to be pretty close to airtight, about 1.5 percent of the merchandise walks off by itself every year. Lopuszynski figured she was starting this Open four dollars in the hole. The feeling in her stomach was a lot worse, though, than the four-dollar loss.

On the same day that Lopuszynski was dealing with shoplifters and fires, Roger Harvie and the ever-present Barker were in nearby Plainview training the marshals. Of all the volunteer jobs at any golf tournament, the one that may be most important and the one that is most often fraught with troubles is marshaling.

Marshals are part of the playing field. They are inside the ropes. They are expected to help find wayward golf balls. They are expected to keep spectators out of the way of the players and to keep people safe from golf balls, from weather, and from each other.

"Put simply, if we didn't have marshals, we couldn't have spectators," Harvie said in his opening comments.

In all, there were three training sessions for the marshals, meaning about 600 marshals were expected at each session. Training was held at Mattlin Middle School because there was no place at Bethpage large enough to hold that many people, not to mention Harvie's slide show. The sessions actually began in the school cafeteria with the marshals lining up to receive their packages. Each was required to show a photo ID before being given a credential. Once that was done, they walked down the hall to the school auditorium to learn how to be marshals.

For Harvie, these training sessions would be more poignant than the ones he had done in the past. Harvie was sixty-two and had worked as a professional firefighter in Rochester, New York, until 1984, when he had been offered a full-time job as a regional representative for the USGA. He had done marshal training for sixteen years but never before had 267 of them been firefighters. Both the Farmingdale Fire Department and the Nassau County Fire Academy had been selected as marshals long before 9/11. Six men who had been expected to marshal at the Open had died that day. Now Harvie found himself in a jam-packed room in which many of the men and women were wearing shirts with NYPD and FDNY insignias. Many wore shirts that said simply Gone, but Not Forgotten.

Some of the questions asked during the marshal training sessions seemed almost silly except when one realized that no one in the room had ever done this before.

"Can we bring friends with us when we're working?"

"Sure, as long as they have a ticket."

"When we're finished working, can we go inside the ropes at another hole?"

"Absolutely not."

"If we're working a hole that is a long way from the clubhouse, can we get a cart ride out to our holes?" (See answer just above.)

Harvie tried to keep things as light as he could. "The champion of this event will get one million bucks," he said. "And the first thing he will say is it's not about the money. Fine, he can give us the money, right? He can keep the trophy."

He went down a lengthy list of do's and don'ts: Do not offer players help with rulings; do not start conversations with players, particularly once the championship begins; do not get caught up in watching the golf and forget what you are doing; do insist on fans leaving bleachers if there is a weather warning sign posted; do help find golf balls, but do not step on them.

He urged the marshals to be patient at all times. "Be courteous till it hurts," he said. "There are going to be times when you are going to have to swallow your pride," he said. "That's the toughest part of the job. Don't confront. That isn't what you are there to do. You have a problem with a spectator, find us. We'll take care of it."

Barker finished by telling the marshal trainees a story about being asked at Olympic in 1998 by volunteers if, in return for their work, they would be given a chance to play the golf course. The answer, of course, was no.

"This one is yours," he said. "This is your U.S. Open on your golf course. And I'll tell you one thing I'm sure of: The golf course is going to hold up. Anyone tells you the winning score will be better than five-under, take the bet right now. And when it's over, you better believe you can play the golf course."

15

Welcome to Bethpage

THE LAST DAY that anyone could drive into the Bethpage parking lot without a credential was Thursday, June sixth, exactly one week before the championship would begin. Several players had driven over from Westchester earlier to check out the golf course, and word was beginning to make its way around the driving range there that the Black was everything it had been cracked up to be, and more.

The final lull before the storm was on that Thursday. Those who were playing Westchester were now fully engaged with the tournament under way. By Saturday, players who had missed the cut there would start showing up. Until then, the golf course was empty.

Almost.

Brad Lardon had been the second alternate at Westchester. He had finished tied for twenty-third at the PGA Tour's Qualifying School the previous November, earning his way back on tour after an eight-year absence. When the last group had teed off at Westchester on Thursday afternoon and he hadn't gotten into the field, he decided to drive over to Bethpage and see if he could play a few holes.

For Lardon, being in this U.S. Open was something straight out of Fantasy Island. He had grown up a few miles away, in Hunting-ton, and his first memories of playing golf dated to early morning trips to Bethpage with his dad. "When I was young, I wasn't a good enough player to try the Black," he said. "We would play the Red and the Green most of the time. But when I was about eleven or twelve, I started shooting in the low 80s, even breaking 80 some of the time, and my dad said it was time to try the Black.

"I can still remember driving over here at four o'clock in the morning to get in line for a tee time and how validated I felt as a golfer teeing it up for the first time on the Black. It was really a big deal back then."

This was a bigger deal. Lardon was thirty-seven, a graduate of Rice University. He had turned pro after college and played mini-tours and the Hogan Tour. Twice, he had made it to the PGA Tour (1991 and 1994), and each time he had failed to make enough money to keep his playing privileges. After scuffling around on the Nike Tour for a couple more years, he decided it was time to go home, midway through 1997.

"I was thirty-two," he said. "I was going through a divorce, and I was completely burned out. I didn't even like playing the game anymore, and I certainly wasn't playing very well. I needed to get out, needed to get off the road and start over again."

He landed in a club pro job in Austin, and when Ben Crenshaw opened the Austin Golf Club, he went to work for him there. Being around Crenshaw, playing with him on occasion, watching him prepare to captain the 1999 Ryder Cup team, Lardon felt his pas-sion for the game stirring once again. He was playing better, doing well in local tournaments, but he knew that was a long way from playing well enough to make it back to the tour. Then, in the sum-mer of 2001, he took a group of his members to play another Crenshaw-designed course, Sand Hills, a course in Nebraska that was receiving rave reviews from top players. Many had played the golf course. In fact, the course record, 66, was held by Nick Faldo and Mark Calcavecchia.

The first day he was there, Lardon shot 61. "That told me I was playing pretty well," he said. "When I got home, my friends were saying, 'You're almost thirty-seven, you're playing well, ride the wave one more time while you can.'"

Lardon was remarried by then, and he sat down and talked to Kim, his wife, about how she felt about him going through the three grueling stages of Q-School — and putting up $5,000 of their money just to sign up to give it a shot. "I'll caddy for you," was her response.

Off they went. Each stage was an adventure. At the first stage, Lardon played the last eleven holes in seven under par, to qualify with two shots to spare. On the last day at second stage, he shot 40 on the front nine. Convinced he was choking, he turned to Kim in despair and said, "What in the world am I doing here?"

She proceeded to lecture him on not feeling sorry for himself. He played the back nine in four under and qualified on the number for the finals. That meant he would have the chance to play on at least the Buy.com Tour even if he didn't make it through to the big tour. "I went in with a big-tour-or-bust attitude," he said. "I've kind of been there, done that with the Buy.com [now Nationwide]. I like what I do in Austin. If I was going to give that up, it was going to be for the PGA Tour."

Kim was able to retire from caddying for the finals because John Stubee, who had been part of the caddy program Lardon had started in Austin, volunteered to caddy for him — under the condition that Lardon take him to the tour if he made it through. Lardon was cruising until late in the last round when a couple of bogeys put him in jeopardy. Walking down the 17th fairway, he saw Kim and his brother Mike standing a few yards away. Mike Lardon is a psychiatrist. He had caddied for Brad many times at Q-School. He and Kim were taking a very unemotional, scientific approach to the situation.

"They were holding hands and praying," Lardon said. "I walked over and said to them, 'I'm not going to screw this up.'"

He birdied the par-five 17th hole and figured a par on 18 would put him back on tour. He had 177 yards to the hole on his second shot, and he absolutely flushed a seven-iron. "It was one of those shots where I could feel the blades of grass underneath my club when I hit it," he said. "When the ball was in the air, I had this feeling of complete elation. I knew I'd hit it perfectly and I was back on tour."

The ball stopped 10 feet from the hole, and Lardon rolled in the birdie putt. Of course, as a Q-Schooler he didn't get to play every week (Westchester being an example), and he was still struggling to cash the big check he knew he needed to avoid a return trip to Q-School. But when the chance to qualify for the Open came, Lardon was absolutely determined to make it to Bethpage. He had played in Open qualifying twelve times and had never made the Open. In fact, after thirteen years as a pro, after playing in more than 200 events on the Hogan/Nike/Buy.com Tour and more than sixty events on the PGA Tour, he had never played in a major.

"Closest I came was in '92," he said. "I lost a playoff to Bob May [who later went on to lose the classic playoff in the 2000 PGA to Tiger Woods] and never came that close again. I just had to make it this time."

He probably caught a break when he missed the cut at the Kemper Open. That gave him a chance to play a couple of practice rounds over the weekend at Woodmont. He decided to change putters because he had putted poorly at Kemper. He shot 69 in the morning on the tougher North course but was only five under par for the day when he got to the 16th hole in the afternoon. Brother Mike had been running in to check the scores and reported back that six under would probably play off and that seven under would almost surely get in. Lardon had two par-fives — 16 and 18 — to play. He birdied 16 and came to 18 knowing a par would do no worse than play off. "I didn't want to play off," he said. "Been there, done that. I just decided I had to birdie the hole."

His third-shot wedge stopped eight feet from the hole. His putt was dead center.

"I had tears in my eyes when it went in," he said. "To finally get into the Open at my age at the most special place I could think of to play in the Open. It's just the ultimate. But the thing I don't want to do is come here and think I've reached my goal. I want to play well here."

For some players, especially first-timers, that is often easier said than done. Just being in the Open means so much that it can be difficult to get the adrenaline flowing or to ignore all the nerves you are feeling. Walking onto the first tee on Thursday afternoon, a pristine, late spring day, Lardon was amazed by where he was and by what he saw.

"I was the only person playing the Black Course," he said. "You have to understand, in my experience, *no one* plays the Black alone. You have three foursomes on every hole, that's just the way it is. I walk out there, and the only people I saw were a trooper they sent to walk around with me (all the players who arrived early were being given security escorts) and Tom Meeks, who came driving over to say hello. That was it. I actually felt lucky not to have gotten in at Westchester, because I knew this was a once-in-a-lifetime experience.

"It's funny, when I was a kid, getting onto the Black was a benchmark in my life. Now, twenty-five years later, it still is."

The golf course was just about as empty the next afternoon when David Fay arrived. By this time, almost everyone from the USGA staff and the executive committee was in town. Most were staying a few miles away, at the Melville Marriott, where most of the week's meetings would be held. Fay had to attend some of those meetings and — much to his chagrin — a lot of the social events scheduled for each night. But before he dealt with all of that, he had made the same turn off the Southern State Parkway that he had made almost eight years earlier, driven the four miles up Bethpage State Parkway, flashed his green parking credential, and driven onto the circle right outside the clubhouse door.

Just as he had done on that blustery November afternoon, Fay walked around the clubhouse to the first tee. It looked considerably different now than it had then. There were grandstands behind the tee and to the players' right. All around, Fay could see additional grandstands and roping and corporate tents. He could also see a golf course that was about as far from what he had seen in '94 in terms of conditioning as one could possibly imagine.

Again, Fay began to walk. The chills he felt this time had nothing to do with the weather. The temperature was in the 70s. "The place just looked great," he said. "I had thought we could make the place come back to life with some money and with Rees and Tim and Craig doing their thing, but I can honestly say I never imagined it could become what it had become."

He retraced his original walk: down one, through the tunnel, up two, back down three, and then up four. By then he had seen enough. He crossed onto the back nine and back across the road. He looked up 15 and knew the hole would play plenty hard, that Meeks's belief that there was no need for the Currier-Bodington back tee had been correct. He stood on the 17th tee and looked at the grandstands surrounding the green and pictured what it might look like in nine days when the last groups came through with the Open on the line. Then he walked up 18, a completely different hole than it had been before the redesign, stood at the top of the hill, and took a deep breath. He felt completely satisfied with what he saw.

This is going to work, he thought. It's going to more than work, it's going to be great. And no one is going to tear this golf course up. It will hold up just fine.

At that moment, he decided that one of his goals had already been met. "We'll come back here," he said a couple of days later. "I wanted to walk out of here with people saying this should be part of our informal rota, right along with Shinnecock and Pebble Beach and Pinehurst. That's going to happen. I really think we got this one right. In fact, I *know* we got it right."

Winning score? he was asked.

He thought for a moment. "Four under," he said.

Tom Meeks did not have nearly as good a day as his boss. He and Tim Moraghan spent the afternoon beginning their course setup. The plan was to do nine holes on Friday, then nine holes on Saturday. Meeks had been making notes on potential hole locations for more than a year. The two men, armed with putters, used cans of spray paint, which would later be used to "dot" the greens at each potential hole location. Then they putted at the cans, keeping in mind that the greens would be considerably faster — they were now rolling at about 11 — by the time play actually began in six days.

The plan was to pick five locations on each green, the fifth being for a possible playoff on Monday, and rank them. Most players mistakenly believe that the hole locations get more difficult with each passing day of a tournament. Thus the term *Sunday flag*, meaning that the hole is in the toughest possible location on a green.

That's not the case at the Open. Meeks and Moraghan designate each location 1, 2, 3, or 4, the highest number being the most difficult. Their goal each day is to have the eighteen hole locations add up to as close to forty-five as possible. Most days the number is either forty-four or forty-six. For example, on Thursday there would be four 4's, five 3's, four 2's, and five 1's. Total: 44. On Friday it would probably be five 4's, four 3's, five 2's, and four 1's. Total: 46. The same formula is repeated on Saturday and Sunday.

"You don't want to start out with the eighteen easiest hole locations on Thursday and have the eighteen hardest ones on Sunday," Meeks said. "You want balance. Sometimes you have to make adjustments because you might not want to go in the same part of the green two days in a row." Meeks did have a few locations that he called Sunday specials, certain holes on certain golf courses where there was a traditional Sunday location. Since the Open had never been played at Bethpage before, there weren't any traditional spots, but Meeks had a couple of locations in mind.

He would also show his list of potential locations to Tommy Roy and allow Roy to suggest a location or two for the weekend. "It's got to be from my list, though," he said. "At Oakland Hills, in '96, he wanted us to put the flag on the front center of the 13th green on Sunday, right in a little bowl where the ball would roll right toward it. I told him if we put the hole there, we might as well put a clown's mouth behind it." Once, in 1989, the USGA had put a flag in the middle of a bowl on a green, the sixth at Oak Hill, and there had been four holes in one on the same day. That wasn't likely to happen again anytime soon.

The interaction between Meeks and Roy was quite different from the relationship the USGA had previously had with ABC. In the ABC days, Frank Hannigan would quietly go through the locations with P. J. Boatwright and select certain hole placements because they were thought to be better for TV. "I never told anyone at ABC what I was doing," Hannigan said. "If I had, Jim Jennett [the director] would have had kittens because they were hyperconscious of not being accused of influencing the outcome of the U.S. Open in any way."

That wasn't the case with NBC. The relationship between NBC and the USGA was far more collegial than the relationship between ABC and the USGA had been. Every year at the U.S. Amateur, the two organizations staged what they called the Marr Cup (named for the late Dave Marr) with NBC personnel — notably the ex-pros like Johnny Miller, Mark Rolfing, Roger Maltbie, Bob Murphy, and Gary Koch — taking on the USGA brass — Fay, the Mikes, Meeks, Moraghan — in a match play competition.

"Basically, it's just a day of bonding and fun," said Jon Miller, the NBC programming vice president. "We have dinner afterward and a good time is had by all."

That wasn't likely to happen in the ABC days. Terry Jastrow, ABC's golf producer, was a lot more businesslike and less outgoing than Roy. He was married to Anne Archer, an actress, and according to the USGA folks had a star's mentality. For example, he always insisted on having a portable toilet that was designated just for him right near the truck — complete with a security guard to make sure no one but Jastrow entered at any time.

"It's just different," said Mike Davis. "I liked the ABC guys, and they were very good at what they did. But there is definitely a little more of a laid-back approach with NBC. Especially now when they've been doing it for a few [eight] years. They have confidence in their approach, and so do we."

They also clearly exerted more influence than ABC ever did. When Hannigan heard that Roy and Fred Ridley had been on Meeks's call list on the day he did the pairings, he was indignant. "A TV producer and a volunteer [all the executive committee members are volunteers] have a say in the pairings? Are you _____ kidding me? That's an outrage! P. J. [Boatwright] and I would sooner jump off a cliff than have people like that telling us who to pair with whom."

Fay laughed at Hannigan's indignation. "So how many pairings got changed?" he asked. "One? Big deal. Frank may not have consulted with TV, but he knew what their needs were, just like we do now."

It was almost five o'clock by the time Meeks and Moraghan finished. Meeks got in his car, which he always calls a rig, and headed back to the Melville Marriott. About a mile from the hotel he was slowing at a traffic light when the car in front of him stopped very suddenly. Meeks hit the brakes and stopped in time. The car behind him did not. He was rear-ended. He felt some pain in his back. The guy in the car was apologetic.

"Are you okay?" he asked. "I just couldn't stop."

Meeks told him he was okay, although the rear end of his car clearly was not. The man gave him his insurance information, and Meeks and his car limped the rest of the way to the hotel. That night, Meeks told Ridley and Reed Mackenzie, the president of the USGA, what had happened. Both men are lawyers. Mackenzie's firm specializes in personal injury.

"Did you tell the guy you needed to see a doctor?" they asked.

"No."

"Did you tell him that your back hurt?"

"No, I told him I was okay."

Both lawyers shook their head. "Tom, you screwed up big-time."

Meeks was cackling the next afternoon as he drove around the golf course, his back a little bit sore. "I guess I bogeyed," he said.

"Double-bogeyed," Mackenzie said later.

That night, Meeks woke up in a cold sweat. He'd had the same dream that he had every year at this time. It was Thursday morning. The Open was set to begin. But there were no hole locations. "I'm standing there, and all the players are screaming at me, 'Where are the hole locations, Tom?' And I have no idea what to tell them."

Meeks finally rolled over and went back to sleep, hole locations rattling through his mind over and over again.

The first withdrawal took place at about the same time that Meeks was being rear-ended. Bruce Fleisher, exempt by virtue of having won the Senior Open in 2001, called Mike Davis to say he wasn't going to play.

"I really think my first obligation right now is to the Senior Tour," Fleisher said. "I'm going to go play in Nashville next week. I'm needed more there. Besides, my withdrawing will give the first alternate a chance to play, and it will probably mean more to him than to me. It's the right thing to do."

Fleisher had come out and played the golf course a week earlier. When he had played on the regular tour, the one thing that had kept him from being a star had been length. Playing the shorter golf courses on the Senior Tour, Fleisher had become a star. The Black was going to be too much golf course for his game, and he knew it.

The first alternate was Felix Casas, a Filipino who had been the first alternate in the qualifier at Lake Merced Golf and Country Club, outside of San Francisco. Roger Harvie, who had about a hundred different jobs during Open week, was assigned to find Casas and tell him the good news that he was in the Open. Harvie called the contact number Casas had left at the qualifying site. No answer. He called IMG, which he had listed as his representatives. They had the same contact number. He sent a fax to the office of the Australasian Tour, which was where Casas normally played. They responded by saying they would try to track him down.

Casas would be the first player from the Philippines ever to play in the Open. "I've got half the world out looking for him," Harvie said. "If he doesn't turn up by Monday, we'll have to call the second alternate."

While Harvie was searching for Casas, Davis had a completely different kind of problem: where to put three massive RVs. John Daly had traveled on tour in a custom-built RV for several years because he hated to fly. Davis Love III had bought an RV at the start of the year and, more often than not, brought it with him to tournaments and parked right next to Daly. Jay Don Blake had also gone the RV route shortly after he and his wife had become parents. A week before the tournament, Love called Mike Davis. There was no place close to Bethpage to park the RVs, and given the expected problems with traffic and security, neither he nor Daly was eager to stay very far away from the park. He wondered if there was any place *in* the park where they could set up headquarters for the week.

Davis went to the one person who would know: Dave Catalano. At that moment, almost every square inch of the park was being used for something, parking or corporate tents or drop-off and pickup spots for shuttle buses. There was, however, an open area just behind Catalano's house that could probably house several RVs. Catalano didn't need the headache of having a couple of families camping in his backyard during the most important week of his life, but he was willing to do it if it would help the USGA.

"There's just one condition," Catalano said. "I want a picture with them before the end of the week."

That, Davis figured, would be no problem.

When the championship committee met on Saturday morning, the members wanted to know about the rough. Meeks and Moraghan said it was about three and a half inches and that Craig Currier was inclined to not cut it again before Thursday unless it rained. Both Currier and Moraghan were of the school that believed a shot hit into the rough should incur a penalty of some kind. Both also knew that, on the modern PGA Tour, players had grown accustomed to playing shots from the rough — especially the first cut — almost as if they were on the fairway. The same was true of bunker play. If a bunker wasn't absolutely smooth and perfect, if the sand on one hole was a little softer than on another, players were guaranteed to scream.

"Our approach has always been a little bit different," Moraghan said. "The rough is a hazard. A bunker is a hazard. You hit a ball in there, you shouldn't expect a perfect lie. I know a lot of guys today do. I hope we never get to the point where we give in to them on that."

The committee members disagreed. They wanted the grass cut to be sure it didn't get any longer than three and a half inches, and they wanted to be certain that the golfers would have some kind of play if they hit the ball in there.

Meeks and Moraghan were both inclined to side with Currier's plan. All three men understood that the committee didn't want to hear too much moaning and groaning from the players, who tended to start calling a golf course tricked up the minute they made their first practice-round bogey. When Moraghan delivered the news to Currier about cutting the rough Saturday afternoon, Currier rolled his eyes and started to argue.

Moraghan held up a hand. "Craig, I'm just the messenger now," he said. "It's Saturday. We've got the entire golf world showing up here Monday. From here on, it's their show. We do what they tell us to, regardless of whether we agree or disagree."

Currier nodded. "I guess everyone's feeling a little bit tight in the throat right now, huh?" he said.

Moraghan smiled. He wasn't going to agree or disagree, but Currier was pretty sure where he stood. They were sitting in carts on the second fairway as they talked. Moraghan took two golf balls and tossed them into the rough. Both disappeared. "That's three and a half inches right there," he said. "Don't worry, Craig. The golf course will be tough enough."

*   *   *

Since the 18th green was closest to the clubhouse, Meeks and Moraghan worked their way backward on the back nine that afternoon. They were joined by Irv Fish, a longtime friend of Reed Mackenzie's. When they walked onto 17, they encountered Trey Holland, who had stepped down as USGA president earlier in the year. For years, Holland had worked with Meeks and Moraghan in his role on the championship committee, setting up the golf course. Now he was in for a brief prechampionship visit from his home in Indiana. He was completing his first tour ever of the Black.

"This place is unbelievable," he said as he shook hands with his old companions. "I'd heard it was really something, but you've got to see it. I mean, wow!"

Holland is not a man given to hyperbole. He is a urologist who rarely raises his voice and has a sharp, biting wit that he keeps to himself except around friends. "I walked off 14," he said, "thinking that 13 and 14 were a little bit easier and maybe the golf course wasn't so tough coming in. Then I crossed the road and saw 15 — Heartbreak Hill! I mean, what a hole that is!"

Holland is best known in U.S. Open lore for a moment he would prefer to forget. In 1994, as the walking rules official with the last group on Sunday, he had given Ernie Els a drop on the first hole that he wasn't entitled to because he believed a TV crane that could have been moved out of Els's line of sight was not movable. It was that incident as much as anything that had driven a stake into the heart of the David Fay–Frank Hannigan friendship. Hannigan, on air as the rules expert for ABC, had calmly explained the mistake Holland was making.

"He had a USGA walkie-talkie right there," Fay said. "He could have prevented it from happening if he had wanted to."

"I was on the air the whole time," Hannigan said. "ABC was my employer. I couldn't just walk away from the microphone at that point."

The two men are never going to agree on the issue. Fay thinks Hannigan could have pulled away for a few seconds and warned someone that Holland needed help. Hannigan says his first chance to do so came after it was too late. In any event, Fay points out that

Els made bogey on the hole even with the drop and that, in his opinion, Holland's mistake didn't affect the outcome. It did, however, affect a friendship.

Holland survived his mistake — he also survived a crash in his private plane a few years later — and went on to become a highly respected president. Now, with Mackenzie in place as his successor, he planned to get off the stage before the first ball was hit.

A handful of players had arrived that morning. Scott Verplank had gone out to walk a few holes and had run into Currier on the first green. After they had introduced themselves, Verplank said to Currier, "Where do you keep the sheep?"

"Sheep?" Currier asked.

"Yeah," Verplank said, pointing at the rough. "I figure you've got sheep out here fertilizing this stuff. Otherwise, how would you keep it looking so good and so tough all at once?"

Currier suddenly felt a lot better about the three-and-a-half-inch edict.

A little earlier, Bernhard Langer, a two-time Masters champion, had walked into the clubhouse and asked if someone could show him where the first tee was. Absolutely, he was told, and a volunteer was assigned to show him where to go. Langer followed his escort out the back door of the clubhouse, turned to the right, walked a few yards, and was told, "Good luck, Mr. Langer, enjoy the week."

He said thank you, then looked at the fairway. All he could see were corporate tents. "Are you sure this is the first tee?" he asked.

Whoops. Wrong first tee. The volunteer had taken him to number one on the Green Course, which was now the Tillinghast Village. That would have made for a tough opening hole. Langer made it to number one on the Black a few minutes later.

Vijay Singh and Scott McCarron had no such trouble finding the first tee. The fairway was another matter. Singh launched two drivers into the rough — one left, one right. McCarron did the same before taking out a three-wood and hitting a shot that stopped in the fairway — with a good six inches to spare. McCarron looked at the sign. "Warning: The Black Course Is an Extremely Difficult Course Which We Recommend Only for Highly Skilled Golfers." When the bleachers first went up, the sign had been left on a fence that was covered by the bleachers. Mike Davis, realizing it was out of sight, had ordered it moved to a prominent spot right near the players' entrance to the tee.

McCarron pointed at the sign. "Why do I think," he asked, "that they put that sign there for me?"

Singh had missed the cut at Westchester, and McCarron had flown in early that morning, figuring that Bethpage Black was probably a lot different from his old high school girlfriend Beth Page and he needed a look at it. They are two of the longer hitters on the tour. McCarron surprises people with his length because he isn't very big — 5 feet 10, 165 pounds — but can hit it as far as almost anyone on tour. Singh calls him Big Ball because of his length off the tee. When he led the Masters after thirty-six holes in 1999, someone asked him about his ability to hit the ball to distant places.

"I've always been able to hit the ball a long way," McCarron said. "It's just recently that I've been able to find it."

Meeks and Moraghan drove up just as McCarron walked onto the 12th green with a half smile on his face. "Is it true," he asked Meeks, "that when we cross the road to 15, it gets *tougher?*"

"I'd say so," Meeks said.

"Do you know what I hit into this green?" McCarron asked. "Driver — *good* driver — two-iron. Vijay crushed one off the tee and hit four-iron."

Meeks nodded, fighting a smile.

"I'm telling you right now," McCarron said, "this is the toughest U.S. Open golf course I've ever seen."

Meeks waited. He knew a complaint was coming. McCarron looked at Singh. "But we were just talking on the fairway," he said. "And we agree it also might be the *fairest.*"

Meeks gave up the fight against his smile. "Scott," he said, "you just made my day."

16

Tiger's Coming!

IF THE BETHPAGE regulars had walked into their clubhouse on Sunday morning, June ninth, they might not have recognized it. Every piece of golf equipment had been placed in storage — "Looking at this place is just killing me," Joe Rehor, the longtime pro moaned jokingly. Rehor's pro shop was now the player and family hospitality area, complete with a long buffet table, tables for people to eat at, and comfortable chairs and couches for lounging and relaxing. The lighting had been changed, the walls had been decorated to look like a den, and players, wives, moms and dads and kids — lots of kids — had taken over for the week.

Out the door and across the walkway, the Tillinghast Room had become the player registration area. Registration at a major usually involves a few more steps than at a normal tournament. For one thing, players at the Open are asked to sign the scroll.

The scroll is just that — a scroll — that reads slightly differently each year. In 2002, it said, "In Appreciation of the Hospitality of Bethpage State Park (Black Course) for the 2002 United States Open Golf Championship Conducted by the U.S. Golf Association." Below that were the words "The Players." Each player was asked to sign his name in the order in which they registered —

except for Retief Goosen, the defending champion. His spot on line number one was reserved, regardless of when he checked in. The scroll would be hung in the clubhouse once the Open was over.

The first player to sign in was Scott Verplank, who walked into the Tillinghast Room precisely at ten A.M., when registration officially began, and seemed a bit nonplussed to be the first arrival. Actually, Shigeki Maruyama had been there a few minutes earlier but had been told by Ron Read that he was a little bit early. Maruyama had shrugged and gone to eat breakfast. He was still in player hospitality when Verplank walked in.

Read was the USGA's western region director. During the Open, all the regional directors take on different assignments: Roger Harvie had marshals and roping and tracking down lost alternates. Bill McCarthy, who ran the north-central region, was coordinating the shuttle service to the 10th tee and would be the point man for any evacuations — removing players from the course during a thunderstorm. Jim Farrell, the director of the northeast region, would be the 10th-tee starter.

Read would be the first-tee starter from Thursday to Sunday, but right now it was his job to guide players from table to table in the room, making sure they signed everything that needed signing and received everything they needed to receive, most notably badges for family and friends. Players were entitled to up to four family badges, which allowed access to the hospitality area. The other badges were essentially grounds passes, although a lot of people who received them just assumed that since they said Player-Guest, they could go anywhere they wished.

The first thing a player was asked to do was sign his name and hometown on the registration sheet. This was more important than one might think. Many players had deals with resorts or golf clubs that required them to be introduced as coming from a particular place. For years Hale Irwin, who lived in Missouri, had been introduced as being from a resort in Hawaii. Once, Ian Woosnam, the 1991 Masters champion, had put down the small town in England where he lived as his hometown. Read introduced him as being from there for three days. On the fourth day, Woosnam took him aside and told him he was to be introduced as coming from Wales. Read was baffled. Later he learned that Woosnam was paid by the Welsh board of tourism to represent them and they had apparently been very unhappy when word got back that he was listing a home across the border.

Others put down the address of their agents. John Daly, who probably hadn't set foot in Washington, D.C., a half-dozen times in his life, was listed as being from Washington, D.C. A number of IMG-represented players put down the company's Cleveland office under the home address listing on their entry form. Tiger Woods, an IMG client, put down his street address in Windermere, Florida. Greg Norman did the same for his home in Jupiter, Florida.

Read would also double-check with players how they wanted their names pronounced. This was an especially sensitive topic with the defending champion. For years on the European Tour he had been called Retief Hoosen. That was not, he insisted, the way his name was pronounced. "Goosen," he said. "I've always said Goosen."

Ron Read would say Goosen.

Once a player had signed in and been given all his various credentials, he would be asked where he wanted his player gift sent. Every golf tournament in the world gives a player gift, usually crystal. In fact, most golfers have received so much expensive crystal in their lives that they roll their eyes when someone tries to give them some more.

Jon Barker remembered when he had given Nick Faldo his player gift — crystal — in 1998 at Olympic, Faldo had shrugged and said, "One year, why don't you guys just give us a fishing rod that says U.S. Open on it?" So when it came time to come up with a player gift for Bethpage, Barker thought long and hard about how to come up with something different. "I thought about a fishing rod," he said. "But even though most of the guys fish, not all of them do." (In fact, if you read a PGA Tour media guide, it seems as if 99 percent of the players list hunting and fishing as their outside interests. Brad Faxon, one of a very small handful of players who didn't hunt or fish, liked to list "all sports except for hunting and fishing" as his outside interests.)

Barker finally came up with an idea for something he thought would be different. He hired an artist to do a drawing of the Black Course to look the way it might have looked when Tillinghast first drew the plans seventy years earlier. The artist had drawn the routing as if it were the 1930s and even forged Tillinghast's name in the bottom corner. Barker then had the drawings framed to present to the players. Most thought it was a wonderful idea.

Almost as good as a fishing rod.

Everyone was wondering when Tiger would show up.

"He's kind of the one everyone wants to meet, but also the one everyone's a little bit nervous about," said Elizabeth Body, the cochairman of the player hospitality committee. "I just keep telling them, treat him the way you treat everyone else. Of course, that's easy to say."

Woods wasn't expected until Monday, when most players would arrive. As a result, Sunday was going to be the last easy day for everyone. Because the public still wasn't on the grounds, security was relatively light, there was no traffic, and once players had parked their cars it didn't take them very long to get through registration, into the locker room, and onto the practice tee or the golf course.

That would all change the next morning when more than 40,000 ticket holders would show up. That was why what could best be described as the crisis-management committee held its first meeting on Sunday afternoon. This was a meeting that would be held for the next seven afternoons for the specific purpose of figuring out what had gone wrong, what could go wrong, and what was about to go wrong. Even though the meetings always began with a collegial air and would be filled with encouraging words and pep talks, they were bound to get tense as the week went on.

For many years, Mike Davis had run the daily meetings. He had decided this year to turn that role over to Jon Barker. He was doing that in part because it freed him to deal with other problems and not be stuck in a meeting that could run as long as two hours in the middle of the day. He also did it, though, because Barker was being groomed for bigger things by the USGA, and this was one way to add to his experience.

As might be expected, not everyone was thrilled with the idea of Barker, who was only thirty-one, running a meeting that would be attended by a lot of people who were older and more experienced than he was. Barker was aware of this and tried very hard to tread as lightly as he could. "I knew as soon as Mike told me he wanted me to do it there were going to be people unhappy about it," he said. "But what was I going to say? He's the boss."

The meetings were held in the trailer that normally served as the park's tennis office. Depending on the day, up to thirty people might be squeezed into the conference room. Every USGA department was represented — corporate, admissions, will-call, security, media, operations, accounting, rules, tournament management, and the various regional directors who were in different troubleshooting roles for the week. The state was represented every day by parks director Bernadette Castro; Brad Race, who held the title of general tournament director; their assistants, Nancy Palumbo and Tara Snow; Dave Catalano; and the police, led by Bob Nuzzo and his supervisor, Colonel Greg Sittler. The other key people in the room were Joe Scariza from the Department of Transportation, who was up to date on traffic flow and parking problems, and Joe Corless, the USGA's security consultant. Technically, Corless was in charge of seeing to it that the players could move around the golf course as easily and safely as possible. In reality, he was Tiger Woods's bodyguard.

Barker began the meeting by asking everyone to introduce themselves. When it was Dave Catalano's turn, he said, "I'm every-

one's landlord this week." He added: "To put this in sports terminology, we finished last in 1995 and got the number one pick in the
draft. Tomorrow we start playing in a seven-day Super Bowl. We're
ready."

Barker's first job was a tough one: convincing everyone to turn
off their cell phones. Every person in the room had one, and most
were constantly ringing. "We're just not going to get anything done
if we have phones ringing the entire time, and I know they will,"
Barker said. It was agreed, finally, that Nuzzo would keep his on in
case of emergency.

On hand were now 400 state troopers who had come in from
around the state. They had been briefed that morning and were in
the process, as Nuzzo put it, "of trying to find their way around
here."

There weren't any major problems on Sunday. ESPN was complaining because the police had decided to shut down Round
Swamp Road, the main road into the golf course, after six A.M.,
beginning the next morning. "They feel they need in-and-out
access all day," Craig Smith told Nuzzo.

"So does everyone else," Nuzzo answered.

The only people who would be allowed on Round Swamp after
six A.M. were the players. Most were staying at the Huntington
Hilton, which was a couple of miles down Round Swamp from the
golf course. In order to ensure that no one had to venture onto
Route 110 or the Long Island Expressway en route to a tee time,
players with the proper parking sticker would be allowed onto
Round Swamp.

Nuzzo had no problem with that. But he couldn't understand
why they had to be allowed to use Round Swamp when they were
leaving the golf course.

"Because they'll get lost," Steve Worthy had told him. "And if
they get lost, they'll get pissed off at us. It isn't that many cars, and
it is easier for everyone to do it this way."

"It isn't easier for us," Nuzzo answered.

He had given in, though, in large part because he liked Worthy, and the two men had come to understand that the other wouldn't make a big deal out of something unless it was a big deal.

"Today's the last easy day," Barker said. "Tomorrow, all hell is going to break loose. No matter how prepared we think we are."

The sun was barely up when the problems started.

As instructed, hundreds of volunteers began showing up well before the gates were to be open to the public so they could go through their pat-downs, get on their buses, and reach their posts in plenty of time to start work shifts.

The pat-downs were supposed to be done by the private security company hired by the USGA for the week, Beau Dietl & Associates (BDA). Dietl was the retired New York City policeman who had made a name for himself as a private detective and as a regular guest on Don Imus's radio show, where he often fractured the language in ways that would make Yogi Berra wince. His company had been one of five to bid on the Open contract. Every year the USGA hired a private security company to do the nonpolice security work that was needed: check badges at corporate tents, media areas, and in the clubhouse; guard the grounds at night; and, in the case of this Open, conduct the pat-downs that were being required of everyone before they got on shuttle buses.

There had been some concern among the operations people when Dietl had come back after his initial bid and said there had been a miscalculation — he probably called it a miscalculus — and he was going to need more money. His original bid for the week had been $300,000. He now said he needed $400,000 to supply all the people who would be needed for the pat-downs. Worthy and Bussey sighed and agreed to the extra money.

But Monday morning came, and a lot of the BDA people did not. Some had failed to get clearance on their background checks. Others simply didn't show up. As a result, the volunteer lot was filled to overflowing shortly after sunrise with people waiting in long lines to get patted down. Barker had told the volunteers during their training session to figure on needing a good thirty minutes from the time they parked their cars until they reached their posts. On Monday morning, many of them needed ninety minutes to get where they were supposed to go.

Worthy was furious — on two counts. First, he was furious with BDA for not producing the people it had promised. Second, he was upset because the police, who were out in force as Nuzzo promised, refused to help with the pat-downs. On Monday afternoon at a meeting that was — as Barker had predicted — quite a bit more tense than Sunday's session, Worthy demanded to know why the police could not, would not, help with the pat-downs.

"They're standing right there, people are standing in line waiting and waiting, why couldn't they help out?" he asked Nuzzo.

Before Nuzzo could answer, Colonel Sittler jumped in. "A pat-down is a search when it's done by police," he said. "We can't do it without cause."

"Even if people agree to allow it?" Worthy asked.

"Right. What if we find something illegal on them that should lead to an arrest? What if someone claims we didn't conduct the search properly in some way? That makes us liable. We just can't do it."

Worthy didn't like that answer, but not liking it wasn't going to change it.

He and Nuzzo were also battling over another issue: Laura Southerland. Specifically, Nuzzo was insisting that the police needed a USGA representative in the police command post to deal with questions that arose over who should or should not be granted access to the park or to certain areas of the park. The police, as Nuzzo pointed out, were perfectly happy to say no to everyone. It was easier and made traffic-flow problems — which now included cars, trucks, golf carts, and pedestrians — a lot simpler. But he also knew that wasn't the way the USGA wanted it, that there were times when different vendors had to get things onto the property during the day. Rather than having to track down Worthy or Bussey, or in some cases Mike Davis, he wanted someone in the command post who would know exactly who needed to get in and why. The logical person was Worthy's assistant, Southerland. She had been working in the operations trailer since December and was familiar with virtually every person who would need access. The problem was that her expertise also made her invaluable to Worthy.

"If you want Round Swamp open to the players going *out* when I don't think we should have to do that, you need to do something for me," Nuzzo had told Worthy. "I want someone from your group in our command post."

Worthy understood Nuzzo's thinking but didn't feel he had anyone he could spare, especially Southerland. "If Laura is with you guys all day, that really hurts my operation," he told Nuzzo.

"Round Swamp is important to you, this is important to me," Nuzzo answered.

Most of the other issues were of the fixable variety. When Love and Daly had showed up with their RVs in Catalano's backyard, Currier had been called to shave down a couple of trees so they could get through to their parking spot. More than 400 cell phones had made it to the front gate — meaning they had not been detected during the very slow parking lot pat-downs.

Everyone was in agreement that the cell phones had to be banned. Warnings had been sent out with all tickets telling people not to bring cell phones. Still, they brought them. There were reports coming back from Jones Beach that people who were discovered with cell phones during pat-downs were just tossing them into bushes rather than going back to their cars and then lining up again. At the end of the day, some people were spotted getting off buses, walking to the bushes where they and many others had tossed cell phones. They would pick up the first phone they found and dial their own cell-phone number, then follow the ringing until they found their own.

Nuzzo shook his head at that one. "Gotta give people credit for being innovative," he said.

There were also some fanny pack problems. People had been told they could bring fanny packs with them, small bags containing things like diapers and purses and other small items. "I've seen some fanny packs [that were allowed in] that could sleep two or three on a camping trip," Nuzzo said.

As expected, there had also been trouble getting some players to the clubhouse. Jean Van de Velde had made the mistake of not filling out his player registration information after he had qualified at Purchase. As a result, he showed up Monday morning without a parking pass and without the gate pass that had been sent to the players. He thought that his PGA Tour ID badge would get him in, because most weeks it did just that.

Not this week. The police, especially on the first day, were very much in Checkpoint Charlie mode. By the time they had contacted the police barracks and the barracks had contacted the USGA and the USGA had determined that Van de Velde had indeed not filled out his registration form and that it probably *was* Van de Velde trying to get in, two hours had passed. Van de Velde was finally escorted into the clubhouse, where he was able to register and receive all the ID he would need for the rest of the week.

Colin Montgomerie, who had flown in from Europe on a red-eye that morning, also had some trouble getting through security. He was driving a Lexus as part of one of his corporate deals and had not picked up his parking pass or one of the Hertz SUVs being held for players at all the local airports. Fortunately, he did have his gate pass, and unlike Van de Velde, the police recognized him. Eventually, he got through.

"I wasn't about to fool with any of them, though," he said as he was registering. "I had the sense that they were not men to be trifled with. Very polite, but also very firm."

Nuzzo would have liked hearing that.

Mike Muehr, the survivor of the twelve-for-one playoff at Woodmont, arrived with all the correct paperwork and was told, for some reason, that player registration was on Central Avenue in Bethpage. Knowing that couldn't possibly be the case, he managed to talk the policeman into calling the USGA office in the clubhouse. Ellen McMahon, Davis's assistant, took the call.

"Bethpage?" she said. "Central Avenue? No. Registration is here. If he has all the right ID, send him up here right away."

Finally, there was the case of Woody Austin and the New York accent. Austin, who had qualified at Woodmont, arrived in the correct car with the correct parking pass, a gate pass, photo ID, and everything else that could possibly be asked for. But when the police officer at the checkpoint went down his list of players, he told Austin he was sorry, but his name wasn't on the list.

"Honest, Officer, I qualified," Austin said. "How do you think I got all this paperwork and ID?"

Still skeptical, the officer agreed to call the USGA office and see if there had been some kind of mistake. This time it was Davis who took the phone call.

"I got a guy here named Woody Watson, says he's in the field," the policeman said. "I've got no one named Watson on my list. I know Tom Watson isn't playing, so who is this guy?"

When the policeman said Tom Watson, Davis started to laugh.

"Do me a favor," he said. "Ask the guy how to spell his name."

In the background, Davis could hear the policeman ask Austin to spell his name and heard him saying very slowly A-U-S-T-I-N.

"Got anyone under that name?" Davis asked.

"Oh, yeah," the cop said, "right here." He turned back to Austin. "Sorry, buddy, I thought you were saying Watson, not Austin."

It was late in the afternoon when the player everyone had been waiting for arrived. Tiger Woods had no trouble getting into the parking lot. A small entourage awaited him when he got out of his car: caddy Steve Williams, Corless, and two state troopers. All the top players had been assigned police escorts to help them get around the grounds, and Woods was certainly no different. He was whisked into player registration, the police clearing a path for him so quickly that he was past most people before they realized who it was they were being cleared out of the way for.

As soon as he walked into the Tillinghast Room, everything went quiet. Elizabeth Body, who had been preparing for Woods's arrival, more or less took charge once Read had greeted Woods and started him on his way around the room. "I just tried to keep him moving," Body said. "He was quiet and polite, but I didn't want him feeling as if people were staring at him when he was just trying to register. Then I looked up and saw that all the people working in hospitality had come across to gawk."

Body got Woods to sign the scroll and sign up for a practice tee time — he didn't really need to since he habitually showed up first thing in the morning — and sent him up to the locker room to get settled and on his way to play a few holes. Then everyone breathed a sigh of relief.

Woods was registered. Almost everyone in the field had arrived. Most of the mishaps had ranged from minor to amusing.

And Felix Casas had been found. Roger Harvie had gotten an e-mail at nine-fifteen Monday morning from IMG's Manila office. They had tracked Casas down in San Francisco. He was on a plane en route to New York. Tricia Solow was desperately trying to find a hotel room for Casas. The best she could come up with was a motel in Cutchogue, about fifty miles east of the golf course.

But he was in the U.S. Open. Casas landed and took a very expensive cab ride to Cutchogue. Tuesday, he would see the golf course for the first time and get his courtesy car. *If* he had enough cash to pay for another long cab ride.

17

Final Preparations

ON THE FRIDAY before Open week began, Jon Barker left the office before midnight for one of the first and last times of the spring. He had no choice. He was sick. That afternoon, during a training session, he had started to feel dizzy to the point where he thought he was going to faint. He had gathered himself and finished the session. By the time he got back to his office, he felt even worse. His throat was swelling, and he was having trouble swallowing. Tricia Solow told him he needed to see a doctor. Barker didn't argue.

The doctors ran some tests and told him, "You look like you've been gargling with broken glass." He had something called strep pharyngitis, a virus usually brought on by exhaustion. That certainly made sense. He was sent to the hospital for a couple of IVs — one filled with steroids, the other with a saline drip — and soon felt better. The doctors recommended a lot of rest, which, of course, was completely out of the question. He did, however, leave the office early enough that night that he had time to stop at Sweeney's for dinner.

While Barker ate, someone came over to his table and said there was a person in the restaurant who wanted to meet him. Barker nodded and began to prepare his sorry-but-we-just-don't-have-any-tickets-left speech.

The person who wanted to meet him didn't ask for tickets. Her name was Donna Hickey. Her husband, Brian, had been scheduled to marshal on the 18th hole at the Open. On the morning of September 11, he had been filling in for another firefighter on the Rescue 3 squad in the Bronx when the call from the World Trade Center came in. He had gone in with the rest of the members of Rescue 3 and never came out. He was identified by DNA taken from his mangled helmet, which had been found during the Ground Zero search.

Donna Hickey had scheduled her husband's funeral for Tuesday, June 11, the Tuesday of Open week. "I did it for two reasons," she told Barker. "It would have been his forty-eighth birthday. But also, I thought by scheduling it then, maybe he would still be a small part of the Open. I hope it won't cause you any trouble. He was just so excited when he thought he was going to be a part of the Open."

"He will be, Mrs. Hickey," Barker said. "He will be."

The funeral was held at St. Martin of Tours Roman Catholic Church in Bethpage, less than two miles from the entrance to the park and just around the corner from the Bethpage Fire Department headquarters. Firefighters came from New York, Massachusetts, Pennsylvania, Delaware, Maryland, Connecticut, Ohio, and Washington, D.C. All 600 seats in the church were filled an hour before the noon service began. Another 400 people watched a closed-circuit telecast in St. John Baptist de la Salle next door. And close to 2,000 firefighters, all of them in uniform, lined the blocked-off streets outside the church, listening on loudspeakers.

A giant American flag, suspended from two ladder trucks, flapped in the breeze throughout the two-hour service. Shortly after noon, a police escort led two Bethpage fire trucks, followed by an FDNY truck from Rescue 4, the squad in Queens where Brian Hickey had been a captain, and then a ladder truck from

Rescue 4, which carried Brian Hickey's casket. Three limos followed, carrying Hickey's family, including Donna and their four children, ranging in age from twenty-four to ten.

As the casket was lowered from the truck, the forty-member FDNY pipe-and-drum band played "Amazing Grace." The silence as the last note was played was deafening. One of those who eulogized Hickey was Tim Kelly, a lieutenant at Rescue 4. "Brian was supposed to work as a marshal at the Open this week," he said. "I don't know how they'll get along without him."

If you were in the church that day, there was little doubt that Brian Hickey would be part of the Open.

Back at the golf course, reviews on the Black were now coming in from all corners.

"This is the best golf course I've ever played, period," said Billy Andrade, a twelve-year tour veteran. "Not the best public course, not the best U.S. Open course, the best course. It has everything you could ask for. The fairways are perfect, the greens are spectacular. The rough is hard but not impossible. Every single hole out there is a good hole."

Tom Lehman, the 1996 British Open champion who had played in the last group on Sunday for four straight years at the Open (1995 to 1998), was more succinct: "This place makes Augusta look like a dog track."

Jeff Sluman was the last player to arrive. As he drove in on Round Swamp Road on Tuesday afternoon, Sluman was slowed to a crawl because of cart and pedestrian traffic all around him. That gave him time to look at the golf course as he passed through. "I'm not sure exactly why, but when I saw those holes [15 and 17] on my right, I just caught my breath," he said. "I've played a lot of golf in a lot of places, but just driving in there was a feel that was special. Then, when I actually got on the course, I understood why."

It is worth noting that golfers do not rave about a golf course unless they really mean it. In fact, they are more than willing to criticize any golf course, whether it is Augusta or Pebble Beach or St. Andrews, if they don't like it. These compliments were genuine.

There were, as expected, a couple of legitimate concerns. First and foremost was the 10th tee. Several players simply couldn't reach the fairway. Others could reach it only if they hit a near-perfect drive. "That's just not right," Johnny Miller said after he had gone out and walked the course with his son Andy, who had qualified for his first Open. "There should always be a place where you can land a ball without having to hit it 250 yards and have a shot. That hole doesn't have one."

There was also grumbling about the rough behind the bunker on number 12 — the problem that Mike Davis had noted back in May. And there was the ongoing issue of supersizing the golf course. A lot of players believed that a large chunk of the field had no chance to contend on a par-70 golf course that was 7,214 yards, the longest in Open history.

In all, though, the players were having a ball. The atmosphere on the golf course during the practice rounds was carnival-like, the fans interacting with the players constantly and the players, for the most part, enjoying every second of it.

On Monday, Craig Stadler couldn't fly the bunker on number 12. When a couple of fans began heckling him good-naturedly, Stadler turned to one of them and said, "Here, you try it." The guy ducked under the ropes, grabbed Stadler's driver, and smoked a ball over the bunker. The crowd went nuts. Stadler couldn't stop laughing. He had the man walk down the fairway with him as a reward.

Brad Lardon, who spent a lot of time reminding people he had grown up in Huntington and needed local support, was walking off the 12th the next day, shaking his head about how tough the hole was, when a fan walked up to him and said, "Brad, no offense, but I can't tell you how much we're all enjoying watching this golf course kick your butts."

There was concern, naturally, about the proximity of the fans to the players. At Tuesday's three o'clock meeting, Joe Corless complained that a lot of the roping between greens and tees didn't give the players sufficient room to walk without coming too close to the fans. He was worried first and foremost about Woods, who was, as always, drawing huge galleries everyplace he went.

Woods was also, as might be expected, getting a lot of tabloid attention. New York isn't London when it comes to tabloids, but it does have its share of screaming headlines. Woods's girlfriend, Elin Nordegren, had already made the front page of the *New York Post* a few weeks earlier after some photos she had done as a bikini model began making the rounds. On Tuesday, the *Post* had a story revealing that Tiger and his glamorous bikini-model girlfriend were renting a castle near the golf course, complete with full-sized swimming pool and every amenity you could possibly want. The cost, according to the paper, was $150,000 for the week.

Terrific story. Not exactly true. Woods was sharing a house about two miles from the golf course with Mark O'Meara. It was a comfortable home with no swimming pool. Cost for the week: $6,000.

What was perhaps most remarkable was how the story got into print. One of the young women working in the clubhouse was a nineteen-year-old college journalism major. She had introduced herself to several reporters early in the week, hoping to get advice on how to advance her career. She mentioned to a couple of those reporters that a friend of hers had heard from another friend that Tiger Woods was renting a castle for $150,000.

Presto, instant story. When she read the story, the journalism major was embarrassed. "I just figured," she said, "that you always double-checked on something like that."

Not always.

The best pretournament stories, as is almost always the case, had very little to do with Woods or any of the other stars in the field. They had to do with players for whom just being in an Open was the thrill of a lifetime.

No one fit into that category more than Derek Tolan, a sixteen-year-old high school junior from just outside Denver. Tolan was one of twenty-two players who had made it through both local qualifying and the sectional. He had earned his spot at a sectional at Columbine Country Club in Littleton, the Denver suburb whose name will always be connected with the awful high school shooting spree of 1999, by holing a 50-foot chip on the first playoff hole to win a three-way playoff for the last spot. One of the people he had beaten in the playoff was Mike Reid, a twenty-five-year tour veteran, who had won twice in his career and had almost won the PGA in 1989.

Sectionals have little to do with résumés, though, and Tolan's chip-in earned him a trip to Bethpage, a good deal of publicity as the youngest player in the field, and a new car, courtesy of his father, John, who had promised it to him if he qualified for the Open. "He said to me, 'Hey Dad, if I make it to the Open this year or win the Colorado Open, will you buy me a new car?' I said, 'Sure, son, go for it.' I never dreamed I'd end up paying off."

John Tolan was a club pro at a nine-hole executive course and driving range and appeared to be just about as thrilled as his son was to be standing on the range. At one point, looking around him at the pros lined up, hitting balls, Derek turned to his father and said, "This is so cool! I'm hitting balls with tour guys!"

Jerry Haas was a few years older than Derek Tolan but felt almost the same way. He had once been a tour guy himself, playing for three years in the '90s with mixed success, before dropping back to the Nike Tour, where he played well enough to win three times and make a decent living. But in 1997, at the age of thirty-four, he was offered the chance to coach at Wake Forest, his alma mater, and decided to get off the merry-go-round. He had played in three Opens, but the last one had been in 1988.

Haas had always been known on tour as Jay Haas's little brother. Now he was back on the range, with his brother a few yards away hitting balls — preparing to play in his twenty-third Open. Jay Haas was forty-eight, one of those rare guys who could still compete with the big hitters even as the Senior Tour loomed. His longevity was defined, in many ways, by his Open record. He had finished fifth in 1977 at Southern Hills and fifth again in 1997 (with a fourth at Shinnecock in 1995 in between) at Congressional.

Jerry had spent most of the week trying to convince himself that he could handle the Open again, that he could control his nerves. "On the way home after Woodmont, I started thinking to myself, what have you gotten yourself into here? I'm a golf coach, I haven't played under conditions like this or this kind of pressure for years. The Open is always about driving it in the fairway, though, and if I have a strength, that's it. So if I can stay out of my own way in terms of nerves, I might be able to play pretty well."

He was talking about dealing with Open pressure when his brother walked by. "Hey, Jay," he asked, "how do you prepare for what it's like out there the first day of an Open?"

Jay Haas laughed. "Easy. Just walk through a door and have it hit you in the face over and over and over again."

Most of 2002 had been one slammed door in the face after another for David Duval. He had broken up with his longtime girlfriend, Julie McArthur, less than a year after the two of them had announced they were engaged. Then, in Los Angeles, at the Nissan Open, he had felt a twinge in his back during the third round and had been forced to withdraw prior to the final round. He kept playing tournaments even though his back hurt but didn't play very well. He had already missed four cuts in half a year, the same number he normally might miss in about two years. He hadn't seriously contended to win a tournament since his breakthrough victory the previous summer at the British Open. He had finally taken time off after missing the cut at the Masters — this after finishing second, sixth, third, and second there the previous four years — to rest and was slowly starting to feel as if his game was coming back.

"I know I got my swing messed up because of the pain in my back," he said. "I'm just now getting to where I can swing without pain and feel as if I'm swinging the way I need to swing. But it still comes and goes. I went out on the range today [Tuesday], and for a while I started to hit the ball great. Then I started hitting it not so great. So I stopped."

Duval may be the least understood player on tour. The sunglasses he wears all the time to protect his light-sensitive eyes from getting dust and dirt into his contact lenses make him appear distant and unemotional. He is quiet in a way that can come off as aloof. He is blunt, not willing to simply hand out easy TV sound bites to TV sound bite questions. He laughs when people describe him as an intellectual because he has been known to read things other than *USA Today*.

Winning the British Open had lifted a huge burden from him emotionally, if only because he would never have to answer the questions again about being such a good player — thirteen titles — but not having won a major. He knew how Phil Mickelson felt when the questions came up, because he had been there, done that.

The U.S. Open had a special place in Duval's heart even though he had never really come close to winning it. It had been his first major. In 1990, as an eighteen-year-old college freshman, he had qualified for the Open at Medinah, beating, among others, Davis Love III, in a qualifier at Bay Hill. "I shot 75 66," he said. "I played so poorly the first eighteen holes I was thinking about leaving to get to a college match. But I stuck it out and made it. When I got to Medinah, I was just playing along, and on Sunday I made three birdies early and looked up after seven holes and saw I was on the leader board."

He smiled. "Never should have looked."

He played the last eleven holes in 10 over par and finished fifty-sixth. He hadn't forgotten the feeling of being in contention, even if it was just for an instant, and badly wanted to be there again.

Duval had arrived at Bethpage Sunday and gone out to play by himself in the afternoon. "I got halfway around the golf course and started laughing," he said. "I was thinking, wait a minute, people sleep in their cars so they can go through *this* torture? What in the world are they thinking? The place is amazing. The rough is like peanut butter when you put your club through it — really, really hard. I lost three balls on Sunday in there.

"They've got it close to perfect. The rough is the same on every hole. The greens and fairways are great. I'd have put in a couple more yards of fairway on some of the holes because the rough is so penal, but I don't think, overall, I've ever seen a better course setup than this."

Duval was also enjoying the New York fans. He had played on Monday with Andy Miller, Johnny Miller's son. Naturally, many in the crowd were far more familiar with the father than the son. "They kept yelling 'Come on, Johnny,' at him," Duval said. "So finally I said to this one guy, 'The guy's name is Andy. You're watching Andy, not Johnny.'

"The guy kind of nods and says, 'Yeah, okay, right, he's Andy.' Then I get up over my ball and he yells, 'Come on, Ernie, give it a ride!' I liked that."

Like many other players, Duval had been besieged, walking from green to tee, by people asking the same question: What do you think of the golf course?

"They want to know what we think because they're so proud of it," he said, smiling. "All I can say is they damn well ought to be."

On Wednesday morning, Fred Ridley was given a tour of the golf course shortly after sunrise by Tom Meeks and Tim Moraghan. As the chairman of the championship committee, it was up to Ridley to give final approval for the hole locations that Meeks and Moraghan had selected.

Ridley and Reed Mackenzie were the two most visible representatives of the volunteer arm of the USGA. While it was the staff, led by David Fay, that was charged with all the torturous details of getting an Open played, it was Mackenzie and Ridley who technically had final say — much to the horror of Frank Hannigan — over any and all major decisions that affected the tournament.

On first blush, the two men might appear to be the stereotype of the USGA committeeman, generally considered to be middle-aged to old, white, wealthy, and stuffy. Mackenzie, who was fifty-

nine, and Ridley, who was forty-nine, were white and were successful lawyers, Ridley in real estate development, Mackenzie in
personal injury.

The stereotype ended there. Mackenzie had been born in
Brooklyn in 1942, the product of a brief wartime romance. His
father, whose name was Reed King, enlisted in the navy in 1943
and was killed in a pilot training exercise later that year. His
mother then moved to Minneapolis to live with her parents. When
Reed was six, she married Ian Mackenzie and moved to Eau
Claire, Wisconsin.

Reed was a very good young player. By the time he got to college, he had a handicap of plus two and was playing regularly in
elite amateur events. He enrolled briefly at Dartmouth, wasn't
very happy there, and returned home to finish school at Wisconsin
State at Eau Claire. It was while he was in college that he qualified
for his first — and, as it turned out, last — U.S. Amateur in 1963.
"Been first alternate four times since then," he said. "But I haven't
gotten in."

For a while he thought his future might be in broadcasting. He
had worked as a PA announcer in high school for the Eau Claire
Bears, a Class C Northern League affiliate of the then Milwaukee
Braves, a team Henry Aaron had once played for. In college, he
worked at a local radio station doing everything from reading the
farm news to calling high school football and basketball. Still
unsure what direction he wanted to go in, he enrolled in law school
at the University of Minnesota but continued to work in radio.

"I eventually decided that radio and TV was a business in which
a few guys did very well financially at the top, but there was no
middle," he said. "The hours were very inflexible, and at the time
the pay wasn't very good, certainly not as good as it was as a lawyer
once I graduated."

By the time he graduated in 1968, he was a member at Hazeltine, then a fledging club (it opened in 1966) with lofty ambitions.
He went to work at a law firm specializing in personal injury cases
and watched in dismay when the Open came to Hazeltine in 1970

and the golf course was almost universally blasted by the players. Mackenzie became active in the club's efforts to figure out what it needed to do to change the golf course in order to get the Open back. In 1977, after the USGA had brought the Women's Open there, he was in charge of the scoring committee. One of his fellow Hazeltine members who was a member of the Minnesota Golf Association asked him to be the association's representative on junior events. As a result, he went to the Junior Amateur that year, where he met Tom Meeks.

"Tom encouraged me to come to the rules forum the next January," he said. "I liked golf, I liked being involved in tournaments. I figured, why not?"

He did so well on the rules test at the end of the forum that P. J. Boatwright invited him to work as a rules official at the '78 Open at Cherry Hills. "They gave me a gold committee badge and everything," Mackenzie said with a smile. His only bad moment came when Bob Murphy hit a ball into a water hazard at the hole he had been assigned. "There were trees in the hazard, I remember that," Mackenzie said. "When I pointed out to Murphy where his ball had crossed the line of the hazard, he became very grumpy."

Mackenzie survived Murphy's grumpiness and moved up the USGA ladder. He was Hazeltine's liaison to the USGA in the effort to bring the Open back there. When it did finally return to the club in 1991, Mackenzie was the general chairman. The success of the championship that year, both in terms of the improved golf course and the marketing, got him some attention, and his name came up a year later as a potential candidate for the executive committee. There was, however, some resistance to his candidacy.

"I had a reputation as a club thrower," Mackenzie said. "That's sort of frowned upon, as you might expect. I heard some stories about my feats later that were amusing. You know, a lot of club throws are actually tosses. I don't throw clubs as much now because I'm not nearly as flexible as I used to be. I also have trouble conjuring up that sort of emotion for my golf game [he is now a five-handicap] these days."

Although Meeks, who frequently plays with Mackenzie, will rattle on about how upset he gets when Mackenzie throws (tosses?) a club, Mackenzie has a sense of humor about it. Ask him when the last time he threw a club was and he will look at his watch.

In spite of the club-throwing specter, Mackenzie was named to the executive committee in 1992. When Fay first brought up the idea of going to Bethpage in 1995, he and Ridley were both among the skeptics. "I knew from my own Open experience that you need the cooperation of the club," he said. "In this case, that would be the state, and our biggest problems had always been dealing with state agencies on permit issues. Plus, you had the question of what could happen if a new administration came in after an election. I just thought it would be too difficult. Fortunately for us, people didn't listen to me."

Mackenzie didn't argue against the concept all that hard once he heard Fay talk about it. "When David talked, you could see his passion for the idea," he said. "His face actually got a little red during his presentation, not with anger, with enthusiasm. He kept saying it was a people's place and we [the USGA] needed to connect more with people, with the public golfer."

Mackenzie and Ridley were both a little concerned about how thick the rough was. That was why Ridley had checked the rough almost as carefully as he had checked the hole locations during his Wednesday morning tour with Meeks and Moraghan. He was certainly a good enough player to understand the difference between pitch-out rough and shot-makers rough. He had grown up in Lakeland, Florida, the son of two teachers. His first passion was baseball, specifically the Boston Red Sox, who played their spring training games in nearby Winter Haven. Ridley became a batboy there, and his greatest thrill came when Carl Yastrzemski gave him a pair of spikes one day and said, "Here, kid, break these in for me."

"I put three pairs of socks in my shoes so they'd fit and walked around in them until they were broken in," he said.

To this day, Ridley can rattle off the names of every player on the 1967 Red Sox team that came from nowhere to win the American League pennant, although he didn't actually set foot inside Fenway Park until the summer of 2001.

He played baseball and basketball until high school. By then, having learned the game on a public course in Lakeland, he had become a top junior golfer. He was offered a scholarship at Florida, one of the elite college golf programs, and accepted, thinking that was the best way to find out just how good he was. "I never played higher than fifth most of my college career," he said. "We had some really good players. When I graduated [in 1975], I decided to devote myself to golf for one full summer before I went to law school."

The devotion paid off. That summer, he beat Curtis Strange in the round of 16, Andy Bean in the semifinals, and Keith Fergus in the final to win the U.S. Amateur. That achievement made it tempting to pass on law school and turn pro, but he decided to finish law school and then decide. He went to Stetson, continuing to play amateur golf in the summers. He had some success but nothing like the Amateur, and that convinced him he probably wasn't cut out for the tour. He went to work for IMG for three years after law school, then moved back to Florida and got involved in developing golf-related real estate.

Several years later, in 1987, he was asked to captain the Walker Cup team (the amateur version of the Ryder Cup). Doing that reconnected him with the USGA, and in 1993 he was asked to join the executive committee. In 1995, when Bethpage had first come up, he, too, was skeptical.

"I thought it was a noble idea," Ridley said. "I had heard of the golf course and knew it was kind of worn out. I was worried about the politics that would be involved in getting it fixed up. In the end, though, especially after I saw the golf course, I could see that there was a lot more upside potentially than downside. It was worth the risk. Now we all look like geniuses."

Ridley's feelings about how the Open was going to go at the

Black were never more evident than at one of the many pre-Open parties. This one was a formal sit-down dinner at Bernadette Castro's house, complete with toasts from both the state and the USGA. When it was Ridley's turn, speaking for the championship committee, he held up his glass and said, "We fully expect that this will not be a one-act play."

18

Last Rehearsal

ON WEDNESDAY AFTERNOON, NBC and the USGA held their annual production meeting. This was as much a pep rally as a meeting. The USGA was represented by Tom Meeks, Mike Davis, and David Fay. By this time, everyone from NBC had seen the golf course, but Meeks was there to walk them through it one more time and answer any questions. Davis and Fay stood in the back of the production trailer where the meeting was, with big grins on their faces, listening to Meeks.

"We rolled a couple of greens last night because they were getting a little soft," he said. "That's not the way we want 'em, as you fellas know. We're hearing we may get some rain this afternoon and, of course, that's not good. But we think the golf course is in pretty good shape right now."

NBC's Roger Maltbie, who had played the course a couple of weeks earlier and watched the practice rounds, wondered about the drive on number 12. "You concerned about guys not being able to reach those bunkers at 12, Tom?" he asked.

Meeks had been working on his answer, especially since a lot of players were talking about how ludicrous the notion of a 500-yard (okay, 499) par-four was.

"There is no place in the manual where it says you must reach a par-four in two shots," he said.

That line brought a mixture of stares and hoots. "That's my story," Meeks said, breaking into his cackle, "and I'm sticking to it."

The two-tee start, he said, was going to work. The players, he pointed out, had been asked to start at least one practice round from the 10th to get a feel for what it was going to be like getting shuttled out there and starting from there. "The average practice round has been an hour shorter," Meeks said. "The players like this very much."

As he spoke, Craig Currier, who had been asked to come to the meeting, too, walked in a few minutes late. "Sorry I'm late," he said. "I was working on getting some extra help." He glanced at Meeks and added, "I hadn't thought I'd need to cut the rough every day."

The remark went past the NBC people. It did not go by Meeks, who launched into an unsolicited explanation of how much the rough was being cut and why.

The rest of the questioning was mundane, more along the lines of who was going to win (Woods) and what the winning score might be. Meeks predicted it would be between five and seven under par. "He was predicting 10 under a month ago," Currier said softly. True. But after talking to players who had played the golf course, Meeks felt better, especially since they were almost unanimous in saying that the greens seemed to have a lot more slope than most people had expected.

"It's subtle," Currier said. "These guys will notice it quicker than other people will."

They had certainly noticed. A number of players were predicting that if the rain held off, the winning score might be over par. Tommy Roy wrapped up the meeting by asking Fay if he had anything to add to the Meeks treatise. "David B," he said, invoking the name everyone at NBC called him by, "you got anything to add?"

"No need," Fay said. "I know the pictures, the presentation, and the preaching will be perfect."

Certainly the preaching. Throughout the NBC trailers a sign had been posted: "This is a championship, not a tournament."

There would also be no pins anywhere to be found once NBC was on the air.

The one true nongolfer among the NBC people in the trailer was the man in charge: Dick Ebersol. "I play golf twice a year," he said. "I play for four days at the Players Championship, and then I play a few times in August on a six-hole golf course on Chappaquiddick with my younger sons," he said. "That's it. But I *watch* golf all the time."

Ebersol was fifty-five, one of those rare production people who was as well known to the public as those who work in front of a camera. He had been a coproducer of the original *Saturday Night Live* and was married to actress Susan Saint-James. He wore his still-brown hair long, almost '70s style, and seemed to have a cigar in his hands at all times.

The Open was one of his proudest achievements, because he remembered where NBC's golf coverage had been when he took the job as NBC Sports president in 1989. "The first day I was on the job I found out that Lee Trevino was leaving to play the Senior Tour and Vin Scully was also leaving," he said. "I had no 18th-hole analyst or lead guy. ABC had just re-upped with the Open, and the Masters was untouchable. But I really wanted to get us into golf in a big-time way.

"Tommy Roy and Johnny Miller were the keys. Having them in place made it possible for us to get the Open. Now I'd put our golf up against anybody. Tommy plans for this every year as if he's planning the Normandy Invasion."

In that sense, D-Day was now just hours away.

Back at the tennis trailer, the D-Day metaphor seemed like a pretty good fit when that day's three o'clock meeting convened. Steve Worthy and Bob Nuzzo were now in full battle mode over the issue of Laura Southerland. Worthy had initially agreed to send her over to Nuzzo that day but had decided later there was no way he could spare her. Nuzzo was not happy.

"I'm not going to start anything in the meeting," he said. "Steve and I will talk about it later . . . in private."

Private, no doubt, if you weren't within five miles of the conversation.

Worthy had other major concerns, notably the continuing problem with Bo Dietl. The no-show rate had gone down Tuesday but was back up to 40 percent on Wednesday. He and Felix Sorge were now contacting other security companies to see if they could bring in more people.

"If you do that, will there be time to do background checks?" Romaney Berson asked.

"For some," Nuzzo said. "Maybe not for all. Does that make you uncomfortable?"

"If you're okay with it, I'm okay with it," said Berson, who had reached the point where she thought if she had to deal with one more background check she would jump out a window.

There were other problems. The volunteers were complaining loudly about the length of the walk to the volunteer tent on the 15th hole. Most of them had less than an hour to eat, and by the time they made their way through the crowds to 15, got themselves into the jam-packed tent, got something to eat, and trekked back, they were practically sprinting to get back inside an hour. Some had simply not come that day. Others were threatening not to show the next day.

"I think we need an auxiliary tent of some kind," Dave Catalano said. "Because it's going to be even worse tomorrow."

Jon Barker looked at Worthy. "That possible?" he asked.

"I'll find out," Worthy answered.

There were other concerns. The Green Course was already starting to sink under the crush of all the cars, and this was *before* the predicted rainstorms. One stretch limousine bringing corporate customers had bottomed out and had to be towed free. There had also been the rather comical sight of four Anheuser-Busch clients who were scheduled to play corporate golf walking through the gate from the Green Course parking to their tent with their golf clubs slung over their shoulders. No one had stopped them.

So much for fanny packs.

But the major issue — again — was player security. Joe Corless was very unhappy with the way the golf course was roped. He wasn't happy with the way those BDA employees who had showed up were being deployed. He delivered a fairly impassioned speech about the need for things to get better by Thursday. Midway through, Sorge walked out.

Corless was especially upset with the number of people inside the ropes on the putting green. There were, he said, people wearing USGA guest badges. Clearly, they didn't belong there. He also thought there were far too many media people.

"They should only be in there if they have an armband," said Craig Smith.

"I see a lot of them without armbands," Corless said.

That led to a lengthy conversation about who should and should not be allowed on the putting green and about media access to players who finished their rounds on the ninth hole. Smith wanted to be sure that when a group finished on the ninth, one player wasn't standing around talking to the media while the other two were waiting in a van to get back to the clubhouse.

"Just don't let the media talk to anyone out there," someone suggested. "Let them do it back at the clubhouse."

After much debate, it was finally decided to give reporters at least a minute or two to make arrangements to talk to a player back at the clubhouse if there wasn't time to conduct an actual interview. "Just do me a favor, and tell your guys not to get rough with any of the guys out there," Smith said to Nuzzo and Sittler.

Sittler smiled. "I promise we won't shoot anyone," he said.

Smith did not appear comforted.

When the meeting broke, Roger Harvie followed Corless into the parking lot. "You aren't being fair, Joe," he said angrily. "Felix is doing the best he can under the circumstances, and you're in there killing him. You say we haven't done the reroping you asked for. It's been done. Go check it for yourself."

"I'm just telling you what I've seen," Corless answered. "That's what I was hired to do."

He turned and walked away. Harvie started to answer, thought better of it, and stalked away angrily.

There was a simmering problem here. Corless was not on the USGA staff. In fact, his full-time job was with the PGA Tour. He had been hired as a consultant by the USGA shortly after the tour had hired him in 1998. Some staff members found his approach condescending. They also resented the fact that almost everything he suggested seemed to be in the name of protecting one player: Woods. Corless didn't make any bones about Woods being his number one priority. He walked all eighteen holes with him every day and made it clear that he considered him to be his personal responsibility.

Woods would tee off the next day at 1:35. Corless would be right there with him. That meant he wouldn't make that day's three o'clock meeting. Which was probably good news for everybody.

From the moment the gates had first opened on Monday morning, the most chaotic spot on the grounds had been the merchandise tent. When people come to a U.S. Open, they want to take something home so they can show people they were there. Often, they come armed with lists given to them by friends who have asked them to make a purchase on their behalf.

Mary Lopuszynski had her volunteers ready to roll. All day, the tent appeared to be jammed, but somehow the lines for the forty-four cash registers kept moving. And Lopuszynski was already reordering early in the week because it was clear that the $10 million worth of merchandise she had ordered wasn't going to last until the weekend.

On Wednesday afternoon, Lopuszynski was working near the front of the tent discussing reorders when she got a call on the cell phone she kept constantly wrapped around her ear (to the point where her ear was actually swollen) telling her she was needed in the center of the tent right away. The Nassau County executive was there, and he wanted to meet her — right away.

"I just figured it was one of those deals where I had to go and shake hands, thank him for his hospitality, and that would be it," she said. "As soon as I walked up, I had an idea it wasn't going to be that simple."

Standing in the middle of the busiest aisle in the tent, Lopuszynski found county executive Thomas Suozzi. With him was a small entourage that included Suozzi's mother, an assistant, a photographer, and two men in suits who Lopuszynski assumed were his security people. Suozzi was talking on his cell phone. He paused long enough to be introduced. Lopuszynski asked if there was anything at all she could do to help him.

Suozzi barked "Hang on" into his cell phone and then turned to Lopuszynski. "Do you know what county you're in?" he asked, his tone telling Lopuszynski this was not a geography test.

"Yes, I do," she answered. "We're in Nassau County."

"And do you know that you aren't paying the taxes you owe Nassau County?" he said, his voice now raised.

"You're wrong," Lopuszynski said. "We've been paying our taxes. I know that for a fact."

Every year when the USGA goes into a jurisdiction to conduct the Open, it works out a plan through its legal and accounting departments with both the state and the local governments to pay taxes on the merchandise it sells. Now Suozzi, photographer at the ready, was claiming that the USGA was somehow ripping off the people of Nassau County. "It's a good thing I came over here," Suozzi said to the invisible person inside his cell phone, "or we'd have been ripped off for millions — again."

Lopuszynski sensed a grandstand move and knew she had to stay calm, not give Suozzi anything to work with, and get him out of the tent without allowing him to cause a scene.

"Sir, you're wrong, and I can show you exactly how you're wrong," she said. "You aren't being ripped off."

"Okay, fine, prove it."

Lopuszynski took Suozzi and friends straight to the USGA's accounting office. Pam Martin, the USGA's controller, wasn't there but John Hynds, the director of finance, and Carrie Cardace, the assistant accounting manager, were. Lopuszynski started to explain the problem to Hynds, saying that Suozzi was convinced the USGA wasn't paying taxes to Nassau County the way it was supposed to be doing.

"That's just wrong," said Cardace, who was sitting across the trailer and heard what was being said. "I did all the paperwork myself. We've been paying taxes exactly the way we're supposed to be paying them. If you want, I'll give you our taxpayer ID number, and you can check it yourself."

Suozzi went a little bit pale. "I'll call you back," he said to the cell phone.

Then he circled the room, shook everyone's hand, thanked them for their help, told them to enjoy their stay in Nassau County, and left.

Earlier in the day, the USGA's legal department had gone through the annual ritual of getting off-site vendors to cease and desist selling merchandise with the U.S. Open logo on it that was not actually licensed U.S. Open merchandise. This happened every year at every site.

"It isn't so much a concern because of any loss of income," Romaney Berson said. "Obviously, people come into the tent and spend plenty of money. The concern is that someone buys something with our logo on it, they tend to assume we're responsible for it. The lettering on the shirt runs, the cap falls apart, whatever it may be, they're going to blame us. It makes us look bad."

The USGA does not take what would be called a hardball approach to most unlicensed vendors. During the winter, when B. K. Sweeney's had started selling items with the Open logo on them, they had received a very polite letter explaining that they really couldn't sell Open merchandise without being licensed and would they please stop. No threats, no deadlines, just a request to stop. They stopped.

The approach to vendors on the street was similar: please stop. The only problem came when Anne Kellstrom, who was representing the USGA, wanted to take possession of the property being sold to ensure that it wouldn't be sold in the future.

"You can't do that," Bob Nuzzo told her. "We'll make the arrest, and we'll seize the property."

"But we don't want anyone arrested," Kellstrom said. "We just want them to stop."

"Okay, that's fine," Nuzzo said. "But if there's no arrest, you can't seize property. They may not have a right to sell it, but you don't have a right to take it."

A true conundrum.

A compromise was finally reached. There would be no arrests. The offending vendors would be told by the police that they were guilty of copyright infringement, but if they packed up and didn't return, they wouldn't be charged. If they did return, they would be charged.

Everyone seemed satisfied with that.

There was one other issue that needed to be resolved: the ongoing Worthy-Nuzzo battle over Laura Southerland. Nuzzo had been so angry when Southerland did not report to his command post on Wednesday that he threatened to shut down Round Swamp Road to departing players.

"I feel like I'm being taken advantage of," he said. "I understand that there are parts of the USGA's job I don't understand. But there are parts of our job they don't understand. Not having someone in there really hurts our operation."

Nuzzo and Worthy finally sat down on Wednesday afternoon after the three o'clock meeting and talked the whole thing out. Fortunately, the two men liked and respected each other enough that there were no hard feelings. Worthy actually felt — hoped — that

with the championship under way on Thursday and everything —
he hoped — in place, he might be able to get by without Southerland, although he still wasn't thrilled with the idea.

"I'll send her over first thing in the morning," Worthy said.

"I'll send someone to pick her up first thing in the morning,"
Nuzzo answered.

Worthy sighed.

It was time to start playing golf.

19

D-Day

FINALLY, IT WAS REAL.

Seven-and-a-half years after David Fay had walked the golf course by himself and dreamed that a United States Open championship could be played on the Black Course, the best players in the world pulled into the parking lot where Fay had parked his car and prepared to compete in the 102nd U.S. Open. In the midst of an early planning meeting, Mike Butz had said, "Sometimes we forget that what really matters is getting 156 players around the golf course for four days and making sure one of them gets the U.S. Open trophy on Sunday night." Now those 156 players were warming up on the range and making their way to the golf course. After all the planning and preparing and wondering and worrying, they were ready to begin identifying, as Sandy Tatum had once put it, "the best player in the world."

The best, at least, for one week on one very hard golf course.

The morning had dawned cool and overcast, the temperature in the 50s, when players with early tee times began heading to the range shortly after six A.M. Among the first players to arrive on the range was the one player on the property who did not have a tee time, Trip Kuehne. Once Felix Casas had been found, Kuehne had become the first alternate. When Roger Harvie tracked him down on Tuesday, Kuehne had decided to fly to Bethpage to be there in case there was another withdrawal.

"It's the U.S. Open," he said. "If there's any chance you'll get to play, you have to take that chance."

Kuehne had arrived on Wednesday, grabbed a cab at La Guardia Airport, and asked to be taken to the Hampton Inn, where Tricia Solow had found him a room. Thirty minutes later, the driver pulled up and told him the fare was $155. Welcome to New York.

Since Kuehne had no idea if a spot might open up in the first groups at seven-fifteen A.M. or in the last groups at two-fifteen P.M. or someplace in between, he had no choice but to be at the golf course, warmed up and ready to go by seven-fifteen. He arrived knowing he could be in for a long, frustrating day. Most withdrawals take place prior to Thursday. It is rare for players to show up, register, play their practice rounds, and then withdraw. Still, until the last threesome was off the tee, Kuehne had hope, and he had to try to be ready.

Everyone else knew exactly when he was expected on the tee. The only difference, of course, was the two-tee start. Players had been told to be at the staging area for the shuttles that would take them out to the 10th tee at least twenty minutes before their tee time. Players were, of course, welcome to leave earlier if they felt they needed to stretch themselves a little longer after the van trip. Most preferred to linger on the putting green until the last possible minute.

In order to be sure that the players got to the shuttles in plenty of time, Robbie Zalzneck had been assigned to patrol the putting green and let players know when it was time to head to the shuttles. Zalzneck was Jon Barker in the years that Barker wasn't Barker. In other words, he had done everything in Tulsa in 2001 that Barker was now doing at Bethpage and was preparing to do all those same things again in Chicago in 2003. Then it would be Barker's turn again at Shinnecock in 2004.

Zalzneck was twenty-nine and had been hired by the USGA

after the Open at Pinehurst in 1999 when it had been decided that having an advance man on-site at every Open at least a year in advance was a good idea. He had worked for Club Corporation, which owns Pinehurst, and had been the USGA's main contact leading up to the Open there. He had impressed Butz, Davis, and Meeks with his know-how and maturity. So when it was decided to hire a second Barker, Zalzneck got the job.

At the initial three o'clock meeting on Sunday, when everyone had introduced themselves, Zalzneck had said simply, "Robbie Zalzneck, not my year."

He had no idea how accurate that line would prove to be. On Tuesday afternoon, he had parked a cart outside the clubhouse, gone in to get some work done, and come back to find that the cart was gone. It had been "stolen" by Roger Harvie, who had mistaken it for his cart. Zalzneck had no choice but to walk to his next meeting. On Wednesday, when the golf course had been cleared late in the afternoon because of a rainstorm, Zalzneck had helped out in the evacuation process. He had parked his (now recovered) cart by the side of a fairway and, just to be sure, had left it right next to a state trooper, telling him not to let anyone drive it away who wasn't him.

He went and gathered the players, pointed them to the waiting vans, and headed back to his cart. Sure enough, it was still there, the trooper standing right next to it. What was missing was his umbrella, which Zalzneck had left on the seat while he sprinted onto the fairway to tell the players they needed to cease play.

"Where's my umbrella?" Zalzneck asked the trooper.

"How should I know?" he answered.

Now, Ron Read's voice in his ear counted down the time until the first group would tee off. "Time check," Read would say. "It is 6:55 . . . now. Twenty minutes until game time."

That time check was Zalzneck's signal to get the first group to the shuttle stop and into the vans. He walked onto the putting green to let Steve Pate, Dudley Hart, and Paul Stankowski know that it was time for them to make the 50-yard walk from the putting green to where the shuttles were staging.

Zalzneck got about three steps onto the green when he was cut off and grabbed by the arm by a state trooper. "Players and caddies only on the putting green," he said, dragging Zalzneck away from the players.

Apparently, the message to limit access to the putting green had been taken a little further than intended. The instructions the police received were supposed to inform them that those with USGA guest badges no longer had putting green access. Somehow, it had been translated into *all* USGA badges. Zalzneck was wearing a USGA staff badge, which gave him access to every inch of ground on the property. Except, at that moment, the putting green.

Once the policeman had pulled him off the green, Zalzneck calmly explained to him that there'd been a miscommunication and asked him to either call the command center or Nuzzo to confirm what he was saying. The policeman eyed him skeptically, but seeing his walkie-talkie and USGA-authorized cell phone, figured it was worth a check. When word came back that, yes, staff was allowed on the green, Zalzneck was able to get back to shooing players to the shuttle buses.

Clearly, though, he had been right when he introduced himself on Sunday. This was *not* his year.

At 7:09, Ron Read checked the PA system on the first tee to make sure he could be heard. Then he continued his radio countdown so all the USGA staffers who weren't being dragged off the putting green would know precisely when the championship would begin.

Paul Goydos walked onto the tee at 7:10, wearing an uncharacteristic smile. Goydos's nickname among his fellow players was Sunshine, given to him when he was a tour rookie in 1993 by Jeff Sluman because of his ability to find the dark cloud in every silver lining. Once he had shot a 63 in a U.S. Open qualifier at Woodmont. When someone complimented him on the round, he shook his head and said, "I didn't make a putt all day." He liked to tell people he was the worst player in the world because there were times when he — like anyone else who played the tour — was convinced that he was just that.

Thirty-eight years old, the onetime Long Beach schoolteacher brought a different mentality to golf than most of his fellow players. He was a Democrat, something seen on tour about as often as snow, and was often at the center of arguments on the driving range or in locker rooms on subjects ranging from terrorism to the national budget to the play of his beloved Long Beach State 49ers basketball team. On more than one occasion, referees had threatened to eject him from Long Beach State games for heckling them.

He had won once on tour — in 1996 at Bay Hill — shortly after growing a scruffy goatee. During the awards ceremony, he had asked Arnold Palmer, the tournament's host, if he would play a practice round with him at the Masters. Back then, a victory earned you an automatic spot in the Masters. "Only if you get rid of that thing on your face," Palmer told him. He got rid of it. In fact, he even got the artist who drew the portraits of all the Bay Hill champions that hung in the clubhouse to airbrush the goatee out of his portrait.

Goydos had struggled with his game in 2001, finishing 132nd on the money list, the first time since his rookie year he had not been in the top 125. He had been playing better in 2002 and was looking forward to leading off the Open. He had played most of his golf growing up, and even now as a grown-up, at a muni in Long Beach that was known to locals as "the bone yard" because so many older people played there that you could almost hear their bones cracking early in the morning on the first tee.

Right behind Goydos came Mike Muehr and Jerry Haas. Both looked a little bit dazed walking onto the first tee at such an early hour and seeing the grandstands, behind and to the players' right, packed with people. The air crackled with anticipation as it always does on the first morning of a major, but this was a little different. It wasn't just the players who were brimming with pride and pumped full of adrenaline, it was everyone from volunteers to officials to spectators.

"I felt like a five-year-old kid waking up for my first day of school this morning," said Glen Zakian, who would be the standard-bearer for the first group. "We've all waited a long time for this to happen." Zakian was thirty-six, a high school football and basketball coach who, like so many others, had volunteered as soon as the call had gone out two years earlier. He appeared to be at least as fired up to be standing on the tee as the players.

They went through the preround rituals: handshakes with Read, with officials standing on the tee, with Zakian and the walking scorer, and finally, with Jerry Stahl, who would be their referee. They were handed scorecards by Read and grabbed tees and some fruit or water from the table set up by the side of the tee. Haas looked as if he didn't know whether to laugh or cry.

"I woke up in the middle of the night having an anxiety attack," he said. "I mean, I'm a golf coach. How can I possibly be prepared for something like this? I think I slept two hours total." He smiled. "I keep telling myself this is going to be fun. I just wish I could get myself to believe it."

Just before seven-fifteen, Read stepped to the microphone and delivered the same sort of speech he has delivered on the first tee of every Open since 1989. "Ladies and gentlemen, welcome to the 2002 United States Open golf championship, conducted by the United States Golf Association. The championship will be contested for seventy-two holes of stroke play. This year, 8,468 golfers have entered our national championship; 156 of them have qualified to compete here."

He paused for applause, took a breath, and said, "Player number one, from Coto de Caza, California, Paul Goydos!"

Goydos had waited until the last possible second to take off his jacket. He gave a quick wave and a smile in response to the applause, stepped to the tee, and hit an ugly hook deep into the rough on the left side of the fairway. "Steer job," he said later. "I wasn't *too* nervous."

Muehr, clearly just as nervous, hit it even farther left. Read introduced Haas, who was wearing a black Wake Forest pullover.

Just as he stepped to the tee, the first cell phone rang. Haas ignored it, stepped up, and became the first player in the championship to find the first fairway. As the players started off the tee and down the hill leading to the fairway, Read said, "A friendly reminder: *No* cell phones, please."

Yeah, sure, no cell phones.

None of the players in the first group could get anything going as the morning wore on. Haas and Muehr each saved par on the first hole. Muehr's tee shot ended up right in front of Mary Lopuszyn-ski's satellite merchandise tent and he somehow got the ball out of the trampled-down rough there, then got up and down for par. Haas hit his second shot into the right-hand bunker, blasted to six feet, and made the putt. Goydos had to make a five-footer for bogey.

That set the tone for the round. Goydos, easily the most accomplished of the three players, played one of his worst rounds ever on tour. He was eight over par after nine holes, scrambling to make bogey on most holes. Muehr was mixing birdies with bogeys, and Haas was hanging in, thanks to a remarkable short game. On the 12th hole, he got back to just two over par when he holed out for a birdie from the right, front bunker, drawing one of the louder roars of the early morning.

"Wow!" he said, walking off the green. "That may have been my all-time shot. I told [caddy] Billy [Harmon] before I went in there that it would be unreal if I could get up and down from there. Then I holed it."

Maybe the birdie got Haas too pumped. Or maybe he was just drained from working so hard the first twelve holes. Regardless, he double-bogeyed 13 and 14, arguably the two easiest holes on the golf course, and limped home from there with a 78. Muehr wasn't much better, shooting 77, while Goydos rallied on the back nine to shoot 80.

"I accomplished my goal on the back nine," he said. "No head injuries among the spectators." He smiled wearily. "I know the

USGA is trying to identify the world's best player this week. The good news is, clearly they've already identified the worst."

Actually, Goydos wasn't even close to being the worst player on the golf course. The rain the previous afternoon had created what should have been favorable conditions. The greens were a little softer than they had been in the practice rounds, and the weather was ideal: cool and comfortable, with very little breeze. Even so, the Black was winning the opening round with the world's best golfers.

There had been a lot of pretournament talk that players starting on the front nine would have an advantage because the first few holes offered more birdie opportunities than the first few holes of the back nine. That wasn't proving to be the case, though, because no one was making many birdies. By day's end, a total of six players — the lowest number since the first round at Shinnecock in 1986 — would break par.

Three players shot 69: Billy Mayfair, Dudley Hart, and Jeff Maggert, who had contended often in the past without winning. One player shot 68: Sergio García, the brilliant but temperamental twenty-two-year-old Spaniard. He was trailed around the golf course all day by his girlfriend, Martina Hingis, the Swiss tennis star who had won seven major championships by the age of twenty-one. Hingis was injured and not playing, so she was spending the week with García.

"It's good to have someone to talk to who understands what this sort of thing is about," García said. "You know, most of the time with a girl, you talk about your frustrations when you are competing, and they just kind of look at you. She knows what I'm saying and what I'm feeling. That helps."

It helped him enough on Thursday that he trailed the leader by only one shot. But the name of the leader had to be daunting to García and everyone in the field: Tiger Woods.

To say that Tiger Woods is the most dominant figure in the game of golf is a little bit like saying that being president is an important job. Whenever he tees it up in any golf tournament, it is as if there are 155 other guys and then there is Tiger. Every move he makes is closely observed; everything he says is scrutinized. At the age of twenty-seven he is by far the most famous athlete in the world. When he arrived at Bethpage, he was two months removed from winning his second straight Masters (third overall), giving him seven major titles. In the Open field, only Nick Faldo (six) and Nick Price (three) had won more than two majors. Both of them were in their midforties and not likely to add to that total. Woods was just beginning. His goal was simple: break Jack Nicklaus's all-time record of eighteen professional major titles. He had been up-front about that since the day he turned pro in 1996, and there were very few among the original doubters who thought he would not someday surpass Nicklaus.

Being the most famous athlete in the world in this media-saturated time is not always easy. What's more, Woods made it clear that neither the media nor the public were major priorities for him. He did what he felt he had to do. He signed autographs on occasion but always felt burdened by the need to do so. He showed up in the media tent every Tuesday and almost always talked after he had played a round of golf. (Every once in a while when the golf course didn't cooperate, he still stormed off without comment. When he first came on tour, he had done that on a regular basis. Now it only happened two or three times a year. Of course Woods didn't have that many poor rounds in the first place.)

Woods had two basic goals that drove everything else he did: surpass Nicklaus and surpass Michael Jordan. The latter competition was almost as tangible as the first. Jordan had become the world's wealthiest, best-known athlete in his prime. Woods had taken him as a role model. In one sense that was good, because there was no better competitor in the history of sports than Jordan, no athlete who won by using his brains and his toughness as much as he used his body, the way Jordan did. But Jordan, at least to outsiders, appeared to have no soul. Everything he did off the basketball court appeared to be motivated by money or how it affected his image — which went straight back to the issue of money. His approach to life was perhaps best summed up when friends in his home state asked him if he would campaign on behalf of Harvey Gantt, who was running for the Senate against Jesse Helms, the ancient Republican who had spent a large part of his political career working against desegregation. Jordan refused to help. When he was asked why, his answer was, if nothing else, honest: "Republicans buy sneakers, too."

Woods was a registered Independent. Beyond that, almost no one knew anything about his political leanings, because, like his role model, he worked hard to be completely apolitical. In addition to selling golf shoes, he was also selling golf clubs and balls, cars, credit cards, the wonderful world of Disney, and a golf magazine. Woods often complained about his lack of a private life, about the constant burdens of being Tiger. But he always had time for his many sponsors.

He had matured considerably, though, since the famous lunch he'd had with Arnold Palmer in Augusta in 1997. He had complained to Palmer then about the fact that he couldn't be a normal twenty-one-year-old.

"Tiger," Palmer had answered, "normal twenty-one-year-olds don't have fifty million dollars in the bank. You want to be a normal twenty-one-year-old, give the money back. Otherwise, quit complaining."

Woods had learned from Palmer and from Nicklaus about handling stardom. He chafed less in public now and had learned how to talk in the predictable clips that TV loved, usually punctuated by his million-watt smile. He had a quick, sharp wit — one that often turned biting when he was with friends — and he could use that more often than not to deflect serious questions. The fact that he almost never sat down for one-on-one interviews with print reporters also allowed him to keep a comfortable distance.

Those who worked for him had learned that they had better not give away too much of Tiger, either. Mike (Fluff) Cowan, his first caddy on tour, had lost his job because Tiger felt he was enjoying the notoriety of being Tiger's caddy just a little too much. Hughes Norton, the snarling IMG agent who had represented him "unofficially" as an amateur (in those days Tiger's father, Earl, was on the IMG payroll as a junior talent scout) and in his early days as a pro, also got the boot for not knowing when to keep his mouth shut. Girlfriends, even plain old friends, knew that to give up anything about Tiger's private life would jeopardize the friendship because Tiger would see it as a betrayal.

Now, his agent was a young IMG operative named Mark Steinberg whose main job was to simply repeat the word *no* several million times a year. Caddy Steve Williams was more than happy to snarl and growl at anyone not a member of the inner circle who ventured near his man on the range or the putting green. In short, Tiger had created the perfect insulated world for himself, exactly what he felt he needed to chase Nicklaus and Jordan.

Woods was now in his sixth full year on the PGA Tour. He came to the Open having already won thirty-two PGA Tour events, a staggering number for someone in his midtwenties. Every other player in the field knew that if Tiger played well on Thursday at a major, there was an excellent chance he would walk away with the trophy Sunday. Most of the time when he didn't win majors, it was because he got too far behind early and couldn't quite rally on the weekend.

García's 68 was already on the leader board by the time Woods, Chris DiMarco, and Darren Clarke teed off at the 10th hole on Thursday afternoon. Woods, who admitted later that he was still a little bit stiff from the van ride, pulled his tee shot on number 10 but managed to scramble for par. From that moment on, he was resolute. He birdied the 13th and 14th, stumbled briefly with a bogey at the 16th, and then rolled in a 20-footer for birdie at the 18th. He had played his first nine holes — the tougher nine holes according to everyone — in two under par. His name went to the top of the leader board, tied at that moment with García. Seeing that, everyone nodded their head knowingly: It was going to be a Tiger week at the Open.

Woods was, for him, almost loose. Walking down the hill from the 14th green to the 15th tee, he made a stop in a Porta-John reserved for players. The area on both sides of Round Swamp Road was probably the most crowded part of the golf course on most days. When Woods came out of the Porta-John, a huge crowd was waiting for him. When he stepped outside, everyone began to applaud.

"What, you didn't think I was toilet trained?" Woods asked.

That scene actually made TV. The next morning, reading a newspaper description of Tiger's one-liner, Kip Ingle told his family, "That's it! That's the one I helped set up."

Ingle was a friend of Steve Worthy's who worked as a volunteer every year at the Open and had been drafted to help set up the 682nd and last Porta-John on the golf course. That was the one between 14 green and 15 tee. When he read the account, he called Worthy and said, "Did you hear what happened? Tiger used *my* Porta-John."

Yes, Woods thrilled people in many different ways.

On the front nine, Woods played calmly and steadily, again finishing with a birdie, this one a 15-footer at the ninth. He had shot 67, but the most significant number of the day was seven — that was the number of putts between 10 and 20 feet that he had holed. When Woods putts like that, there is no one in the world who can beat him.

"When he's making those putts he's on a different level than the rest of us," said his pal O'Meara. "You don't like to think that way, and you don't just throw in the towel, because anything can happen, but let's face it, he's just playing a different game than the rest of us."

Every player was being watched at all times, more so than anyone really knew. In addition to the very visible 893 uniformed police officers — the total of state and local police on hand — there were plainclothes officers all over the grounds, undercover officers, bomb experts, and even experts trained to deal with any kind of chemical weapons. There were also surveillance cameras posted at strategic points around the park, most notably at all the entrances, to keep an eye out for anyone entering who might look suspicious.

For Woods, though, it went a good deal further than that. As soon as he pulled his car into the parking lot, he was greeted by a coterie of people. One was Steve Williams. Another was Joe Corless. There were also two uniformed policemen, with others available to move crowds if need be.

And, there was a nondescript-looking middle-aged man wearing a credential that said Scoring. His name was Dan Hoban. He worked for the Secret Service.

Hoban's scoring credential was legitimate. He wasn't a very good golfer, but he was an avid one and he had worked as a volunteer when the Open was held at Congressional in 1997. He was assigned there to be a scorer and enjoyed the work, the interaction with the players, the atmosphere. Not long after that, Hoban met David Fay, who filed Hoban's background in his mind for future consideration.

Hoban was forty-seven. He had grown up in New Jersey and had dreamed of being a frogman as a kid because he was fascinated by the show *Sea Hunt.*

"I can honestly tell you that I ended up doing what I do because of Mike Nelson [the Lloyd Bridges character in the show] and the idea of working underwater the way he did," Hoban said. "I started out as a [Navy] Seal, working as a bomb technician. Then a friend of mine told me the Secret Service was looking for some bomb techs, and I applied. That was eighteen and a half years ago."

In 1999, Hoban again worked as an Open volunteer, this time at Pinehurst. Early in the week, Fay pulled him aside and asked him a favor. "I'd like you to walk around with Tiger one day," he said. "Take a look at what we're doing [securitywise], and tell me if you've got any ideas or suggestions."

Hoban laughed, remembering the conversation. "What I didn't know was that he was baiting the hook."

Hoban did as Fay asked and thought there were more than enough people in the security detail. Corless was there by then, in addition to police, security people, and plainclothes officers walking outside the ropes. "There were a lot of people," he said. "But what I noticed was that while Tiger was being watched a good deal, golf was also being watched a good deal. I thought there was a need for someone who, in truth, never really looked at Tiger and certainly never looked at the golf. Someone who would just keep an eye on the crowd, watch for anyone who looked out of place inside the ropes. Joe was doing that, but he was just one person, and he needed to keep an eye on Tiger, too. They needed another set of eyes and ears. Someone who was trained to know what to look for."

Gee, Fay said, I wonder who would fit that profile?

With that, Fay reeled in his fish. When the week was over, Fay told Hoban he wanted him to be involved on a more official — but still unofficial — basis the following year at Pebble Beach. "We're talking about the most recognizable athlete in the world," Fay said. "Dan's my security blanket. When he's out there with Tiger, I feel better about things."

When Woods arrived at Pebble Beach, Corless introduced him to Hoban and said that he would be walking with them throughout the week. Woods eyed Hoban's credential and said, "Why? I don't need another scoring guy."

It was then that Corless explained who Hoban was and what his role would be. "I'm a little bit like the advance guy," Hoban said. "Joe stays with Tiger on the range. I'll go ahead to the first tee and check the route and see what it looks like there. Here, for example, on the first day, I noticed that the railing leading around the clubhouse to the tee was on the left — that was the side the public was on. So I walked up to Tiger before he left the range and just said, 'Tiger, when you get to the walkway around the clubhouse, please stay on the right; let Joe walk on the left.' He doesn't ask me why on things like that, he just does it."

Hoban is not one of those security people who thinks of himself as being best friends with the star he works with. "I'd like to think Tiger has faith in what I'm doing," he said. "I enjoy doing it. But it's a business relationship. He comes to the golf course each day to do a job, and so do I."

The difference being that Woods is paid handsomely for what he is doing. Hoban does it because of his loyalty to Fay.

After four Opens with Woods, Hoban felt he knew his habits well enough to get where he needed to get to before Woods did, even on the golf course. "I've reached a point where I have a sixth sense about where he's going to hit the ball on most holes," he said. "I know where the potential trouble spots are, and I try to work with the police to make sure extra people are there. The other day, walking to the seventh tee, some guy with a penknife cut the rope, intending to walk inside, I guess, and ask for an autograph. Before he could move, there was a tap on his shoulder — plainclothes policeman. He had to turn over his driver's license and the penknife. He got them back when he left the property."

It is a long day. Each evening when Woods and his coterie reached his car, Elin Nordegren and Kultida Woods would climb in while Williams loaded the golf clubs in the trunk. Corless and Hoban would simply say, "What time tomorrow?" Woods would tell them — usually sixty to ninety minutes before his tee time — and they would be there waiting when he pulled up.

"There's a certain tension to the whole thing, because if you aren't constantly alert, looking around, making eye contact with certain people, you might as well not be there," Hoban said. "I'm always glad to see him when he pulls up, but I'm even gladder at the end of the day when he gets in that car and drives away. Then, I can relax."

Woods leading the golf tournament (whoops, championship) was going to be the big story of the day, but there were plenty of other story lines by nightfall on Thursday.

The big one was Bethpage itself. There was now no question that it could stand up to the greats of the game. What's more, no one was complaining that the scoring was the result of a tricked-up golf course. There was some grumbling about 10 and 12, and there were a few complaints about the hole location on the 11th. Tom Meeks had made the point during one of the pretournament surveys that he thought 11 was an underrated hole, in part because the green had a little more slope to it than any green on the golf course, other than 15. He and Moraghan had picked what they knew was a slightly risky hole location for the first day, a front, left spot that could cause problems if players were too aggressive.

In fact, a couple of players, including PGA champion David Toms, had misread the slope and putted their ball off the green. Another player who made that mistake was Andy Miller. That made his dad a tad unhappy. When Johnny Miller arrived at the NBC tower a short while after watching Andy putt the ball off the 11th green, his opening comment to Fay was, "I didn't think very much of that hole location at number 11. But since it's the first day, I'm going to give you a mulligan."

"Don't want it," Fay answered. "Take your best shot. I may need the mulligan later in the week."

Later, Fay, Meeks, and Moraghan would all agree that the hole location was close to the edge. "Close," Fay said, "but not over the edge. A lot of guys got off that green without the trouble that Andy [Miller] had."

Even though he bogeyed the 11th, Andy Miller managed to shoot 76, which was shaping up as a reasonable score — three shots better than the score produced by the defending champion. Retief Goosen, who had played in no fewer than forty events around the world since his Open victory, shot a tired-looking 79. David Duval, who had no reason to be tired, shot 78. Hale Irwin, perhaps proving that his fellow senior golfer Bruce Fleisher had known what he was doing when he withdrew, shot 82. Felix Casas, who had managed to get out of Cutchogue, was no doubt wondering, after he shot 88, if it had been worth the trouble to fly in and get a tour of eastern Long Island.

Derek Tolan, on the other hand, had to be pleased with his 78, a respectable score on a brutally difficult golf course in his first round ever in a U.S. Open. Darrell Kestner, playing in his eighth Open and hoping to make his first cut, shot a disappointing 77. He did get one good laugh, though, when, as they waited on the first tee, Kevin Warrick, a twenty-one-year-old amateur who was in his group, turned to him and said, "So, is this your first Open, too?"

Phil Mickelson, still looking for that elusive first major title, shot a solid 70 and pronounced himself quite satisfied with where he was positioned. Nick Faldo, Fay's choice for an exemption, made him look good by shooting 70. Jean Van de Velde, recovering from his long wait on Monday, shot 71. So did Charles Howell, although he probably didn't look at any scoreboards along the way. Jeff Sluman — Fred Ridley and Tommy Roy's favorite golfer — shot 73. Lee Janzen, the man who had replaced him in Mickelson's group, shot 76.

Off the golf course, there had been few major problems. The only scare of the day for anyone from the USGA had come in the middle of the afternoon when Nancy Bennett and Ann McNamara, the gurus of admissions and will-call, were en route to the three o'clock meeting. As they steered their golf cart in the direction of the tennis trailer, a police car came up behind them, siren and lights on. They pulled over, figuring the police needed to get past them. No, the police wanted them.

"I didn't think we were going *that* fast," Weiler said later.

It turned out that the police surveillance cameras had picked up two men coming through one of the gates who they thought might be wanted on felony warrants. They asked Bennett and Weiler if they could run the tickets — whose bar codes had been recorded going through admissions — to see if the names on the tickets matched up with the men wanted on the warrants. As it turned out, the police tracked the men down later and learned they were not wanted men.

"Scared the heck out of us, though," Bennett said.

Roger Harvie had been given a scare when representatives of the state turned up after a report had been filed Wednesday because an NBC tractor had backed into a grandstand. There had been a few minor injuries — mostly cuts and scrapes — but the incident had brought the state out, wondering about the security of the grandstands. In all, there was seating in the grandstands around the golf course for 23,962. The last thing the USGA needed at this stage was someone going through the golf course testing every one of them.

Harvie assured the inquisitors that the grandstands were quite sturdy, had been tested on numerous occasions, and that the accident had been one of those flukes that occurs on occasion. He then made sure both Brad Race and Bernadette Castro knew what was going on in case the state decided to take the issue any further.

There was also the ongoing Bo Dietl problem. Attendance by security staff had not improved as the week went on — in fact, it had dipped after cresting at 70 percent on Tuesday. Worthy and Romaney Berson had informed Dietl that they were negotiating with another security company to bring in extra people for the weekend. The lines in the volunteer lot for pat-downs continued to be a problem, as did lines at the train station. That was partly good news though: the lines were long because so many people had actually heeded the pleas of the USGA and everyone else and chosen to ride the train rather than drive. Prechampionship calculations had been for perhaps 12,000 people a day riding the train. The number was turning out to be closer to 20,000.

There was also a request from a frustrated Amy Mickelson. The crowd following her husband was so thick that her parents, trying to follow along, could see very little of the actual golf. Amy was able to see because she was allowed inside the ropes. Why, she wondered, couldn't her parents walk inside the ropes with her?

The answer, of course, was simple: Let one set of parents inside the ropes and any parents requesting the same access had to be accommodated. Mike Davis was sympathetic but adamant. "I understand that it's difficult when you're related to one of the big-name players," he said. "But we've already got half the world inside there with the big-name groups. We said wives only, and we have to stick to it."

They didn't *exactly* stick to it, try though they might. On Sunday afternoon, Leonard Shapiro of the *Washington Post* was kneeling next to the third tee as Sergio García prepared to tee off. He slipped a little and bumped into the person kneeling next to him.

"Sorry about that," Shapiro said.

"No trouble," said a somewhat accented female voice. "It is very tight in here."

Shapiro glanced at his neighbor. It was Martina Hingis. He did not demand that she be removed since she was not García's wife.

Neither did anyone else.

20

Rain, Rain, Go Away . . .

TOM MEEKS AND Mike Davis got their first surprise of Friday when they arrived for their morning setup a few minutes after five A.M. Checkpoint Charlie had been dismantled. Or, at the very least, security had taken a breather. Both men were able to drive into the clubhouse lot without being stopped at all.

"I coulda driven an atom bomb right up to the clubhouse if I'd a wanted to," Meeks reported to Bob Nuzzo.

"I think you might have been stopped before it got to that," Nuzzo said. But he wasn't happy. Clearly, someone on the overnight watch had let down their guard. Access to the clubhouse and golf course area — places like the maintenance barn and vendor areas — was less restricted before six A.M. A number of trucks with equipment and cars making deliveries had temporary passes that allowed them to get through to those places before the six A.M. shutdown of Round Swamp Road. But they were all supposed to be checked.

"An atom bomb," Meeks repeated to anyone who would listen — and a number of people who weren't listening.

Since Meeks wasn't carrying an atom bomb, it soon became apparent that the biggest problem of the day was going to be the one thing completely out of human control: the weather. The report for Friday called for rain in the morning, slackening off to showers in the afternoon. At least there were no thunderstorms in the forecast. The last thing anyone wanted on cut day was a delay that would force the second round to be completed on Saturday. That had happened the last two years at the Open, and it made no one happy.

"It can rain all day as far as I'm concerned as long as we get the cut made by dark," said Tom Meeks. "From what we hear, it shouldn't be too bad. And this golf course drains well."

The rain was already coming down hard when the first groups teed it up at seven-fifteen, and as the day progressed it was apparent that the "slackening to showers" part of the weather report had been wrong. If anything, it rained harder as the day wore on, and the question became how long the USGA would keep the players on the course under such conditions.

The answer was, a lot longer than the PGA Tour would.

"It's an outdoor event," David Fay said when the question was posed to him. "It is also not a union [read PGA Tour] event. On tour, the players are the bosses. They want to get off because it's raining, they get off. Here, we make the decision, not them." Since there was no lightning threat, the major problem was keeping some of the greens squeegeed so players could putt on them.

The USGA stance annoyed a number of players. The most vocal on the subject was Sergio García, who had about as bad a day on the golf course as a person can have. It certainly didn't help his mood that, in a reversal of Thursday's tee times, he was being shuttled to the 10th tee just as Tiger Woods was arriving in the warm, dry clubhouse, having shot 68. Woods had started by birdieing the first two holes, then played steady, unspectacular, patient golf the rest of the way around.

"On a day like today, you have to remind yourself that everyone's playing in these conditions, accept the fact that it's going to be a long day, and just plod your way around," Woods said when it was over. "That's what I did today. I stayed patient, took double [bogey] out of play on the holes where I made mistakes, and got through it."

Woods's maturity was in direct contrast to García's behavior in the muck and the rain. The Spaniard's first shriek of frustration came after his opening tee shot at the 10th. His hand slid off the club, he screamed in agony, and the ball flew to the right. He managed to make par by crushing a two-iron onto the green, but then he lost his drive right again at the 11th, and that led to a double bogey. He managed to recover to birdie the par-five 13th but then bogeyed Trey Holland's Heartbreak Hill, the 15th.

The area around 15, 16, and 17 is right in the heart of corporate tent land. It is also close to the Trophy Club, located near the 15th, a large tent where ticket holders who opt to pay $450 for the week (as opposed to $275 for a grounds pass) can go to stay dry on a rainy day and have a few beers. The corporate tents were pouring drinks for their clients all day, too. And, as you might expect on a dreary, soaking rainy day, a good number of people were staying inside, watching the golf on TV monitors, and having a few — or more than a few — pops. Then, when the glamour groups came through the neighborhood, they might poke their heads outside to watch them play a little bit.

Anyone watching on TV could see that García was having an awful time on the first few holes. His golf wasn't very good, his body language was showing a lot of anger, and his infamous preshot waggle, where he picked his club up and down behind the ball seemingly countless times, was out of control. By the time he reached fifteen, the crowd had started to count his waggles. The average was in the mid- to low twenties, with a high of twenty-nine. It was maddening to watch, to the point where those playing with García would make a point of looking away while García was waggling in order not to get dizzy.

García heard the counting. As he made his way through the tent-surrounded holes, the jeering and taunting grew louder. Apparently, the line that really got to him came on the 16th fairway when someone yelled, "Hey, Sergio, how's it feel having a girlfriend who's won more majors than you?" García whirled in the direction of the voice and delivered what appeared to be a middle-finger salute.

"It was a fist," he said later. "Sort of."

The crowd had gotten rowdier as the day went on. Most were cold and soaked, many were inebriated, and a lot of them were covered with mud. According to the police, most of the trouble was in the area around the corporate tents, and almost all of those who were warned, asked to leave, or, in a couple of cases, arrested wore corporate badges.

"Most of the real golf fans were just having a good time out there," Nuzzo said. "There weren't a lot of hecklers in the grand scheme, which was more than 42,000 people."

There was one fairly spectacular arrest. A man who had really had too much to drink decided it would be fun to ride a golf cart. He found one sitting near the second tee, hopped in, and took off. He didn't get very far down Round Swamp Road before he was stopped by the police. He was charged with stealing the golf cart — and with driving that cart under the influence.

García's struggles — the waggling, the heckling — continued unabated most of the way around. He finally holed out on the ninth green almost six hours after starting, with a 74. Remarkably, he agreed to come to the press tent for an interview. As it turned out, that was another mistake.

After patiently going through his birdies and bogeys, he was asked if he thought play should have been stopped at any point.

"I certainly did," he said. "And I don't know if Tiger Woods had been out there, I think it would have been called."

That statement was wrong, wrong, a thousand times wrong. In fact, the USGA had come very close to calling play a couple of times during the afternoon. The key was whether players could putt to the holes on the greens. If a player landed in casual water on a fairway or even in a bunker, he could simply move his ball. If there was so much water around the hole that he couldn't get a putt to it, then play had to be stopped. At one point, Tom Meeks got a call from the 17th green saying there was too much water around the hole for players to putt. He put out a call on the radios saying that if the water could not be removed for the players to putt, play would have to be stopped. There was a similar problem on number two. Both times, the squeegee crew was able to clear enough room around the holes for the players to putt.

"It was close a couple times," Davis said. "I think our thinking was if we polled the players and said would you rather suffer out here a little longer and get this over with or come back here at seven-thirty in the morning to finish, almost all of them would say they wanted to finish. The golf course *was* playable as long as we kept squeegeeing the greens. Was it pleasant? No. But it was playable."

By midafternoon, the golf course had the look of a battlefield after platoons of tanks had moved through it. Tony Zirpoli, taking player scorecards next to the ninth green, looked outside his trailer at one point because he could hear the constantly squealing tires of the shuttles trying to get players back to the clubhouse. "The turning area out there looked like Stalingrad," he reported.

Fay laughed when he heard what García had said. "Actually, this is the way it works," he said. "Tiger and I have worked out a telepathy thing. Wherever I am, he can send me a signal telling me what to do. I never got a message this afternoon saying we should stop play, so I didn't stop play. Of course, if I had, I would have had it stopped immediately. Anything Tiger wants, Tiger gets."

As soon as Johnny Miller got off the air — the telecast had been extended because of the slow play caused by the weather — he had made his way to nine, which was (or so it seemed to Miller) miles from the tower at 18, to watch Andy finish.

"The whole afternoon was torture," Johnny Miller said. "On Thursday, I was able to watch most of his round because he played in the morning. But Friday, I was in the tower the entire time he was on the course. I was following it on the computer and it was killing me because I could see he had a chance, but I knew it was going to be close. As soon as we were done, I headed straight to nine."

By then, the final group of Andy Miller, Kevin Warrick, and Darrell Kestner was in the fairway. Miller needed par to make the cut,
Warrick needed a bogey. Both had driven the ball in the fairway,
and even though they could barely see the green, both managed to
find it and two-putt for par. That made Warrick the only one of the
five amateurs in the field to make the cut and Miller the only son of
an Open champion to make it.

"It's not quite like my dad," Andy Miller said. "His first Open [at
Olympic as a nineteen-year-old amateur in 1966], I think he finished ninth [actually eighth]. Still, this is great. I'm glad I hung on
and made it. I'd like to go out and shoot some good numbers
tomorrow and Sunday."

He was cool, calm, and collected as he spoke. His father was a
wreck.

"I'm really proud of him, shooting 74 today, in these conditions,"
he said. "I know I sound like a dad, but he's a good player. He has
the game to play on the PGA Tour and do well if he can just get
himself there."

Andy Miller certainly had the kind of mindset about golf that
would serve him well if he ever did get to the tour. A year earlier,
playing in the first round of Q-School, he had been well within the
qualifying number on the last day when he missed a birdie putt on
the back nine. Slightly aggravated, he tapped his putter against his
shoe and, unwittingly, bent it slightly. Just after he tapped in, he
noticed what he had done. It was only a small bend, one no one
else would have noticed, but he immediately told his fellow competitors that he had played a stroke with an altered club and disqualified himself.

Now, there was no need to do anything like that. He had made
the cut at his first U.S. Open. Maybe it wasn't as good as his dad,
but it wasn't bad, either.

Most had thought the cut would come at about 147 or 148, seven
or eight over par. But with the conditions worsening throughout
the day, the scores kept climbing. By the time the last groups hit

the ninth and 18th greens at a few minutes after eight o'clock, in near darkness, it was apparent the cut was going to be 150 — 10 over par.

Once the round was over Meeks was dispatched to the press tent to explain why play had continued and to make it clear that who was on the golf course had no effect on the decision. Meeks was also peppered with questions about the tees on 10 and 12, which many players had called virtually unplayable since the rain and the wind made the holes so long. On tour, rules officials will often adjust a tee or the length of a hole, depending on the conditions on a given day. Meeks told the media that the USGA's policy was to not move a tee marker more than five yards forward or backward, regardless of the conditions.

"When they saw the conditions today, they should have moved the tee on number 10 up to compensate," said Nick Price, echoing the thoughts of many players. "You had to hit the ball 250 yards in the air into the wind to get to the fairway. A lot of guys just can't do that. It wasn't fair."

Deep down, Meeks knew Price and the others had a point. When the Open was over, in his postmortem memo on the golf course, he would recommend that if the Open ever returned to Bethpage, 20 more yards of fairway should be created at number 10, and the area over the left side of the bunker on number 12 should also be fairway.

But this was Friday night, at the end of a long, brutal, wet day. Sitting in the press tent, still shivering after fourteen hours on the golf course, Meeks wasn't about to concede an inch to anybody.

"As far as I know," he said, "just about everyone on the PGA Tour can hit a tee shot 250 yards."

He said nothing about 250 yards on the fly or into the wind.

The players weren't the only ones affected by the rain. By the middle of the day, the Green Course parking lot was, for all intents and purposes, washed out. Late-arriving corporate customers were turned away because the lot was nothing but mud. The Polo Fields parking lot was almost as bad. By the time the three o'clock group gathered for its meeting, it was apparent that both parking lots would not be available the next day. The plan was to send as many people who parked at those two lots as possible to SUNY Farmingdale. The rest would have to go to Jones Beach.

This was a crisis. The first group that had to be dealt with were the caddies, who had been parking at the Polo Fields.

"There's no way we're going to be able to get the word to all the caddies that they can't park there," Jon Barker said. "If they show up at the Polo Fields and then have to get back into traffic and park someplace else, especially if it's Jones Beach, they may miss their tee times. And that would be a disaster."

Dave Catalano pointed out that there were small portions of the Polo Fields that could still be used. Perhaps a sign that read Caddy Parking Only could be put outside the Polo Fields lot. That would no doubt anger some others who would be sent elsewhere, but it seemed like the best possible compromise.

That scenario had just been worked out when a very tired-looking Steve Worthy walked in, his clothes caked with mud. "I just got word," he said. "We can't go to SUNY tomorrow. We're having to tow people out of there right now. By the time we get everyone out tonight, there will be no way to safely park people there tomorrow."

That brought a lengthy silence.

"What are our options?" Barker asked.

"I think we really have only one option," Worthy said. "We've got to send everyone to Jones Beach and do everything we can to get the word out to as many people as we can that they all have to go there." He smiled wanly. "I guess the only good news is there should be plenty of parking over there because it doesn't look like much of a beach weekend."

Getting the word out was going to be a major undertaking. Even then, there were going to be people who would show up and try to talk their way into the closed lots; everyone knew that. There would be a lot of volunteers who, on hearing the news, would probably decide not to show up. But there were no alternatives. A second meeting to decide exactly how to carry out the new parking plan was scheduled for later in the afternoon to give Worthy, the police, the people from the state, and Craig Smith a chance to come up with detailed plans on exactly what to do.

The Open makes its cut one of two ways: it either takes the low sixty players and ties or it takes everyone within 10 shots of the leader. This was going to be a low sixty and ties year, since there were a grand total of nineteen players within 10 shots of Woods.

As always, there were prominent names who failed to make it to the weekend. One was David Duval, who fought back on Friday and looked for a while as if he might make the cut before fading to a 73 that left him one shot out at 151. Colin Montgomerie, in spite of the 25,000 Be Nice to Monty buttons handed out by *Golf Digest Magazine* as part of a campaign to get American fans to treat Montgomerie with more respect, also shot 151.

He took missing the cut in remarkably good spirits. He even laughed when Jeff Sluman asked him how much he had paid for the 25,000 buttons and joked about his constant battle with his weight. "When I was a boy, my parents had a rule: I couldn't play any sport until I cleaned my plate," he said. "I got in the habit of always cleaning my plate. Now I need to get out of that habit and stay out of it."

For the moment, he would have plenty of time to contemplate how to do just that.

Retief Goosen, the defending champion, also went home after shooting 79–75. So did two-time champion Lee Janzen (Sluman, by the way, was tied for twentieth at 146), who had shot 76–77; Stewart Cink, who had finished third in 2001, was one of those who simply couldn't handle the Friday conditions, skying from 70 to 82. The same thing happened to Billy Andrade, who went from 72 to 82. The three players who had started the championship on Thursday all went home Friday: Paul Goydos improved from 80 to 78, as did Jerry Haas. Actually, all three players shot 78 Friday, Mike Muehr adding that score to his opening 77. Steve Pate never did recover completely from the gout that had bothered him during the qualifier and shot 82–75. "At least I don't have to walk this course again," he said late Friday. Darrell Kestner shot 77–86. Felix Casas, no doubt worn out by all the flying, cabbing, staying in motels, and the rain, was 10 shots worse on Friday than Thursday, shooting 92, the high round of the week. He left, saying he was still thrilled to have played at all.

Derek Tolan said the same thing after shooting 88 on Friday. "I knew right away that this was going to be too much golf course for me," he said. "I mean, it was hard enough on Thursday when the conditions were good. Today, whoa, it just ate me up."

Still, Tolan would leave with lots of memories and would have a new car waiting for him when he got home. "The whole week has been so cool," he said. It didn't end on Friday, either. Saturday morning, still sporting his player badge, he was on the range, hitting shots with the pros. And why not?

The press releases were handed out just as play was ending. Everyone coming to the U.S. Open by car on Saturday, except for players and caddies, was to consider Jones Beach the one and only available parking lot. Fans were encouraged, urged, begged to take the train if at all possible. All the local radio stations had been contacted and asked to make the announcement as often as possible through the night. All the local papers would print announcements. Volunteers were being contacted whenever possible by phone or by e-mail. The Department of Transportation, which had fifty-two different traffic signs directing people posted throughout the area, would have all of them direct people to Jones Beach.

Almost all the shuttle buses would be sent to Jones Beach, as would most of the available security people. Steve Worthy and Romaney Berson had signed a contract that day with Securitas, the company that owned Pinkerton, to supply another twenty-four guards for the weekend at a cost of $25,000. Worthy would deal with Bo Dietl and the no-show issue when the event was over.

"I should have known it was going to be a long week with those guys when I was driving past the 15th fairway on Tuesday night and saw one of their guys out there hitting a shot into the green," Worthy said. "If there was any doubt at all about whether things were going to get better, it should have been gone right then."

The guard did not get a second attempt to hit the green.

For the moment, BDA had become a minor concern. The biggest question to those running the Open on Friday night was not can anyone catch Tiger (the consensus was no) but can we get people out here to *watch* Tiger?

Woods had a three-shot lead on Friday night over Ireland's Padraig Harrington and a staggering seven-shot lead on everyone else. K. J. Choi, Davis Love III, Sergio García, and Jeff Maggert — who was almost as steamed as García at the USGA for not halting play — were tied for third at 142. Phil Mickelson, Billy Mayfair, and Shigeki Maruyama, who shot a miraculous 67 in the afternoon, aided by a hole in one at the 13th hole, were another shot back, at 143.

Brad Lardon had made the most of his first major, shooting 73–73 for 146 and a tie for twentieth. He would play with Sluman on Saturday. Lardon was one of six players who had made it through both local and sectional qualifying who had made the cut. Each had beaten remarkable odds to play the last two days at the Open, and by doing so, they made themselves exempt from the locals in 2003. "Now *that's* a bonus," said Jason Caron, who had shot 75–72 to make the cut, the 72 being one of the low rounds shot in the afternoon.

Caron was a month shy of thirty, a slightly built New Englander (Hyannis, Massachusetts) who was in his second year on the Buy.com Tour. He had benefited from his pairing, playing with Tom Gillis and Todd Rose the first two days. Gillis, who was thirty-three, had the distinction of being the only American playing as a full-timer on the European Tour. Caron and Gillis were friends from 1995, when both had played on the Hooters Tour, a minor league a step below the PGA Tour–controlled Buy.com Tour. Caron had called Gillis about playing a practice round together when he saw they had both qualified and then a day later was delighted when he learned they had been paired together. Playing together seemed to relax both of them. Gillis also made the cut at 147, and as luck would have it, they were paired again on Saturday.

This was Caron's first major and he admitted to being somewhat in awe of the whole thing. "I think I've gotten a little better with it each day," he said. "Monday, I walked out on the range, looked around, and saw wall-to-wall people. I mean, I don't care what anyone says, just qualifying for this thing is a big deal. At least to me. I mean, how many people in the world can say they qualified for the U.S. Open?"

He was also somewhat in awe of the course. "I couldn't believe the rough when I first saw it. I mean, they must fertilize and fertilize and fertilize. I've seen rough, played a lot of golf, but I've never seen anything like this. I kept telling myself to work some of my nerves out each day. By Thursday, I was okay, except at the beginning. Then I had a chance to really have a good round until I played the last four, five holes in four over. That didn't make me happy."

He recovered to play those same five holes in one under on Friday when the back nine was his first nine. He had talked that morning to Brett Quigley, a close friend who had played in several Opens. "Brett told me that if you start trying to figure the cut on the front nine on Friday, whatever you figure, it's going to be a shot or two higher than that because guys get nervous and the conditions are so tough," he said. "Before I went out I was watching the telecast, and they were saying the cut looked like eight, so I figured, maybe it will be nine. I never thought it would go to ten. When I hit the last hole at seven over, I thought I was in pretty good shape."

Caron, Gillis, and Rose were in the second-to-last group of the day (night?), and when they had arrived at the ninth green the crowd in the soaked grandstand was exactly twelve, all of them friends and family of Caron. When he had made a pretty chip to four feet and holed the par putt, the twelve of them had stood up and done the wave. Caron's grin was just about as wide as the wave itself.

21

Homestretch

WHEN JON BARKER arrived at his office at a few minutes before six on Saturday morning, he found several messages. One had been left on his desk. It was another request from Amy Mickelson. No, she wasn't asking that her parents be allowed inside the ropes. This time she wanted to know if New Jersey Nets star Jason Kidd, who wanted to see Phil play, could be allowed inside the ropes, since he would be mobbed if he walked outside.

Barker knew the answer, but he checked with the powers that be anyway. Kidd would have to take his chances outside the ropes.

Barker then checked his phone messages. One came from a woman in Arizona who wanted to make sure the USGA let NBC know that her grandson had won a long-drive contest by hitting a ball 372 yards. She thought it would be very nice if NBC would pass this information on to its viewers during Saturday's telecast.

The next message came from a man in Spokane, Washington, who had read Sergio García's comments about the weather and Tiger Woods. He said he saw no reason why García should not be penalized for his unsportsmanlike comments, that it would be entirely justifiable to add two strokes to his Friday score since he had embarrassed himself and the game with what he had said.

That would definitely be a new one for the rule book: "trash-talking, two-shot penalty."

Finally, there was a call from someone in the office of Manute Bol, the former NBA player who had been doing a good deal of charity work in his home country, Sudan, since he retired. Mr. Bol, the woman explained, was planning to come to the Open on Sunday, but because he was 7 feet 7 it would be impossible for him to squeeze into any kind of shuttle bus. Therefore, he needed a clubhouse parking pass.

Barker called Steve Worthy on that one. Worthy, being an ex-basketball player, was very familiar with Bol and could understand why riding a shuttle bus might be difficult for him. But there was simply no clubhouse parking available, especially with the governor and various state politicians planning to show up on Sunday. "Tell him he can ride the handicapped shuttle," Worthy said. "That's the best I can do."

The good news that morning, at least in terms of logistics and security, was word from New York senator Hillary Clinton's office that she wasn't planning to attend on Sunday. Earlier in the week, Kathy Paparelli, Mike Butz's senior executive assistant, had taken a call from Senator Clinton's office. She was informed that the senator might want to come to the golf tournament on Sunday. "If she comes," Paparelli was told, "the Senator is planning on bringing her husband with her."

That would be the former President of the United States or, as he is apparently known in Hillary Clinton's office, the senator's husband.

But now neither the senator nor her husband would be coming Sunday, which meant the only member of the Secret Service who would have a role to play would be Dan Hoban. That would make everyone's life simpler.

The other good news was the weather. The rain had finally cleared off in midmorning and the weather was still cool enough — the high would be 63 — that Jones Beach would not be inundated with beachgoers. That meant that if people got the word to go there to park, they would not arrive to find parking lots that were already full.

Most fans and volunteers seemed to have gotten the word about the parking change. The larger problem was telling the corporate people who showed up expecting to park at the Green Course that they couldn't. Notifying corporate folks that their VIP parking stickers now entitled them to park with everyone else at Jones Beach and ride the same shuttle buses as everyone else was bound to cause some screaming and yelling.

"Oh, yeah, we heard about it," Mimi Griffin said. "Part of our package is VIP parking. A lot of people were angry that, all of a sudden, they didn't have it anymore. The mistake we made was not putting into the package that if there was a major rainstorm, the VIP lot might have to shut down. I think in the future, if we're parking people on grass rather than concrete, we'll certainly do that."

Live and learn.

There was also some confusion among the players about the Saturday pairings. Normally the rule in re-pairing after the second round is that ties are broken by a first in, last out formula. In other words, if ten players shoot the same score, the player who posted that score first gets the latest tee time, the player who came in last, the earliest. But with a two-tee start, it was basically impossible to determine exactly who finished when, so players with identical scores were simply placed in a blind draw and assigned tee times randomly by the Unisys computer used to compile scores and statistics.

This surprised the players, because on the PGA Tour, where two-tee starts are the norm on Thursday and Friday, first in, last out is simply determined by tee times. "Who came up with this?" asked Vijay Singh, who made the cut on the number and then found himself in the first group out at 9:10 A.M. "You tell the guy it was a bad idea and I'm not at all happy about it."

No doubt the USGA would reconsider the system for next year on that basis.

On the range, which was still quite muddy after all the rain, there was a lot more room for players warming up, even if Derek Tolan was still hanging around. The field was now down to seventy-two players from the original 156, and with everyone going off in twosomes from one tee, the preround atmosphere was far more relaxed, at least in terms of getting players where they needed to go.

The caddies had come up with the trivia question of the week: Next to Tiger Woods, who among those still left at Bethpage had the most lucrative clothing and shoe contract?

Answer: Martina Hingis.

Hingis's boyfriend had started his day by leaving a note in Woods's locker apologizing for his comments of the day before. To his credit, he did not make the oft-used, smarmy claim that he was somehow quoted out of context, he simply said he had spoken from frustration and he was sorry. It was a noble effort but almost not worth the time. Woods is not the forgiving sort. And even if he isn't angry at you, he is going to try to step on your neck on the golf course anyway. It is part of his greatness.

One person who wasn't contrite about anything was Jeff Maggert. Maggert was thirty-eight, a very solid player, a three-time Ryder Cupper who had top-tenned in the Open five years out of six, including a pair of fourths. He had spent most of the opening round on Thursday complaining to Jim Reinhart, who was the rules official with his threesome, about the course setup this year and in past years. Reinhart found this baffling since Maggert had played so well in the Open.

"I was thinking, doesn't this guy realize that he's made more money playing Open course setups than at just about any other event in the world?" he said. "Finally, on the 12th hole, he started in again, and I just walked away and said something like, 'Please take your case to someone who cares.' I'd just had enough."

As luck would have it, Reinhart, who is one of the USGA's top rules people, was assigned the Maggert-García group on Saturday, the third-to-last group of the afternoon. Maggert had arrived on the tee in a fairly grumpy mood, telling Ron Read, "I don't want anyone from the USGA coming anywhere near me the rest of the week." Read, always polite, noted that might be somewhat difficult since the USGA was, in fact, still running the championship.

Shortly before the players were introduced, Reinhart went through the ritual of shaking hands with everyone who would be in the group: walking scorer, standard-bearer, players, and caddies. García, a big smile on his face, greeted him warmly. Maggert turned and walked away before Reinhart could offer his hand or open his mouth. Oh, boy, Reinhart thought, this is going to be fun.

As it turned out, it was fun. Both men played superb golf all day, and García was like a new man, laughing at the occasional heckler, clearly enjoying himself. Maggert, even though he didn't make a bogey all day, never cracked a smile. He was still seething over Friday's conditions and over David Fay's comments about why play had continued.

Walking off the 10th tee, Reinhart had no choice but to be a USGA person who came close to Maggert, since he had to return his scorecard to him so he could keep García's score on the back nine. (The cards are checked after nine holes, then returned to the players.) Reinhart waited until Maggert had played his second shot to the 10th green, then walked over to hand the card to Maggert.

As he accepted the card, Maggert said to Reinhart, "Oh, and you can tell David Fay I said he's a f—— idiot." Reinhart wrote down the quote, leaving out the profanity, and said he would be sure to pass Maggert's regards to Fay. When he heard the comment, Fay shrugged. "Maybe he's mad because a couple of years ago I told someone that I was concerned that, the way we were setting up our golf courses, we might end up not identifying the best players in the world but the Jeff Maggerts of the world."

Yes, that might have upset him just a little.

The golf course was in remarkable condition, considering all the rain that had been dumped on it. Outside the ropes was still a muddy mess, but inside the ropes, the fairways had drained well, and the greens, amazingly, were rolling 14.5 on the Stimpmeter when Meeks, Davis, Ridley, and Moraghan went out to set the holes in the morning.

"I told them the greens weren't going to be a problem," Craig Currier said as he took his midmorning drive around the golf course with girlfriend Joanna Ryan next to him and his dog Tilly — named, of course, for Tillinghast — in the back. "Actually, the entire course held up well." He smiled. "I don't even want to think about what they've done to my fairways on the Green Course. But at least they shut it down today. I'll worry about that when this is over."

Currier made no bones about who he was rooting for to win. "Tiger," he said. "You have the Open once in your life at the golf course you've worked on, why not have the greatest player of all time win? Plus, we have the same birthday — December thirtieth."

But if Currier was way past feeling nervous about the golf course, he was still a little bit jumpy. For weeks, he had been planning a huge Sunday night party at the maintenance barn to celebrate the end of the Open. Everything was in place, including the engagement ring for Joanna. Currier was planning to propose to her in front of about 300 people the next night.

"I'm afraid I may choke when I get up there," he said earlier in the week. "I mean, what if she turns me down? How embarrassing would that be?"

Currier was a man who exuded self-confidence, someone who, as Catalano had put it, had bounded into the room for the biggest job interview of his life. When he talked about Sunday night, though, his mouth twitched a little bit and he readily admitted, "I'm scared to death."

In other words, the rain on the Black Course was, at that moment, the least of his weekend worries.

The bad news as the day wore on was that there still weren't enough security people. Securitas had promised twenty-four guards; eighteen had showed up. The BDA attendance continued to run at about 70 percent. The good news was that it appeared most people had gotten the word about Jones Beach, and with Felix Sorge concentrating a large chunk of the guards he did have available in those lots for pat-downs, people had been able to get on buses and to the golf course with little delay.

In fact, if you walked around and asked most people how they had enjoyed the Open and what problems they had encountered, most said they were having the time of their lives and shrugged off the extra security, the pat-downs, and even the delays.

"I can't tell you how great the people out here have been," Jeff Sluman said as he waited to tee off Saturday afternoon. "Maybe they had trouble with a few drunks yesterday in the rain, but overall, this has to be the greatest crowd I've been around at any major in this country. The British Open is different, those people just *love* golf so much."

"Don't get me wrong," Sluman said later. "I'm exhausted. The Open exhausts you. This course is exhausting. I remember playing my practice round on Wednesday, looking at the green at number three and thinking, gee, I hope they don't put the flag way left behind the bunker this week. Walk out there Thursday and that's exactly where the flag is. They go right to the edge with some of their pin positions. [Tom Meeks: "There are no pins out there, Jeff!"]

"Can you imagine what the course would have been like if we'd have gotten hot, dry weather? My God! We all get on the USGA a lot, and sometimes we're right. They messed up on 10 and 12, and I think they know it. But they deserve credit for doing this. It was a big gamble, and they won. I would think this will change their stuffy, snobby image. I would hope it would."

The players' feelings about the golf course may have been best summed up by Donnie Hammond. "I'd like to come back here sometime and play when I can enjoy the golf course and have fun playing it," he said. Would he be willing, he was asked, to sleep in his car to get on the golf course and play it for fun? "No," he said, "but I'd be willing to pay to sleep in a Hyatt to play it."

The final twosome of the day, Woods and Padraig Harrington, teed off at 2:50 P.M. By then, everyone had been shuttled over from Jones Beach. All the temporary roads that had been needed to get carts and equipment through the mud were down, and there was just one day left for everyone to survive.

Steve Worthy was standing outside the operations trailer, preparing to deal with one last three o'clock meeting. He looked toward the hill that led from the parking lot down to the operations area, and a look of almost indescribable joy came over his face. Walking toward him was his wife, Diana. Running toward him, at full speed, was his two-and-a-half-year-old daughter, Sydney, named for his late father. The exhaustion that Worthy had been feeling nonstop for ten straight days seemed to disappear as he caught his daughter and held her in his arms for the first time in more than three weeks.

"Hi, Daddy," Sydney Worthy said softly.

Steve Worthy didn't answer. He just held on to his little girl.

There would be other moments at the U.S. Open that would receive a lot more attention than this one. In all likelihood, there wouldn't be any more enjoyable to watch.

A few minutes later, Worthy — and everyone else — was back in the real world of the tennis trailer — for the last time.

In truth, there was a feeling of triumph in the room just twenty-four hours after they had faced the grim reality of the lost parking lots. The sense was that they had gotten through it. The number of people who had been turned away at the closed parking lots had been minimal, and considering the scramble mode they had been in on Friday, they had come through relatively unscathed.

For the most part, other than going over the logistics of the awards ceremony, which would include Governor Pataki, the last meeting had the feel of the last day of camp. The group had only been together for seven days, but they had been seven intense, emotional, and often difficult days. "I just want to thank everyone for their patience," Bob Nuzzo said. "I know we haven't been perfect, but we've tried awfully hard. I hope you've had that sense during the week."

"Let me answer that this way," Mike Butz said. "Do you guys travel?"

That even got a smile from Nuzzo's boss, Greg Sittler.

It was the shortest meeting of the week — under an hour. Someone asked Dave Catalano when the golf courses would reopen. "Everything but the Black will be open on Wednesday," he said. "I might have tried for the weekend with the Black if not for the rain. Now I think we'll shoot for a week from Tuesday." He smiled. "I'm comforted, knowing what deep pockets the USGA has when it comes to repairing golf courses."

The one issue left that had everyone a bit concerned was the late starting times the USGA had agreed to for Sunday. At NBC's request, the last group was not going to tee off until 3:50 P.M. At a normal pace of play, that would get them to the 18th green at about 7:45 P.M., leaving about ten minutes for the awards ceremony and sign-off at eight o'clock eastern time.

This was pushing the envelope in a way that it had never been pushed before. NBC had signed off at eight o'clock eastern time in the past, but not when the event was being held in the eastern time zone. In 1998 and 2000, it had signed off at eight o'clock from the West Coast — meaning a five o'clock finish locally. Now, shooting for eight o'clock local time left just about forty minutes of cushion before sundown. Almost any delay would create the very real possibility of a Monday finish.

Fay was, of course, aware of this. He had been aware of it when Dick Ebersol first approached him about it. He had said yes to Ebersol, knowing the later start would create higher ratings, but with one caveat: "We get any word that there's potential for bad weather and we move the times up."

Earlier in the year, with late afternoon thunderstorms in the forecast, the Lords of Augusta had moved their Sunday starting times up by an hour. As it turned out, the storms never showed up.

The irony in Fay's decision was that he often talked about how lucky the Masters had been through the year, scheduling its finish for seven o'clock in the eastern time zone at a time of year when there was no more than an hour of daylight left at that point. Since the Masters, unlike the Open, uses a sudden-death playoff format, a tie means sending the players onto the course in rapidly fading light. In 1989, when Nick Faldo had beaten Scott Hoch on the second playoff hole, it had been raining and nearly dark when he holed his 25-foot birdie putt for the victory.

"There was no way they could have played another hole that year," Fay said. "Those guys must have a deal with the devil or something, because every playoff they've ever had (five since sudden death was adopted in 1979), they've never needed more than two holes."

Fay didn't have to worry about a playoff, since his would be on Monday over eighteen holes if it occurred. But the Bethpage weather report was worrisome: sun early, clouds midday, thunderstorms late afternoon. When Butz and Davis saw that report, they suggested moving the tee times up by at least thirty minutes. After further discussion with NBC, a compromise was reached: the last group would tee off at three-thirty.

Jeff Hall was responsible for receiving the players' scorecards after they finished their rounds. Normally, players walked into a trailer near the 18th hole to hand in their cards, but at Bethpage, Hall was working in a small room in the clubhouse, right behind the cashier's stations.

Hall had been handling scorecards since 1991 when Tom Meeks had been moved from the scorer's tent to the golf course as the master of roving rules officials. He had grown accustomed to the fact that he was often the first USGA face that golfers encountered when they were angry, frustrated, or simply looking to vent. "I never take it personally," he said. "Because almost all the time, I know it isn't meant personally."

He had caught the brunt of Tom Lehman's anger over the hole location at 18 at the Olympic Club in 1998 and had been gratified when Lehman came back to the golf course later that day specifically to apologize to him. "Shows you what kind of guy he is," Hall said. "I always try to remember what Frank Nobilo said to me one time: 'Jeff, we're not having a go at you, you're just the one who happens to be sitting here.' I understand."

The complaints this year had been predictable: Bob Tway had been disturbed by the hole location at 11 on Thursday; Scott Verplank had barked at Hall on Friday about the tee shot on 10. A number of players had asked exactly what it took to get play delayed during Friday's deluge.

When players arrive in the scoring area, the routine is almost always the same. Most bring their caddies with them. Also in each group is the rules official, the walking scorer, and the standard-bearer. Almost invariably, the players will sign a golf ball or two for the standard-bearer. If the walking scorer asks for one, he or she will get one. The players will sit down and exchange scorecards, since each has kept score for the other. Each player will double-check his card against his memory and then ask the walking scorer to call out his hole-by-hole score to make certain there are no discrepancies on the cards. There have been too many incidents through the years for players not to be extremely careful about knowing exactly what they are signing before they sign the card. Once it is signed, it is final.

No one wants to pull a DeVicenzo. In 1968 at the Masters, Roberto DeVicenzo finished tied for the lead with Bob Goalby. But his playing partner, Tommy Aaron, had accidentally given him a four on the 17th hole when he had actually made a birdie three. DeVicenzo failed to notice the mistake, signed his card, and that became his official score, giving Goalby a one-shot victory.

In a sense, the incident haunted both men, DeVicenzo for the obvious reason of having blown a chance to win the Masters, Goalby because he never felt he was given full credit for being the champion. Years later, there were still people saying and writing that Goalby should have refused victory on those grounds and should have insisted on a playoff. Those people failed to realize that Goalby didn't have that option; the rules of golf don't allow for such loopholes.

On this Saturday at the Open, Hall's assignment, after receiving the cards, was to tell the players about the late tee times for Sunday. Most players were surprised. Nick Faldo, who had made Fay look awfully good after shooting a championship low 66 to move into contention, looked at Hall and said, "An hour later than today? Really?"

"I'm just the messenger," Hall said. "Could be moved up a little, depending on the weather, but that's the plan now."

When Hall gave Brad Lardon and Jeff Sluman the news about the starting times, Sluman smiled and said, "What are we going to do, finish under the lights?"

No one is chattier in the scorer's area than Scott Hoch. He had been paired that day with Jay Haas, his old Wake Forest teammate. "How'd you guys come up with the pairings?" he asked as he reviewed his card.

"Completely random," Hall said, referring to those who had the same score at the end of Friday.

"Really?" Hoch said, smiling. "I thought you put the two of us together because we're old teammates. I told Ron Read on the tee that he should introduce us that way — you know, they played together at Wake Forest — and he said no, he couldn't do that. He's too tight, you know?"

Hall was nodding, Haas was smiling.

"Good job by you guys with the two-tee start, though, especially during the practice rounds. Made a big difference. Didn't it, Jay?"

"Absolutely," Haas said.

Hoch finally came up for air long enough to allow Hall to tell both players about the late start on Sunday. Hoch gave Hall a look. "You guys playing yourselves into a situation here?" he asked.

Hall, as he had been doing all day, repeated his line about being the messenger.

As they got up to walk out, Haas turned around and said, "By the way, Scott will be here all week."

There is nothing more vulnerable than a wet golf course, especially on a day with little wind, and the scores reflected the change in conditions. The rain hadn't slowed the greens, but it had certainly made the golf course softer, meaning the players could fly their shots at the flags, knowing they would stop.

On Friday, the scoring average for 155 players (Toshi Izawa had withdrawn after a first-round 80) was 75.7. A total of six players had shot par 70 or better. On Saturday, the scoring average was 72.1, and twenty-nine of the seventy-two players shot par or better, led by Faldo's 66 and 67s by Phil Mickelson, Sergio García, and Vijay Singh — regardless of their tee times.

Woods had finally turned human, or something close to it. For fourteen holes, even under the relatively benign conditions, he failed to make a birdie, and he was two over par for the day when he crossed the road to the 15th tee. At that moment, the field had closed in on him, led by García and by Mickelson, who had just birdied the 17th to one of the hugest roars ever heard on a golf course, to join García at one under par for the week, just two shots behind Woods. For Mickelson, that margin was amazing, since he had started the round eight shots behind Woods and had seen the margin grow to ten shots after he bogeyed three of the first five holes.

"At that point, getting into contention was the last thing on my mind," he said. "I knew how far I was behind, and I was figuring even if I did make some birdies, if Tiger went low, it wouldn't matter anyway. But then I did get things going and looked up on the back nine and things were looking a lot better."

At that moment, Woods and Mickelson were only a couple of hundred yards from each other, Mickelson walking up the steep hill to the 18th tee, Woods facing Heartbreak Hill on the 15th. Golf tournaments (or championships) are not decided on Saturday, but what happened next was an absolutely crucial moment.

Mickelson hit a two-iron on the 18th, wanting to be sure to find the fairway. He didn't, pushing the shot into the left rough (remember, he's a lefty). While he was trudging off the tee, Woods was bombing his drive to the middle of the 15th fairway. While Mickelson was pitching back to the fairway from an absolutely dead lie in the rough, Woods was hitting what might have been his best shot of the week, a soaring six-iron that settled 12 feet from the flag. Mickelson hit his third shot in to about 12 feet. His putt for par just missed. Woods holed his birdie putt at 15 and gave one of his fist shakes, as if to say "about time."

In those few moments, you could feel the momentum swing. Mickelson walked off 18 feeling good about shooting 67 and getting himself back into contention but disappointed with the bogey at 18. As it turned out, he had also missed a chance to put himself into the final pairing with Woods. Woods, now pumped up, hit another gorgeous six-iron on 17 to within eight feet and made that putt for another birdie. Then he parred 18 to shoot 70 on a day when he was clearly struggling with his swing.

He had started the day with a three-shot lead. Now he had a four-shot lead. The difference was in the pursuers. On Saturday morning, the only player within seven shots of him had been Padraig Harrington, a very solid European Ryder Cupper but not someone who had seriously contended in a major before. Paired with Woods, he had shot 73, the only over-par round among the top eleven men now on the leader board.

García, who had gotten through the day with only a few hoots and hollers directed at him, was in second place, the only player other than Woods under par, at one under for the championship. Mickelson and David Fay's pal Jeff Maggert, who had shot a bogey-free 68, were tied for third at even par. Then came Australian Robert Allenby, Billy Mayfair, and Harrington, one shot further back. Faldo and Justin Leonard were plus two — seven shots behind the leader.

Woods had led seven major championships on Saturday night and had won all seven. Most people figured he had already had his "bad" day for the week, and he still led everyone by at least four shots. But this *was* the U.S. Open. There were quality players chasing him. At one stage on Saturday, Mickelson had sliced seven shots off the lead during a stretch of twelve holes. Certainly, anything could happen. Everyone kept saying that crazier things had occurred on the last day of a major than Tiger Woods blowing a four-shot lead.

Of course, pressed to name one of those things, no one could come up with an answer.

For his part, Woods was taking no chances. After he finished doing his postround media interviews, he headed straight for the range. It was almost seven forty-five by the time he got out there and it was getting cool, but he wanted to try to fix whatever it was that had gone wrong during the day. Somehow, word had gotten around that Woods was returning to the range — maybe Fay used telepathy to pass on the word from Tiger — and the grandstands were packed.

The crowd went crazy when Woods, Steve Williams, Joe Corless, Dan Hoban, Woods's teacher Butch Harmon, and the ever-present state troopers walked onto the empty range. Woods hit balls for about forty minutes and then surprised everyone by lingering to sign autographs for almost half an hour.

He, too, had learned from Jeff Hall after signing his card about the late tee times — he wouldn't hit his first shot the next day until three-thirty in the afternoon, so there was no sense rushing home to get to bed early. He signed for people until it was almost dark, then he and his group went straight to the parking lot where his mother and Nordegren were waiting. He pulled out of the parking lot a few minutes before nine. The place was almost empty by then except for the range rats who were now waiting for buses on the far side of the parking lot.

"About one-thirty tomorrow" were Woods's parting words to his support/security group.

They were surprised. That was earlier than normal. But this was the last day of the U.S. Open. Everyone around was awarding Woods the trophy that night. Everyone except Woods.

22

Wait Until Dark

THE LAST DAY of a major is always a long one. Everyone is tired, running primarily on adrenaline. And the late tee times for the leaders make everyone antsy, leaving jangled nerves just a bit more frayed by midafternoon.

The Open is unique because the final round is always played on Father's Day. If nothing else, that fact gives TV an angle it always plays in some way. Every Open champion is a son; most are fathers.

NBC had a ready-made Father's Day angle in the presence of Andy Miller. Andy Miller would be long gone from the golf course by the time NBC went on the air since he was teeing it up in the fourth group of the day at 10:10 A.M., but they could still talk about him. The first group of the day, which teed off at 9:40 A.M., was John Daly and Kevin Warrick, the amateur. Warrick had shot 84 on Saturday, including a nine on the 18th hole when he had driven it in the rough and, according to his description, had whiffed at least twice trying to get his club on the ball before finally taking an unplayable lie. Daly had shot 81. Having made the cut on the number, it was just about impossible for him to care very much about how he played when he started the third round fifteen shots behind the leader.

Daly's interest in the final round was evident in his warm-up: he hit three wedges, three middle-irons, and three drivers. Then he walked to the putting green and, with a cigarette in one hand, hit three one-handed putts and declared himself ready to go.

The over-under on how long it would take Warrick and Daly to play was about two hours and forty minutes. Daly is fast when he's grinding. When he's got one eye on the exit sign, he does everything but wear a jet pack. As he and Warrick walked off the first tee, Ben Nelson, a longtime PGA Tour rules official who knew Daly well, shook his head and said, "That young man [Warrick] better not bend over to tie his shoes at any point because if he does, he's going to find himself playing in a single."

Johnny Miller was on the golf course long before the first group. He made a habit on the weekends of grabbing a golf cart and driving the entire course. He wanted to check the rough and putt the greens to gauge their speed (they were lightning, rolling at just under 15) while also checking the break from different angles so he could make intelligent observations about which way putts were going to go when the leaders got on the golf course. He worked quickly but meticulously, making notes as he went.

Since Andy was teeing off so early, he had time to watch for a while before he reported to the booth. Once he had finished his survey, Miller headed back across the road and, to avoid the galleries, went down the 12th fairway, then cut back over to the fourth hole, figuring he would come upon Andy and Stuart Appleby while they were playing the third hole. When he got near the fourth tee, he found that the path through the trees that would have given him a shortcut to the third tee was too muddy to steer the cart through. He had to go the long way, up the cart path, and come up on the other side of the bleachers that were behind the third tee.

He was, by his estimate, about a hundred yards away when he heard a massive roar coming from number three. Some roars on a golf course are unmistakable. Miller knew right away that this was a hole-in-one roar, especially at this hour of the morning. It just couldn't be anything else, since no one on the golf course was even close to contention. "I figured there was a fifty-fifty chance it was Andy," he said.

He parked his cart behind the bleachers, walked around it, and was mobbed by fans as soon as they recognized him. "Congratulations, Dad, your son just made a hole in one!" people were screaming. Or, "How about *that* for a Father's Day present!"

Miller had tears in his eyes by the time the crowd pushed him to the teeing area. Andy and Appleby were walking on the green, the crowd down there screaming its approval. When the ball rolled into the hole, Appleby, who had already started walking off the tee when the ball was in the air, had raced back to Andy Miller, a huge smile on his face. He shook his hand and said, "Wow, what a Father's Day present *this* will be!" At that moment, he was like everyone else in the gallery.

Tommy Roy keeps a camera rolling at all the par-threes throughout play in case of a hole in one. He couldn't possibly have dreamed that he'd get a scene like this on tape almost five hours before the leaders teed off.

Walking onto the green, Andy heard the yelling back at the tee. He picked his ball out of the cup and waved it in the direction of his father. Then he turned and tossed it into the crowd.

"Well," Johnny Miller said as Andy and Appleby walked to the fourth tee, "I guarantee that nothing that happens out here today is going to top this for me."

One could certainly understand that sentiment.

Before things got too crazy, Mike Butz made his annual Father's Day call to his dad, not long after Andy Miller's ace. The call was especially poignant for Butz since his parents, both in their mideighties, had been fighting health problems all year.

"The only bad thing about working this tournament every year is never getting to be home for Father's Day," he said. "I'll never forget, though, two years ago, at Pebble, I made the call to my dad and I asked him how he was doing. He said, 'I am doing *great*.' I asked what was up and he told me he had made the first hole in one of his life the day before — at the age of eighty-four. I can remember feeling a chill run right through me, knowing how much my dad has always loved golf and how much time we had spent together on the golf course. A hole in one at eighty-four. His first. Can you imagine that?"

Unlike with the Millers, that was a Father's Day (or day before) hole in one where the son had tears in his eyes.

The fans had arrived early. It was warmer than it had been but still quite comfortable. Many fans went out to walk with the early players, while others took up stations in the grandstands around the finishing holes, wanting to guarantee themselves spots when the final groups arrived. Even before Daly and Warrick sprinted onto the final holes, the grandstands around them were full. When Frank Rossi, one of the many volunteers working on Currier's crew for the week, put the flag in at 18 a few minutes before noon, he received a standing ovation.

Richard Spear was watching as the flag went in. He had been driving around the course helping with the final details of course setup each morning. It had been Spear who had recommended Currier to David Fay five years earlier, and he couldn't help but feel tremendous pride in what had been accomplished.

"I still remember the first call from David asking me to come over and look at the golf course," he said. "There was never any doubt in my mind that you could make this place great again. The only trouble was neglect. The turf here has always been good. The soil on Long Island drains well because it's nothing but a big sandbar."

He waved a hand around. "Now look at the place. It has its majesty back. Craig did great work here because he's such a perfectionist. That's why he was the right guy for the job. But the USGA did a special thing. It was an act of social integrity. To tell you the truth, with everything that has gone into it these last seven years, I think I'm going to be a little bit depressed tonight when it's over."

A lot of people who had worked a lot of hours were feeling that way. Bob Nuzzo, his mission almost accomplished on Sunday morning, still had one thing he desperately wanted to do: Get Dave Catalano into a helicopter so he could see what his park looked like from the air. Catalano had never flown, but he had told Nuzzo he would go up with him on Sunday morning if Nuzzo could arrange it.

Every morning, a state police helicopter made an inspection sweep to check the highways and all the surrounding areas near the park to see if there were any trouble spots. Nuzzo had taken Currier on that trip Friday morning. On Sunday, Catalano was the passenger.

"Getting Dave up there and seeing the look on his face when he saw his place from up above will go down as one of the great thrills of my life," Nuzzo said.

Catalano was understandably nervous getting into the helicopter, but after the first few seconds — "My stomach turned upside down a little," he said — he was fine. "I looked over and Bob was watching me closely to see my reaction," he said. "Once I got past the first few seconds I enjoyed it. And what a sight this place is from the air!"

In a sense, that twenty-minute trip to Jones Beach and back was Nuzzo's Father's Day present to Catalano. And Catalano's to him.

There were eight players who would start the day within seven shots of Tiger Woods. Realistically, they were the only ones with any chance at all to catch him.

But that didn't mean other players didn't have goals. At the Open, the top eight finishers and ties qualify for the next year's Masters. The top fifteen and ties qualify for the next year's Open. There is also quite a lot of money to be made if you can go low on the last day. First place was worth $1 million, but tenth was worth $125,000, which isn't a bad week's work, especially for some of the nontour players who had made the cut. So with only a few exceptions, almost everyone playing on Sunday was playing hard because there was still plenty to play for.

Brad Lardon had been tied for twentieth place going into Saturday. Having achieved one goal — make the cut in his first major — he had come up with a new one that was going to be a little tougher to achieve: make the top eight and qualify for the Masters. "This could be the best chance I ever get," he said. "I'm playing well, I've got some confidence, why not?"

But his nerves, so steady the first two days, finally kicked in on the front nine on Saturday. Even with a very comfortable pairing (Jeff Sluman) and the golf course relatively benign, he hacked his way to a 40 going out. "I was really angry with myself," he said. "I told Powell [Holly, a college buddy from Rice who was caddying for him for the week], I am *not* going to shoot some hacker's 82 out here."

He was as good as his word on that, coming back to shoot 34 on the back nine. Still, the 74 on a day when so many players went low hurt him, dropping him back to a tie for forty-second place. That would make the top eight almost out of the question, although the top fifteen might still be possible with a good day Sunday. "My wife told me if I can start the way I've been finishing I'll do fine," he said with a tired laugh Saturday evening. "I'm going home to watch the baseball game [Rice was playing Texas in the College World Series], put my feet up, and try to come back strong tomorrow."

Jason Caron was also hoping that a strong Sunday might get him to the top fifteen. He had shot 73 on Saturday and was tied for thirty-fifth place. Perhaps the most surprised man in the field to still be playing on Saturday was John Maginnes. The man who had thought he was out of the Open after the Purchase qualifier only to find he was in the Open was pretty convinced he was going to miss the cut after a 79 on Thursday. But he had come back to shoot the third lowest round of the day Friday, a 69, and made the cut with two shots to spare. A 73 Saturday left him tied for fifty-third, but he wasn't complaining.

"I've been playing with house money since I bogeyed the first hole of the playoff at Purchase," he said. "This whole experience has been nothing but good as far as I'm concerned."

The mood around the clubhouse and on the course was almost festive as one twosome after another was sent off by Ron Read, resplendent in the socks his daughter Alicia had given him that said I ♥ Dad.

Governor Pataki had arrived by helicopter shortly after eleven o'clock and was making the rounds on the golf course almost as if this were a campaign appearance — which it was, since election day was less than five months away. He received a huge ovation walking in front of the bleacher at the 17th where the crowd was, to put it mildly, feverish. The only trouble came later in the day when he walked back in to prepare for the awards ceremony and a couple of the policemen who had been trailing him on bicycles tried to follow him up the soggy hill leading to the now-empty first tee.

No way. They slipped, they slid, they fell. Eventually, they got off the bicycles and, somewhat sheepishly, walked them up the hill.

The loudest ovation of the day came when Phil Mickelson, playing in the penultimate group with Jeff Maggert, walked onto the first tee. It was Mickelson's thirty-second birthday, and everyone within a hundred miles of Bethpage was apparently aware of that fact. Just as many people seemed convinced that the perfect storybook ending for this Open would be for Mickelson, the father of two young daughters, to catch Tiger on Father's Day to win his first major title.

The problem was that Tiger didn't seem to read a lot of storybooks.

Nonetheless, when Mickelson walked onto the first tee, the entire crowd, packed into the grandstand and up against the ropes near the tee, burst into a raucous, extremely off-key rendition of "Happy Birthday." It was warm and funny and charming. And it was all of those things the first seven or eight times it happened as Mickelson made his way around the golf course. By the time Mickelson hit the back nine, however, those walking with him probably were hoping never to hear the song again.

Even so, Mickelson was clearly touched by the enthusiasm. Maggert would say later he had never in his life seen a player receive so much support. Part of it was people wanting to see Mickelson lose the no-majors monkey, part of it was people genuinely liking Mickelson, and part of it was people wanting to see someone — anyone — challenge Tiger.

The final pairing was a TV dream: Woods and García. Early in the day, Mike Davis had received word that some of the scoreboard operators were putting up lettering on the message part of their scoreboards that said Tiger vs. El Niño, a reference to García's nickname. No, Davis said, there would be none of that — this wasn't the British Open, where blatantly pro-British messages were the norm on Sunday scoreboards. This was the U.S. Open, where Kevin Warrick was considered — at least officially — to be no different from Tiger Woods.

The tabloids were, needless to say, slobbering over the duel of the girlfriends, Elin Nordegren and Martina Hingis. Someone half jokingly suggested that if Disney, one of Woods's many sponsors, was smart, they would set up a Woods-Nordegren vs. García-Hingis match for their next hokey prime-time Battle at Bighorn or whatever it was called. Now *that* might get a rating.

Woods walked onto the putting green just as Mickelson was being serenaded on the first tee. Dan Hoban was already on the tee, scoping the crowd. Butch Harmon was a few steps behind Woods when he reached the putting green. Roger Maltbie, who would be walking with Woods and García, couldn't help himself when he saw Harmon.

"There he is, golf's answer to Bundini Brown!" Maltbie yelled, receiving a half smile, half grimace in return from Harmon. Bundini Brown had been Muhammad Ali's shadow throughout his years as heavyweight champion. Harmon stayed close to Woods because Woods wanted him to stay close. He was the lone survivor from the original group Woods had around him when he first turned pro. In itself that was remarkable, because unlike most who worked for Woods, he remained friendly and open to most people who approached, even the media. It just wasn't in his nature to snarl and growl the way many on Team Woods often did.

Later in the summer, Woods would announce that although Harmon was still his teacher, he wasn't going to be working with him as closely or as often as in the past. Most of the speculation on this change centered on Harmon's outgoing nature. If he had a weakness as Tiger's teacher, that was apparently it.

But all was well on this shining Sunday as Woods walked onto the tee at 3:27, about a minute after García arrived. Both received ovations so raucous that Maltbie shook his head and made his second boxing reference of the day: "This feels like a heavyweight championship right now."

Reed Mackenzie, who would walk as the rules official with the last group, and Brad Race were both standing on the tee at that moment. Each congratulated the other on the work his organization had done during the week. For once, in politics, each meant what he was saying.

Woods walked over to where García was standing, holding the scorecard Read had just handed him. They shook hands. "Let's have a good one out there today," Woods said. Read handed him his scorecard. García turned back to the table where all the scorecards and pencils and tees and fruit were and picked up some extra tees. He turned to Tiger and offered him some tees. Woods looked at him as if he were a traveling salesman trying to sell him a vacuum cleaner.

"No," he said, waving his hand and walking away.

The niceties were over.

At three-thirty, Read stepped to his microphone for the 124th and final time of the week. "Good thing," he said a few minutes earlier, holding up his wrist. "The official watch is falling apart."

The watch made it to the final starting time. "Ladies and gentlemen," Read said, "this is the final pairing of the championship."

It had taken John Daly and Kevin Warrick precisely three hours to get around the golf course, a little bit longer than most had predicted. Each had played reasonably well — Warrick shot 74, Daly

73. Warrick had a lot of time to kill since he would be a part of the awards ceremony as the low amateur. Daly was heading back to Catalano's house to get the RV rolling almost the minute he finished signing his card.

There was one problem. With all the mud that had accumulated in the yard after the rain, Daly could not get the RV moving. It spun and spun and didn't move. He would need a tow to get loose. He called the USGA office for help. Steve Worthy and Frank Bussey made their way over there to see what could be done. They had the equipment to get Daly free, but there was no way to get it through the throngs following the late groups. Daly would have to wait until Woods and García cleared the second hole, which would be in another two and a half hours. Daly wasn't happy, but he understood. He went back into the RV to wait.

By the time Craig Currier and his crew came to give Daly the tow he needed, a huge buzz was making its way around the golf course. Mickelson had gotten off to the fast start he needed by birdieing the first hole. Woods had come up 50 feet shy of the flag with his second shot on number one, putted up to six feet, and then, as gasps came from the crowd, missed the par putt. One hole, a two-shot swing. García parred the hole. He and Mickelson trailed by three. On number two, Woods hit the green again, missed his birdie putt by about two and a half feet, and then watched his second putt do a 360 around the cup and stay out.

He looked stunned. Everyone was stunned. Maybe the unthinkable could happen. The lead was two, and perhaps most shocking, Tiger Woods looked nervous.

But Woods isn't Woods for nothing. He took a deep breath on the third tee and began to play the kind of resolute golf that has marked his game ever since he won his second major in 1999 at the PGA Championship. His first major, the 1997 Masters, was a cakewalk, a twelve-shot victory during which the final round was little more than a coronation stroll. But in '99 he'd had to hold off a charging nineteen-year-old García at Medinah and had done so by one stroke. Since then, he had been impossible to catch from behind when it mattered.

Now Tiger began hitting fairways and greens, one after another, his swing a near-perfect repeating metronome. He parred the next four holes, then birdied the difficult seventh. The nerves might still be there, but they weren't showing anymore. He was a rock, looking away every time García went into his waggling routine, then planning his next shot. In the meantime, Mickelson, who couldn't afford to make any mistakes, made two, hitting wayward drives at five and six that led to bogeys. By the time they made the turn, Woods led Mickelson — who had recovered briefly to birdie the eighth — by four and Maggert by five. García, struggling with his swing, was six back. Like so many others paired with Woods on the weekend at a major, he simply couldn't get anything going, surrounded by the aura of Tiger.

"I won't be intimidated playing with him," he had said Saturday. "What's intimidating is knowing I have to make up four shots on him in eighteen holes."

Now only Mickelson was within four shots, and there were only nine holes left. The crowd was literally imploring him to try to make a move, and he was trying with every bit of strength, physical and emotional, that he had left. The golf course had worn everyone out, and clouds had started to gather overhead. With nine holes left, everyone was simply trying to make it to the finish. Even Woods.

A late afternoon thunderstorm had been predicted the night before, which was why the tee times had been moved up twenty minutes from the original plan. Now the possibility that good luck would prevail the way it had at Augusta in April had vanished. By four o'clock, Mike Butz began warning the rules officials around the golf course that a delay at some point was likely, and he would keep them posted. By five o'clock, he was telling them it was inevitable. Bill McCarthy and Robbie Zalzneck were dispatched to begin getting the evacuation vehicles ready should players have to be brought back to the clubhouse.

At this stage, many players were already finished. The conditions were tougher than on Saturday. It was dry but breezy and the course got fast in a hurry. A lot of players were simply worn out after four days of battling the Black. Andy Miller, even with the one on his scorecard, shot 75 to tie for sixty-second place at twenty-over-par 300. John Maginnes shot 78 and was one shot better, tied for fifty-ninth with two past major champions, Greg Norman and Bob Tway. Brad Lardon also shot 78 and was alone in fifty-eighth place. The $13,988 he made almost doubled his earnings on tour for the year.

Jason Caron shot 73 to tie for thirtieth and collected a check for $35,639, one of the biggest of his career. "I would hope this will help my confidence," he said. "My goal is to be on the PGA Tour next year. I was thirty-fifth on the [Buy.com] money list last year, and right now all I'm thinking is make the top fifteen and get my [PGA Tour] card. This was an awful lot of fun though, a memory I'll carry with me for a while." He would carry it with him to the Tour in 2003 after surviving Qualifying School in December. Among the six players who had made it through the locals to the weekend, Caron was the highest finisher.

Jeff Sluman shot 73 the last day and tied for twenty-fourth. Scott McCarron birdied the third hole on Sunday by rolling his tee shot up from the front to the back and making the putt, but that was the only highlight in an otherwise awful day as he tumbled from a tie for tenth to a tie for thirtieth with a 78. Davis Love III (who had a much easier time getting his RV rolling off of Catalano's property than Daly) and two-time past champion Ernie Els were among those tied with Sluman at 291.

The cutoff number to make the top fifteen and qualify for the 2003 Open turned out to be 288, eight over par. Steve Stricker and Shigeki Maruyama each missed by one. Charles Howell missed by two. Still, there would be no worrying about the scoreboard for him in 2003. He ended up in the top thirty on the money list at year's end, guaranteeing him a slot in the Open.

Jay Haas clinched a spot in his twenty-fourth Open by shooting 72 on Sunday to tie for twelfth place. Minivolcano Dudley Hart was one of those tied with him, a huge relief. Hart had been one of the last players to earn an exemption in '02, rallying on the back nine on Sunday at the Colonial to make enough money to clinch a spot. There was one week left, but Hart was taking it off because one of his infant triplets, born the previous December, was having surgery the next week to relieve some bleeding on the brain and he wasn't planning to play. The surgery went fine, and Hart's 12th-place finish in the Open meant he did not have to sweat his exemption in '03.

Perhaps the happiest man on the grounds not leaving with a trophy in his hand was Tom Byrum. At forty-one, Byrum, who had won once on Tour in his career (1989 Kemper Open), wasn't even fully exempt in 2002, having finished 129th on the money list the previous year. He had exactly one top-thirty finish in a major in his career — a ninth at the 1997 PGA — and had only played in one Masters. By hanging on and shooting 72 on Sunday, Byrum squeezed out a tie for eighth place at 286 with Nick Price and Padraig Harrington. That put him into both the Masters and the Open in '03, and the $138,000 check put him a lot closer to regaining a full exemption on the tour.

"This is a great feeling," he said. "I'd go out tonight and celebrate, but I'm too exhausted. I'm just absolutely whipped."

He spoke for everyone.

At 5:35 P.M. the weather warning signs went up on the scoreboards. That meant that even though play hadn't been stopped, a storm was imminent. It also meant that the grandstands were supposed to be cleared.

"Please clear the grandstands," the marshals, as they had been trained to do by Roger Harvie, announced as soon as the warning signs went up.

No one moved.

On the radio, Tom Meeks, who was roving near the 17th green, was reporting that no one was leaving the grandstands.

Tim Moraghan heard Meeks and laughed. "Are you kidding?" he said. "Most of those people have been sitting there since ten o'clock this morning. They'd rather be hit by lightning than give up those seats they have now."

He probably wasn't exaggerating by much. The police showed up at 17 and 18, and, grudgingly, fans began moving very slowly from the grandstand. It still wasn't raining, and Mike Butz wanted to keep the players on the golf course for as long as it was safe. He wasn't going to take any risks once the storm started to move into the area, but he didn't want to be premature.

Just before six o'clock, he saw the storm starting to close in. "Everyone out there, get ready to evacuate the course," he said. "Let your players know that the next shot they play may be their last for a while, so if they don't want to play them, they don't have to."

There were nine groups left on the course at that moment — eighteen players. Nick Price and Craig Stadler were walking onto the 18th green. Woods and García were on the 12th green. Mickelson and Maggert were one hole ahead.

At 6:02, Butz told Meeks in no uncertain terms: "Count 'em down and get 'em off, Tom — now."

Meeks began a thirty-second countdown, and at 6:03, air horns went off all around the golf course, stopping play. Everyone except Price and Stadler, who were lining up their putts on 18 and not allowed to finish, was carted off to trailers to wait. Price and Stadler sat out the delay in the clubhouse. The weather interns (Penn State meteorology students hired for the week by the USGA) calculated the storm would last less than an hour. If true, Woods and García would have about ninety minutes of daylight to play the last six holes. At that moment, Woods's lead over Mickelson was down to two shots because Mickelson had just birdied the par-five 13th. Woods still had the advantage of having the par-five left to play, but the ball game was still on.

If the weather would cooperate.

Woods and García took refuge from the storm in one of the

weather trailers, accompanied by caddies, girlfriends, Woods's ever-present agent, Mark Steinberg, and Reed Mackenzie. Woods and García were miffed that there was no water in the trailer, but beyond that, everyone quietly sat and waited. Fay, in the NBC booth, calmly explained on the air how a weather delay was dealt with, noting that the storm was expected to pass quickly enough that there was no reason to bring the players back into the clubhouse.

Nerves were *really* frayed now. Everyone knew that the print media would fry the USGA if the late starts created a Monday finish. "If that had happened, I'd have taken the heat for it, and justifiably so," Fay said. "I made the call to go along with NBC and the late start. If it went bad, it would have been my fault."

Luckily, the rain stopped fairly quickly. At 6:52 P.M., with the crowd now reassembled in the grandstands, screaming for play to resume, Meeks, after doing a roll call to make sure everyone was in place, blew the horn to restart play.

Jim Farrell, who was roving on the final day as a troubleshooter, shook his head as play began and said, "Now it's a race between Tiger, Phil, Sergio, and darkness."

Neither Woods nor García is a fast player. García is quick to get over the ball but then spends forever gripping and regripping. Woods is always deliberate, especially with a major championship on the line. A final pairing of John Daly and Lanny Wadkins would have been much more to the USGA's liking. As it was, all anyone could do now was watch, wait, and hope . . . for a finish.

On the radio, Mike Butz's voice could be heard saying: "Anybody got any Maalox?"

Any real question about who would win the championship was removed shortly after play was restarted. Woods absolutely crushed his drive on 13, hit his second shot on the green, and two-putted for a birdie. Soon after that, even with the decibel level higher than it had been all week, Mickelson bogeyed 16 and 17.

The odds were that Woods wasn't going to blow a three-shot lead at that point, but once Mickelson made those two bogeys any lingering doubt was removed once and for all.

The loudest roar — if it was possible to measure roars — of the week at the 17th had come a few minutes before Mickelson arrived, when Scott Hoch, resplendent in a shirt with an American flag on the front, made the second hole in one of the day and the third of the tournament, with a three-iron. "I was between three and four," he said. "My caddy called for a three, I went along, and I guess he was right." Buoyed by that shot, Hoch finished tied for fifth with Nick Faldo, who made Fay look awfully good with his first top-five finish in a major since his fourth-place finish in the 1996 British Open.

Everyone now knew Woods was going to win — the question was when. While Butz and Jon Barker carted the Open trophy to the 18th green and began setting up the table that would hold it and all the other requisite hardware, Steve Worthy and Frank Bussey were putting together a string of auxiliary lights to use, they hoped, during the awards ceremony but, if necessary, while the last group played the 18th hole.

Mickelson and Maggert finished at 8:18 as dusk closed in and the temperature began dropping. Both parred 18, Mickelson for a 70, Maggert for a 72, leaving them at even par 280 and two-over-par 282. Woods was standing on the 18th tee, having bogeyed the 16th, with a four-shot lead. If his lead had been one, with dusk approaching, he might have refused to play the hole. But, leading by four, he wanted to finish as much as anyone. His drive found the fairway.

By now, the crowd was packed around the 18th green about as tightly as you can be packed. "Hey, cameraman," a woman yelled at an NBC cameraman waiting for Woods and García to come up the last hill. "Look behind you, Rudy Giuliani is sitting over there wearing a Yankees cap!"

"Great," said the cameraman. "I'm a Braves fan."

Worthy had finally rescued Laura Southerland from Nuzzo and the police and had brought her out to the green to watch the ceremony. García missed the green, chipped to eight feet, and missed the par putt. He quickly tapped in and cleared the stage for Woods, who had about a 30-foot birdie putt. It was nearly dark. Woods cozied the putt up to about four feet, but, working quickly for once, missed the par putt. Before he could walk over to tap in, someone in the stands yelled, "Bethpage Black rears its head one last time!"

Actually, this bogey had more to do with the blackness than with the Black. Finally, at 8:28 P.M., Woods tapped in. He had shot his only over-par round of the week, 72, with two bogeys on the last three holes as he coasted home. But he was the only player under par, three under at 277, with Mickelson three shots back, Maggert five, and García, after a 74, six shots behind.

Woods held his arms up in celebration, too tired to do much more than that. He was quickly escorted off the green to the clubhouse to sign his scorecard. Standing just outside the door, waiting for him, was Mickelson.

"Congratulations," he told him. "You played great."

"So did you."

There were some the next day who decided that Mickelson's grace in defeat, his telling the media that he had never enjoyed a golf experience more in his life because of the quality of the golf course and the support of the fans, was somehow a sign of indifference, of being satisfied with second place.

Those people had no understanding of Mickelson. He had given everything he had to give, and it had not been good enough to win. Once it was over, he wasn't going to show his frustration in public. That didn't mean he didn't want to win as much as any player not named Woods. It just meant he wasn't going to let the whole world know it.

The awards ceremony, under the lights, was relatively brief. Reed Mackenzie thanked everyone, beginning with Craig Currier, who stood between Dave Catalano and Woods, beaming.

"Your golf course kicked my butt," Woods told him.

"Not exactly," Currier answered.

Later, Woods signed a flagstick for him.

As Mackenzie went down his list of thank-yous, from Catalano to Bernadette Castro to the 4,850 volunteers, Governor Pataki kept inching closer and closer to the microphone. When Mackenzie looked over his shoulder and saw Pataki, he said, "Don't worry, Governor, you're going to get your chance."

A moment later, he did. Sadly, he did not declare that the state of New York had kept its promise to not fuck this up.

But it had.

Kevin Warrick was given his medal as the low amateur. Mickelson got his silver medal as the runner-up.

NBC's Jimmy Roberts did the ritual posttournament TV interview, and Woods said all the ritual posttournament things about how great the course was, the fans, and how wonderful it was to win the U.S. Open for the second time in three years. "It's especially nice," he said, "to win it here on a public golf course. This was a great week for golf."

As soon as Roberts finished, Woods turned away from him without shaking his hand. The previous year when Woods had gotten off to a relatively slow start to his season (not winning on the West Coast swing), Roberts had made the mistake of referring to Woods's "slump." After Woods had won at both Bay Hill and the Players Championship in March, he had concluded his post-Players interview with Roberts by saying, "Some slump, huh, Jimmy?" Eighteen months later, Woods still hadn't forgiven Roberts.

At 8:38 P.M., bathed in Worthy and Bussey's lights, Woods was handed the trophy by Mackenzie. He gave a short, gracious victory speech, concluding by saying, "I think right about now, I'd like to go have a cold one."

He was certainly entitled.

23

Wait Till . . .

THE END OF the championship and the presentation of the trophy did not mean the end of the evening or that the work was over.

One person who still had plenty left to do was the champion. Woods was taken through the clubhouse and up the back steps to Dave Catalano's office. There, the various TV networks that were granted one-on-ones away from the press tent — ESPN, Golf Channel, CNN — were all given their fifteen minutes with the famous. While Woods was doing TV, Phil Mickelson was brought to the press tent to meet with the masses.

It was nine-thirty by the time Woods got to the press tent, and most of the writers were battling their deadlines. There really wasn't much for him to add. Most of the questions focused on his chances to win the Grand Slam. He was now halfway there, something only Ben Hogan, Arnold Palmer, and Jack Nicklaus had ever achieved. Woods, being Woods, kept insisting he had already won the Slam by winning four straight majors, the last three of 2000 and the first of 2001.

That feat may have been the greatest in the history of golf, but it wasn't a Slam any more than the six straight Grand Slam tennis tournaments won by Martina Navratilova over a two-year period in the 1980s — three to end 1983 and three to start 1984 — was a Slam. It was an incomparable string of success, but it was *not* a Slam. In fact, if one goes by the Tiger theory of Slams, that would mean Navratilova won three Slams, since each time she completed a cycle of four, it would be considered another Slam. Clearly, that wasn't the case. Great as Woods is, he can't rewrite history. Record books, yes; history, no.

As Woods spoke, Bethpage was already beginning to return to normal. Cleanup had started in the now-empty corporate tents. Barriers were coming down. Round Swamp Road was reopened to the public. Buses lined up to take the fans back to their cars for a final time.

The merchandise tent would open again on Monday so that anyone who wanted to come in could buy the few items that were left at 50 percent off retail. One of the prime Monday customers would be Bernadette Castro, who would make a last swing to buy souvenirs for staff and friends. There really wasn't much left to choose from. Lopuszynski and staff would end up moving more than $13 million in merchandise, not including another $3 million for corporate customers — 30 percent more than any previous year.

Steve Worthy, Frank Bussey, and Brant McWilliams were already working on teardown, knowing that the next week would be an absolute mess, with tents being dismantled and equipment and trash being hauled away. Dave Catalano, who would work with the operations people on the teardown, was much too busy Sunday night to think about the future. He had to make sure everyone had what they needed in his office while Woods did his wrap-up interviews. Then he had to remember to get Woods to sign the flagstick for Currier. He made a very brief appearance at the state/USGA celebration party. He never had time to get his photo with Love and Daly.

Then he made his way up to the maintenance barn. Sadly, he

missed the highlight of the evening, Currier's speech to the troops, climaxed by his proposal.

"I want to tell you guys something," Currier said, speaking to everyone who had worked on the golf course before and during the Open. "A lot of people didn't think we could do this five years ago, but, boy, did we do it! Now we can sit back, rest a little, and enjoy. Listen up, though. Drink all you want, stay as long as you want. Celebrate as much as you want. But *please* don't drive home. Sleep here, come to my house — hell, sleep in the bunkers if you want, to because *it doesn't matter anymore!*"

That got a big cheer. Nuzzo, knowing the maintenance party was going to be a blowout, had suggested to Currier that he warn his guys about driving. "We don't want a tragedy in the midst of all this joy," he said.

The next day when Currier drove onto the golf course he found that several members of his crew had followed his suggestion and were sound asleep in the bunkers.

Once he had finished his address to the crew, Currier began to stumble. "Um, there is one other thing," he said. A few hoots could be heard from those in the know. He paused. "Oh, boy, I'm sweating here. I've never done anything like this before."

More hoots.

"Joanna, will you come up here?"

A bit baffled, Joanna walked up to the small podium that had been set up in the open area around the barn. "My mom has always wanted me to do this," Currier said as Joanna's eyes went wide. He began fishing around in his pocket. Finally, he produced the ring box.

"Drop!" they all began screaming. Currier dropped to a knee. "Joanna," he said, "will you marry me?"

Amid the screaming and the cheering no one could tell if Joanna had responded. She appeared to be in a state of semishock, laughing and crying all at once. Finally, someone yelled, "Well, Joanna, what do you say?"

"Yes!" she answered, and the cheering in the maintenance barn sounded every bit as loud as it had been at the 17th green a few hours earlier.

Back at the far more formal "toast to the champion" (without the champion) in the clubhouse, Rabbi Marc Gellman was, arguably, the happiest man in the room. He had walked eighteen holes with Woods and García as the assistant scorer, David Fay's trumped-up title that got him inside the ropes. "I told Marc he was allowed to say hello to Tiger and shake his hand on the first tee," Fay said. "That was it. I even told [Dan] Hoban, if he starts gabbing, tell him to stop. Marc's a great storyteller. The last day at the Open isn't the time for storytelling."

Gellman understood. He was thrilled to be there, thrilled that he finished the walk, and beyond thrilled at what he had witnessed during the week.

"People do not understand how great this is," he said. "For all of us who love this golf course, who see it almost as a living, breathing thing, this was the week we waited for all these years, the week when we would find out once and for all if it was everything we thought it was. And it *was*. One player, arguably the greatest of all time, under par. *One*.

"Everyone had a great time — the players, the fans — even with all the security. The police were great, too. This is an example of something important — you can do well by doing good things. The USGA did a good thing by coming here, a very good thing. And I think it is safe to say it is going to do very well when all is said and done."

If Woods and García had not been able to finish that Sunday night, a large chunk of the good feeling that had been built during the week would have gone down the drain. Making everyone trudge back on Monday morning to watch one or two holes would have been awful. It certainly would have been terrible for NBC, forced to sign off on Sunday night without a conclusion. It would have been brutal for the players and for those volunteers who would have been willing or able to come back. It most certainly would have put a major crimp into the postchampionship victory parties in the clubhouse and at the maintenance barn.

But it didn't happen. Even though some media members clamored for Fay to come to the press tent to explain his thinking on the late tee times, he refused. "If we hadn't finished, I would have gone down there without being asked," he said. "But we finished. It's an issue if we have to play Monday. Then I have to go in there and take all the hits. As it was, it turned out to be a nonstory. Thank God."

As soon as NBC signed off, Fay said his good-byes to Dan Hicks and Johnny Miller and climbed down from the tower next to the 18th green. He drove his golf cart to the cart barn and turned in his key for the last time. He checked to make sure Joan, his wife, and Molly, their youngest daughter, had gotten away from the golf course without any problems. Then he walked back to the clubhouse.

The toast to the champion party was in full swing at the far end of the building. Fay had no interest in any toasts. Instead, he walked into the now-empty Tillinghast Room, which had been the USGA staff dining room during the latter part of the week, and was pleasantly surprised to find there was still food there. "I've been gorging on pretzels all afternoon," he said.

He sat down with a tired smile and glanced up at the TV, which was showing the Mets-Yankees game being played a few miles down the road at Shea Stadium. The Yankees had an early lead, and Fay, the old Yankee fan, was pleased to see the score.

"This is perfect," he said. "I'll get out of here in time to avoid any postgame traffic coming out of Shea. And best of all, I can listen to the game on the radio on the way home."

He was pleased Woods had won. "Best player winning validates the golf course a little bit more," he said. "Not that I think it needs validation after this week."

He stood up to leave. There was no final look around. He walked out the door of the Tillinghast Room. If he turned right, he could walk right past the ongoing party where almost everyone in the room was being toasted. No doubt if he had walked in, he would have received a lengthy ovation once he had been spotted.

Fay turned left. He walked out the door unnoticed into the warm night air. The Mets and Yankees awaited on the car radio. In a few minutes, Bethpage would be in his rearview mirror.

For now.

Epilogue

THE LAST USGA trailers pulled out of Bethpage on August first.

It was left to Laura Southerland, Steve Worthy's assistant, to deliver to Dave Catalano the key to the cabin Jon Barker had worked in when he first arrived in 1998. He was sitting in the clubhouse dining room eating lunch with Craig Currier when she walked in with the key.

"We're all out," she said. "I guess the place is officially yours again."

Catalano laughed. "Well, let me officially say that you are welcome to come back anytime."

Negotiations to make that happen were already well under way. On the morning after the Open ended, a story in *Newsday* reported (accurately) that the USGA was seriously considering a return to Bethpage as early as 2009. Fay's dream, that the Open would be such a success that the Black Course would become a part of the unofficial Open rota along with Shinnecock, Pebble Beach, and Pinehurst, had been realized.

Indeed, Fay was so excited about the way the Open had turned out that he took a serious look at a municipal course outside Boston in the hope that it could be, in his words, "the next Black." Fay knew that the membership at the Country Club in Brookline was taking it for granted that the USGA would want to bring the Open back there in 2013 on the hundredth anniversary of Francis Ouimet's historic victory there. Hoping to add some uncertainty to the negotiations, Fay sent Mike Butz and Mike Davis to Ponkapoag Golf Course in July for a look at the place. Sadly, it wasn't the Black — a good course, a fine thirty-six-hole public facility, but not the Black.

Still, Torrey Pines would be announced as the Open's site in 2008 early in the fall, and if Fay had his way, the Black would be the site in 2009 — meaning the Open would be played on muni courses in back-to-back years.

Many had expected Currier to leave Bethpage soon after the Open for a cushy, high-paying job at a country club. He was clearly a hot commodity in the superintendent business after all the publicity he had received for his work on the Black. But he had no real interest in leaving.

"After preparing a course for a U.S. Open, it is a little bit tough to get all fired up about getting one in shape for a member-guest," he said. "Plus, I come in, maybe for a year they let me do what I want to do, and then I've got some guy running the greens committee telling me what to do every day. I don't need that. I'm happy here."

Garrett Boddington had left to run a new private course on the eastern end of Long Island that was still in construction. It was too good an opportunity for him to turn down, even though he hated leaving the Black Course, Bethpage, and Currier. Currier understood. "He's his own boss there, and he'll be a part of the building process, too," he said. "I told him he better take it or he'd have to answer to me."

At Bethpage, Currier only had to answer to Catalano, who was more than content to let him go about his business of restoring the golf courses. The Green and the Red were still in recovery mode after being buried under corporate tents and would not be ready for full play again until the end of the summer. There was still work to be done on the Black. The good news was, the money was there. The USGA was picking up the tab for the damages and the state was committed to keeping the golf courses in good shape.

Currier's deal with Catalano had been that if he stayed, Catalano could not retire. His reputation had also been greatly enhanced by the Open, and he surely could have landed a well-paying job had he chosen to retire from the state. But it was not to be. "I promised him [Currier] I wouldn't go," he said, smoking a postlunch cigarette. "The bottom line for me, I guess, is that this isn't really a job. It's a way of life. I'm not ready to leave my way of life."

The scroll of Open players — with Retief Goosen's name first and Jeff Sluman's name last — had been posted in the hallway just outside the dining room, a few steps from the pro shop. The regulars sat around the bar talking about what Open week had been like, what they had heard players say, shots they had seen them hit to holes they had just played themselves that morning.

On July second, a new pricing system had gone into effect for the Black Course. As per the contract with the USGA, there was no change in how much in-state residents paid — $31 on weekdays, $39 on the weekends, $27 at twilight, $23 and $29 (weekend) for senior citizens. But if you were from out of state, every fee was exactly double what the in-state residents paid, the legal limit according to state law.

"I haven't heard a single complaint yet," Catalano said. "A number of people have said to me that it's still a bargain. You know what? It is."

There were mornings, he admitted, when, as he made the short drive from his house to the golf course, he would see the now-departed grandstands in his mind's eye, filled with fans, and could hear the screams all over again. "It's almost as if everything that went up really became a part of the place," he said. "Seeing it all come down, there was certainly some sadness to that. But most of the time, we're still so busy, there isn't really time to feel any sadness or emptiness."

Currier had predicted the previous winter there would be enough post-Open work to do that they wouldn't even notice that it was over until "the snow starts to fly."

On this hot summer day, Catalano was fully aware that it was over. "And the feeling we all have about it," he said, "is still almost like a dream. It turned out better than we could possibly have dreamed. If it was a one-shot deal, well, it was one hell of a one-shot deal. We can all walk away from what we did with no regrets."

Almost one year after Mike Davis and Mike Butz had convened the postmortem/planning meeting for the 2001 and 2002 U.S. Opens, they convened the 2002-2003 meetings in the same conference room, just off the main lobby at Golf House.

Most of the same characters were there. A couple of Mary Lopuszynski's lieutenants had left, worn out no doubt. Robbie Zalzneck sat front and center at the conference table (it was now his year) while Jon Barker and Tricia Solow, relocated to Shinnecock and planning already for 2004, sat in the auxiliary seating just behind the table.

Other than that, the gang was all there.

Steve Worthy, Frank Bussey, and Brant McWilliams sat to the right of the Mikes, with maps of Olympia Fields in front of them. One of Lopuszynski's first comments when she turned to discussing the '03 Open was to request an extra trailer for her vendors to work from during the week. "You know, something 8 feet by 32 feet where they can set up computers and stuff," she said.

"Absolutely not," Bussey said. Then he laughed and wrote it down.

But not everything was the same as it had been a year earlier. There was a tremendous sense of satisfaction in the room, not quite euphoria — this was not a euphoric sort of group — but clearly a feeling that a very difficult task had been carried out not just successfully but with results that went beyond what anyone could have hoped for.

"I can honestly say this was the best Open I think I've ever been associated with," Davis said. "And I was one of the skeptics. I laughed at the idea in '95 when David [Fay] first took us out there. I would have told you the golf course was in the bottom two percent in the country back then in conditioning. By the time we played, it was as good as you'll ever see. I thought the whole thing was fantastic."

That was the mood, even as they waded through the problems. There had been quite a bit of posttournament theft. Twelve TVs had been stolen from corporate tents. For some reason, 112 chairs had disappeared from the media center. The usual spate of signs and banners had also gone away, never to be seen again.

The best postchampionship complaint had come from one of Mimi Griffin's corporate clients. They had received a $300 bill from Long Island Cablevision for several nighttime pay-per-view events. When they had asked Cablevision for specifics they were told the bill was for a number of pornographic movies and the Mike Tyson–Lennox Lewis fight, which had taken place on Saturday night.

The only people with access to the tents at night were Bo Dietl's security people. Steve Worthy, who had just gone through a fairly rocky negotiation with BDA on what percentage of the bill the USGA would actually be paying, laughed when Griffin reported the Cablevision bill.

"Let me get this straight," he said. "First they watched the porn and the fight and *then* they stole the TVs?"

Worthy was joking; no one had any idea who had actually stolen the televisions. He and Bussey had gone back to BDA after the tournament to let them know how unhappy the USGA was with the attendance throughout the week. Overall, according to Felix Sorge's final report, only a little more than 50 percent of the guards promised in the original contract had ever shown up. Worthy and BDA finally settled on a figure of about $200,000 — roughly two-thirds of BDA's original bid.

In considering a security company for 2003, Sorge and Worthy were looking at national companies rather than local ones as they had done in the past. Five would be interviewed, and a contract would be signed much earlier than the 2002 contract had been signed.

There was no question that the close to 10,000 background checks done on everyone — except for the players — working at the Open had taken their toll. In all, 135 of the people checked, most of them temporary employees hired by various vendors, had shown up with warrants. Most were for misdemeanors. But six people who had felony warrants had been arrested, including one who had been wanted on an explosives charge.

The plan for 2003 was for fewer background checks. Anyone working in transportation would be checked and, as always, anyone working in child care. That would probably be it, unless the Illinois State Police demanded something different. Thus far, they had not.

The volunteer attrition rate for the week had been about five percent — not bad, especially considering that there had been far more volunteers than at any other Open. The rate had doubled on the weekend, largely because of the parking problem. Jon Barker suggested the possibility of a floater committee for volunteers in the future — backup volunteers who would be trained to sub on two or three different committees when there were no-shows. Zalzneck had his work cut out for him to make the volunteer lunch sound as fabulous as Barker had done.

There had been other minor problems. NBC had experienced some technical difficulties because its compound was so far (off the 10th fairway) from the clubhouse. The FCC had shown up on Saturday to make a spot check on equipment, creating more TV headaches. The unions had ended up costing considerably more money than the USGA had hoped. There had been a shuttle bus driver who had started driving east on the Long Island Expressway from one of the hotels early one morning. When a passenger told him he was going in the wrong direction, he insisted that he wasn't.

"Bethpage is west," the passenger said.

"Bethpage?" the driver said. "Aren't we going to Shinnecock?"

Not for two more years.

Some of the computer people from Unisys had been a bit disturbed when they arrived at their hotel and found it was a motel — that charged an hourly rate. They had eventually been moved. "Let's get them something nice next year," Davis said.

And even though Fay had declared it a nonissue, there was an understanding that a bullet had been barely dodged because of the late tee times. Mark Carlson had already passed on an NBC request for an eight-thirty eastern time finish in 2003, which would be seven-thirty local time in Chicago.

"I'm going to talk to David about that today," Davis said when the groans went up at the thought of such a late finish. "He knows we got lucky this time. I don't think he'll mess around with that late a finish again."

Davis was right. Fay told Carlson to tell NBC the latest finish in the future would be seven o'clock local time — for the awards ceremony. That meant the last putt would be scheduled to go in the hole at about 6:50. "Most of the time if you get a rain delay it's at least two hours," he said. "We got away with forty-nine minutes on Sunday at Bethpage. That's rare. Even seven is pushing the envelope a little bit, but I understand why it helps them to do that. But seven-thirty, no, I won't go there again."

During the operations report, Steve Worthy passed out a fact sheet with some remarkable statistics. During the Open, the USGA had laid down 8,200 yards of temporary roads, or enough rock to build a five-foot-wide sidewalk from Bethpage to Manhattan. Close to 200,000 soft drinks had been sold in addition to 163,000 bottles of water. Eighty thousand hamburgers had been eaten. In all, there had been 893 police officers on site each day. More than 1.6 million pounds of trash had been accumulated during the week.

It had been, without doubt, the biggest U.S. Open ever.

"Here's the most amazing stat of all," Frank Bussey said. "I'm not sure I saw one serious word of negative publicity. Not one. If you think about that, with all that went on, that's a miracle."

Amen.

There really wasn't much doubt about the Open returning to Bethpage. When all the numbers were sifted through, Marc Gellman's prediction that the USGA would do well by doing good had proven to be emphatically true. The net profit for the Open at the Black was about $13 million, the highest net figure ever generated by an Open. The USGA, which had been so skeptical about working with the state of New York, found that working with the state, overall, was easier than working with most country clubs. Mike Butz had been joking when he asked Bob Nuzzo if he and his state police traveled, but the USGA did continue to consult Nuzzo unofficially on security matters for future Opens.

Knowing that a return to Bethpage was almost certain, Tom Meeks had already put together a memo with his suggestions for the next time around: move the fairway on number 10 back 20 yards closer to the tee. Move the tee on number 12 up about 10 yards, and bring the fairway on the left side of the bunker in about five yards. Move the tee on number seven up five to 10 yards because in tough conditions (Friday) almost no one in the field had been able to hit the converted par-five in regulation. And, finally, be careful with the hole location at number 11.

"That's the only one we missed on all week," Meeks said. "We missed by two paces both ways. We should have been nine back and seven right; instead we were seven and five." Without much debate, the USGA decided to find out if Meeks was right.

Meeks was planning to retire in 2005 but was hoping he would have an alumni chair in the USGA staff room when the Open returned to the Black. "It's one of the special Open places now," he said. "I think everyone agrees we hit a grand slam there. Next spring, I'm going to call Dave and Craig and go out there and play all five courses."

With luck, they would be able to get him on the Black.

Clearly, the next contract would be different from the first one. The Black no longer needed a $3.5 million makeover. The negotiation went fairly smoothly. Fay and Butz both knew that Pataki wanted the next Bethpage Open announced before election day. On October 10, 2002, they all gathered again in the clubhouse to make official one of the worst kept secrets in history: the Open would return to the Black Course in 2009. When the smoke cleared, the contract agreed to by both parties was for about the same money the USGA was paying Shinnecock for 2004: a little more than $5 million.

The signs began going up soon after. "Welcome to Bethpage. Home of the 2009 United States Open Championship."

Catalano looked at Currier as the announcement was being made. "Less than seven years to go," he said.

Currier nodded. It was time to get back to work.

Acknowledgments

THE SIMPLEST WAY to say thank you to all the people who played a critical role in making this book a reality might just be to reprint the U.S. Golf Association's list of employees here because so many of them went out of their way to make it possible for me to reach the finish line on this project.

Since I can't do that, let me begin where I began when I first conceived the idea: David B. Fay. Everyone agrees that there would have been no U.S. Open at the Black Course without Fay's vision. Just as clearly, there would have been no book on that Open without his remarkable cooperation and patience. Putting aside his inability to find the alleged "I Have a Dream" memo, I never could have gotten off square one without his help and input.

It was Fay who agreed to give me the access I needed to do this book. That meant sitting in on planning meetings, walking the golf course on site surveys, spending time with the people at Bethpage, attending volunteer training sessions, and being allowed to jump around on the property throughout the week of the championship with complete access to anyone and anything as the Open unfolded.

Of course having the boss say, "This guy's in," doesn't mean you are going to get complete cooperation from the staff. They can let you in the room, but they don't have to let you into their hearts and minds and concerns. They don't have to tell you about things that happened when you weren't there. I can't swear that the folks who work for Fay told me everything they possibly could, but I certainly felt as if they tried to. That's where this long list comes into play. So, to begin at the beginning, thanks to . . .

Mike Butz and Mike Davis, the Mikes who have to carry out all of Fay's ideas, no matter how crazy. The irrepressible and irresistible Tom Meeks, whose patience with me was almost unmatched. Tim Moraghan, his inside-the-ropes alter ego, someone who doesn't get anywhere close to the credit he deserves for what happened at Bethpage. Jon Barker, whose life would have been far simpler if I hadn't come into it, and his remarkable assistant, Tricia Solow, not to mention Ellen Gehrman and the two hardest-working interns on the planet, Mike Antolini and Nick Ricciardi. Which brings up other assistants who went way out of their way to help me on innumerable occasions: Kathy Whaley, Kathy Paparelli, Ellie Marino, Margharete Saunders, and Ellen McMahon.

Larry Adamson is one of the great people and great storytellers I've ever encountered. Thanks also to his staff and his successor, Betsy Swain. The last thing the operations people need or want hanging around is a reporter. Steve Worthy is *still* nervous about what's in this book (with good reason), but he and Mayor Frank Bussey and Brant McWilliams and Laura Southerland could not have been any nicer to me. Well, maybe Frank could have been. Robbie Zalzneck will have his year very soon. Others who deserve major kudos: Tony Zirpoli; Roger Harvie; Jim Farrell; Bill McCarthy (haven't forgotten that beer); and Art Spander's biographer, Ron Read. The entire legal staff led by Romaney Berson (every great organization needs at least one Dukie); Pete Bevacqua; Anne Kellstrom; Andrea Davis; and Ann O'Connell.

Thanks also to Mark Carlson, a remarkably fine man for someone who hangs out so much with TV people, and everyone in communications and media relations: Marty Parkes, Craig Smith, Suzanne Colson, Peter Kowalski, Beth Murrison, and Holly Tappen. Also Brett Avery and Rich Skyzinski in publications. It will be readily apparent reading this book that I think Mary Lopuszynski is an amazing human being — even Frank Hannigan likes her for crying out loud — and I hope that someday Bono does show up in the tent. Thanks also to her lieutenants Patterson Temple and Ashley Mohler.

Mimi Griffin was, according to the immortal Dick "Hoops" Weiss, one of the first truly gifted female college basketball players. The work she does for the USGA in corporate marketing takes the gift of great patience, and dealing with my questions on this book also took great patience. I also owe thanks to her staff, notably Jeannie Taylor and Matt Ford. Others: Nancy Bennett and Ann McNamara from admissions and will-call; Kevin O'Connor from scoring; John Hynds, Pam Martin, and Carrie Cardace in accounting. Also, scoring guru Jeff Hall and Dave Donnelly. No one had more on his hands during the Open than Felix Sorge. If he sweated, I never saw it.

Those who work for the state of New York sort of got sucked into this project because the USGA had decided to cooperate with me. From the beginning, the people I dealt with at Bethpage could not have been more accommodating. If it appears that I have great affection for Dave Catalano and Craig Currier, it is only because I do. I'm also indebted to Garrett Boddington, Pete Cash, Bernadette Castro, Brad Race, Tara Snow, and Nancy Palumbo, not to mention fellow Shelter Islander Kevin Carey. Lieutenant Bob Nuzzo could not have been more helpful throughout the process. When we sat down to talk he told me he had become a policeman because "I know this sounds corny, but I wanted to help people." He and his supervisor, Greg Sittler, helped a lot of people during this Open. Including me.

To try to list all the volunteers who went out of their way to help me would be impossible. I hope they will settle for a blanket thank-you.

Players. I probably can't list them all, dating to the local qualifiers I attended, but some must be mentioned: Raymond Floyd Jr., Rick Hartmann, P. J. Cowan, Darrell Kestner, Bob Longo, Jamie Friedman, Jason Pool, Pat Tallent, Loren Roberts, Mike Hulbert, Dan Forsman, Joe Ogilvie, Fred Couples, George McNeill, Willie Wood, Robert Stock, Bobby Clampett, Derek Tolan, Paul Goydos,

Joe Durant, Olin Browne, Steve Pate, Mike Muehr, Joey Sindelar, Billy Andrade, Jim McGovern, Scott Verplank, Lee Janzen, Brent Geiberger, Jim Furyk, Colin Montgomerie, John Cook, David Duval, Vijay Singh, Kent Jones, John Daly, Donnie Hammond, Steve Stricker, Kevin Warrick, Kevin Sutherland, Brad Faxon, Greg Norman, Chris DiMarco, John Maginnes, David Toms, Nick Price, Harrison Frazar, Ernie Els, Brad Lardon, Jeff Sluman, Mark O'Meara, Jay and Jerry Haas, Tom Byrum, Jean Van de Velde, Scott Hoch, Kirk Triplett, Dudley Hart, Charles Howell III, Davis Love III, Scott McCarron, and Phil Mickelson.

Thanks as always to my caddy pals: Jim "Bones" Mackay, Tommy Lamm, Frank Williams, Jimmy Walker, Ryan Scott, Woody Cimarolli, Tony Navarro, and Greg Rita. Thanks also to PGA Tour staffers who helped along the way, notably Marty Caffey, Sid Wilson, Denise Taylor, Joan vT Alexander, James Cramer, Dave Lancer, Henry Hughes (okay, Henry?), Ana Leaird, and my heroes in rules: Mark Russell, Jon Brendle, Slugger White, Ben Nelson, George Boutell, and Wade Cagle. Thanks also to Commissioner Tim Finchem, who still returns my calls if only because Cathy Hurlburt makes him.

One other person played a key role in this book: Wes Seeley. When it became clear to me that I needed another set of eyes and ears at the Open to gather as much information from as many people as possible, Wes was a natural for the job. Having worked for both the USGA and the PGA Tour, he knows golf and he knows golfers, and many of them know him. If there are moments during my recounting of the championship when I appear to be in a meeting at the same moment that something momentous was happening on the golf course, it is because I was, thanks to Wes. He also made himself available on the innumerable occasions when I needed to look things up via computer and was completely incapable of figuring out how to do so.

Esther Newberg is a great agent and a better friend. I've said that before; I'm saying it again because it is still true. She now has the perfect staff in Andy Barzvi and Christine Bausch, and if she lets either one leave she will have to answer to me, among others. Michael Pietsch gets the same boring call as Esther: wonderful editor, better friend. The only thing that makes me nervous about this book is that Esther and Michael both liked the idea right away. Michael's staff at Little, Brown and Company does great work: Stacey Brody, Megan Lynch, Heather Fain, Heather Rizzo, Marlena Bittner, and of course Oprah's favorite model, Holly Wilkinson.

Then there are my friends: Keith and Barbie Drum; Bob and Anne DeStefano; David and Linda Maraniss; Tom and Jill Mickle; Jackson Diehl and Jean Halperin; Lexie Verdon and Steve Barr; Bill and Jane Brill; Terry and Patty Hanson; Terry Chili, Tate Armstrong, Mark Alarie, Clay Buckley (quick, what do they have in common?); Pete Teeley; Bob Novak; Al Hunt; Vivian Thompson; Bob Zurfluh; Wayne Zell; Mike and David Sanders; Bob Whitmore; Andy Dolich; Mary Carillo; Doug Doughty; David Teel; Beth Shumway; Beth Sherry-Downes; Erin Laissen; Jesse Markison; my ever-patient partner, Bob Socci; Pete Van Poppel; Frank Davinney; Scott Strasemeier; Andrew Thompson; Joe Speed; Jack Hecker; Dickie Hall; Jim Cantelupe and Tiffany Bauman; Derek and Christina Klein; Bob Beretta and Mike Albright; Frank "Lew Alcindor" Mastrandrea; Roger Breslin; Jim Rome; Travis Rodgers; Jason Stewart; Mark Maske; Elissa Leibowitz; Mike Lupica; Michael Wilbon and Tony Kornheiser; George Solomon; Bob Edwards; Ellen McDonnell; Jeffrey Katz; Ken and Christina Lewis; Bob Morgan; Hoops (of course); Little Sandy Genelius; Jennifer "Wailin'" Mearns and brood; Joe Valerio; Rob Cowan; and the best golfer you've never heard of, Norbert Doyle.

Basketball people: Mike Krzyzewski; Gary Williams; Mike Brey; Tommy Amaker; Doug Wojcik; Mike Cragg; Cragg's favorite coach, Billy Hahn; Rick Barnes; Dave Odom; the entire Patriot League gang; and the only honest man in the gym, Tom Konchalski. Other golf names: Glenn Greenspan, who had a nice quiet year; gone-but-not-soon-forgotten George Peper, Jim Frank, and Mike Purkey.

Swimmers: Jeff Roddin, Tom Denes, Penny Bates (sorry, Penny, you still make the list); Carole Kammel; Margot Pettijohn; Jeri Ramsbottom; Susan Williams; Mary Dowling; Amy Weiss; A. J. Block; Warren Friedland; Marshall Greer; John Craig; Danny Pick; Mark Pugliese; Peter Ward; Doug Chestnut; Paul Doremus; and the members of the exclusive FWRH club: Clay Britt, the one and only Wally Dicks, and the one and only (thank God) Michael Fell. We all hope Jason Crist comes out of retirement soon, no one more so than Shelley Crist.

The China Doll gang: Red Auerbach, Morgan Wootten, Jack Kvancz, Aubrey and Sam Jones, Silent Hymie Perlo, Peter Dowling (member in absentia), Bobby Campbell, Stanley Copeland, Alvin Miller, Rob Ades, and the rookie, Chris Wallace. To say that we miss Zang Auerbach is a vast understatement.

Last, never least, the family: my wonderful in-law group: Jim and Arlene; Kacky, Stan, and Annie; Annie, Gregg, Rudy, Gus, and Harry; Jimmy and Brendan. Dad and Marcia; Margaret, David, and Ethan; Jennifer, Matthew, Brian, and my favorite player in this year's Open, Bobby. My only complaint with Danny and Brigid is that they are growing up too fast. I have not a single complaint, only gratitude and love, for my remarkable wife, Mary.

John Feinstein
Bethesda, Maryland
November 2002

Index

About the author

John Feinstein is the author of several highly acclaimed bestsellers, including books on golf (*A Good Walk Spoiled, The Majors, Open,* and *Caddy for Life*), basketball (*A Season on the Brink, A March to Madness, The Last Amateurs,* and *The Punch*), football (*A Civil War: Army vs. Navy*), and other sports. He is a frequent commentator on National Public Radio and an essayist for CBS Sports. He is also a columnist for American Online and *Golf Magazine* and a contributor to the *Washington Post* and the *Wall Street Journal*. He lives in Bethesda, Maryland, and Shelter Island, New York.

Look for these other bestselling books by
John Feinstein

The Last Amateurs
*Playing for Glory and Honor
in Division I College Basketball*

"Feinstein's descriptions of the games are intense and exciting."
— Conrad Bibens, *Houston Chronicle*

"There are numerous behind-the-scenes anecdotes that keep the pages turning." — Larry Platt, *Wall Street Journal*

"You'll be glued to the page. . . . Feinstein makes you care."
— Bruce Fretts, *Entertainment Weekly*

A March to Madness
*The View from the Floor in the
Atlantic Coast Conference*

"A basketball junkie's nirvana."
— Charles Hirshberg, *Sports Illustrated*

"A meticulously detailed account of a season of college basketball. . . . Full of insiders' jargon, the drama of personal rivalries, the melodrama of hard-fought contests. . . . Fans will find everything in this book."
— Richard Bernstein, *New York Times*

BACK BAY BOOKS
Available in paperback wherever books are sold

Look for these other bestselling books by
John Feinstein

The Punch
*One Night, Two Lives, and the Fight
That Changed Basketball Forever*

"A chilling book about how a 1977 fight in a Lakers-Rockets game changed the lives of Kermit Washington and Rudy Tomjanovich.... Every NBA player, if not every pro athlete, should be required to read *The Punch*."
— Dave Anderson, *New York Times*

"A wonderful piece of reporting that is required reading for anyone who loves sports, or sports history."
— Mike Lupica, *New York Daily News*

A Civil War: Army vs. Navy
A Year Inside College Football's Purest Rivalry

"An excellent book.... With Army-Navy, you always get your money's worth." — *Wall Street Journal*

"Highly readable.... Feinstein is an outstanding chronicler of the game as a game." — Clay Reynolds, *Houston Chronicle*

"Not only entertaining but also inspiring."
— Henry Kisor, *Chicago Sun Times*

BACK BAY BOOKS
Available in paperback wherever books are sold

Look for these other bestselling books by
John Feinstein

A Good Walk Spoiled
Days and Nights on the PGA Tour

"The golf tour's true heart. . . . Feinstein gets it right."
— *New York Times Book Review*

"A good read rewarded. . . . The best-ever account of life on the PGA tour."   — *Golf Magazine*

The Majors
In Pursuit of Golf's Holy Grail

"The ultimate insider's account. . . . Feinstein examines the hearts and minds of the best players in the world to find what it takes to win the game's most prestigious events."   — *Golf Tips*

BACK BAY BOOKS
Available in paperback wherever books are sold

Caddy for Life
The Bruce Edwards Story

An extraordinary account of teamwork, loyalty, and professionalism in the front ranks of the PGA — the compelling and inspiring story of Bruce Edwards, recently diagnosed with Lou Gehrig's disease, who has been Tom Watson's caddy for more than three decades.

Published in April 2004 by Little, Brown and Company